Beginr
Mac OS®)
Dashboard Widget
Development

Fred Terry

WILEY

Wiley Publishing, Inc.

Beginning Mac OS® X Tiger™ Dashboard Widget Development

Published by
Wiley Publishing, Inc.
10475 Crosspoint Boulevard
Indianapolis, IN 46256
www.wiley.com

Copyright © 2006 by Wiley Publishing, Inc., Indianapolis, Indiana

Published simultaneously in Canada

ISBN-13: 978-0-471-77825-7
ISBN-10: 0-471-77825-7

Manufactured in the United States of America

10 9 8 7 6 5 4 3 2 1

1B/SX/QW/QW/IN

Library of Congress Cataloging-in-Publication Data:

Terry, Fred.
  Beginning Mac OS X Tiger dashboard widget development / Fred Terry.
     p. cm.
  Includes index.
  ISBN-13: 978-0-471-77825-7 (paper/website : alk. paper)
  ISBN-10: 0-471-77825-7 (paper/website : alk. paper)
  1. Mac OS. 2. Operating systems (Computers) 3. Macintosh (Computer)—Programming. 4. HTML (Document markup language) I. Title.

  QA76.76.O63T437 2006

  005.4'4682—dc22

                    2006015521

For general information on our other products and services please contact our Customer Care Department within the United States at (800) 762-2974, outside the United States at (317) 572-3993 or fax (317) 572-4002.

Trademarks: Wiley, the Wiley logo, Wrox, the Wrox logo, Programmer to Programmer, and related trade dress are trademarks or registered trademarks of John Wiley & Sons, Inc. and/or its affiliates, in the United States and other countries, and may not be used without written permission. Mac OS and Tiger are trademarks or registered trademarks of Apple Computer, Inc. in the US and other countries. All other trademarks are the property of their respective owners. Wiley Publishing, Inc., is not associated with any product or vendor mentioned in this book.

Wiley also publishes its books in a variety of electronic formats. Some content that appears in print may not be available in electronic books.

About the Author

Fred Terry has been involved in the computer industry since making a left-hand turn into it from Ph.D. work in medieval languages and literature. He has written a number of software manuals and articles and has worked as a systems and network administrator, web developer, programmer, and quality assurance engineer. In addition to his ongoing love affairs with AppleScript and Perl, his current programming infatuations are Ruby and Ajax. Currently, Fred is a project manager for the Information Management Group at Burns & McDonnell. He has a B.A. in English from Southwestern Oklahoma State University and an M.A. in English from Oklahoma State University. He lives in Lawrence, Kansas, with his family and dog. Fred can be contacted at `pfterry@deadtrees.net`.

For Leesa, who has stood by me through career changes and side projects
without losing her patience or humor

Acknowledgments

No book is produced in a vacuum. I want to thank the developers who let me include their widgets for the example chapters in the latter half of the book: Andrew Welch, Nick Rogers, Jesus de Meyer, Jason Yee, and Simon Whitaker. I can't thank Nick Rogers enough for being a racquetball partner, letting me bounce code off of him, and performing the technical edit. Cleve Devault needs my thanks for giving me some space to work on this book. I also want to thank my agent, Laura Lewin; my acquisitions editor, Katie Mohr; and, most important of all, my development editor, Rosanne Koneval. This book wouldn't have made it over all the hurdles without their capable guidance.

My thanks to Nick Sayre and Andy Rhoades for allowing me to reprint the "Nick vs. Andy" strip (Figure 7-9). Additional "Nick vs. Andy" strips can be found at `http://nicksayre.com/`.

As any writer would say, I have to extend my greatest thanks to my family. My wife, Leesa; my daughter, Sommer; and my son, Keegan, put up with the constant distraction of this book. They are happier than I that it's finally done.

Credits

Contents

Contents

Contents

Contents

Contents

Introduction

Dashboard widgets are based on the technologies that have been powering the Web for nearly two decades. At their simplest, widgets are HTML pages that run inside of Dashboard. There's more to a Dashboard widget than HTML, of course. Cascading Style Sheets provide widgets with style and layout apart from the HTML structure or the content. JavaScript makes the widget dynamic and provides user interaction. Together these three technologies, with some OS X filesystem magic, provide a widget with the look and feel of a standalone application.

In addition to these technologies, Dashboard widgets run on WebKit, the browser engine that Safari is based on. WebKit has two underlying frameworks: WebCore, which is an HTML layout engine, and JavaScriptCore, which is a JavaScript engine. These frameworks are based on the JavaScript engine and HTML layout engine for the Konqueror web browser in KDE. Apple has continued to develop these frameworks and has released them as an open source project where they are maintained and extended by Apple employees. Because Dashboard widgets use these frameworks, they are extendable beyond the three standard web technologies. They can also use plugins written for WebKit. This also means that widgets can make use of all of the features in WebKit, including editable HTML.

Tim Berners-Lee originally created web servers and browsers as a means of sharing information globally. Dashboard widgets bring global information to the Tiger desktop by giving you the information you need at a keystroke. If you want to check the temperature in Melbourne or get the current time in London, that information is only a keystroke away. But widgets provide more than global information; they also give you access to local information. Through access keys, widgets can collect system information from your Macintosh or allow you to connect to and retrieve data from a network database. Widgets can also run any Unix command or AppleScript on OS X. Having instant access to all of your information and OS X services is what really makes the Dashboard metaphor work. You can even see it reflected in the Dashboard icon; each widget represents one gauge on your Dashboard.

Whom This Book Is For

This book is for anyone who wants to create Dashboard widgets or modify existing ones. In it you will find all of the information that you need to begin developing widgets and pointers on how to share your widgets with others. The development tools and resources that you need are part of OS X Tiger, including example widgets and source.

If you are a web developer, you already know HTML and are probably familiar with Cascading Style Sheets. If you don't know JavaScript but know another scripting or programming language, you should be able to pick up what you need as you work through this book. Apple has added extensions to these standard web languages. As part of the WebKit application framework, DOM and Dashboard-specific extensions are available for JavaScript. Additionally, you are able to use the HTML tag canvas to specify a drawing region in your widget. Accessing the canvas as a JavaScript object allows you to draw on it. All of these WebKit extensions are discussed in this book.

How This Book Is Structured

This book takes a stepwise approach to teaching you how to develop widgets for OS X using the Wrox "Try It Out" format. After a new widget element or programming technique has been discussed, you try out the technique by following step-by-step instructions that show you how to apply what you have just learned in an example. You should enter the source code from the examples on your Macintosh as you follow along to help with your understanding of the concepts. At the end of each example is a detailed explanation of the example in the "How It Works" section.

The examples in the book help you gain an understanding of the elements and construction of Dashboard widgets. When possible, the concepts that you learn in one example are incorporated into another widget example so you can see how they are related to each other within a widget. Rather than build one large widget with lots of features over the whole of the book, you work on several smaller examples that convey the concepts you learn in the chapters and show you how they can best be used in your own development.

Chapters 1–12 end with sets of exercises that reinforce what you've learned from the examples and explanations. The answers to the exercises are in Appendix A. As with your high school Algebra text, the answers are just another way that you can check your understanding of the material as well as find a hint whenever you get stuck while doing the exercises.

The following is a summary of the topics covered in each chapter:

❑   Chapter 1, "Tiger, Dashboard, and Widgets," introduces you to Dashboard widgets and explains how they are an integral part of Tiger.

❑   Chapter 2, "The Basics of Widgetry," explains the different parts of a widget. The chapter shows how widgets are constructed by examining the HTML, Cascading Style Sheet, JavaScript, and property list files of the widgets supplied with Tiger.

❑   Chapter 3, "Widget Development Environment," introduces the different development environment options available. In addition to the Xcode development environment supplied with Tiger, you look at using text editors and browsers as your development environment. Third-party development and debugging tools are also introduced.

❑   Chapter 4, "Creating a Widget," details creating your first widget. In addition to creating the main widget components, you see how to create the back side of the widget for preferences. You learn how to add display icons, encoded as PNG files, for the interface, and then bundle the widget.

❑   Chapter 5, "Debugging and Testing," demonstrates how to use logging, printing, and the JavaScript console in Safari to debug your widget. This chapter also looks into using third-party debugging tools and talks about widget testing.

❑   Chapter 6, "Giving a Widget Preferences," explains providing preferences for user interaction. You learn how to flip a widget to give the user access to the back side of the widget and how to save and load user preferences when the widget opens and closes.

❑   Chapter 7, "Widget Events," walks you through the activation, control, and focus events that provide the widget with a Mac-like user interface. You examine all of the events, how you can use them in your own widgets, and how to use control regions with the widget events.

❑   Chapter 8, "Adding to the Widget Interface," shows you how to provide automatic and manual resizing of a widget.

❑ Chapter 9, "Adding Cut, Copy, and Paste to Your Widget," explains how to use JavaScript events to add cut, copy, and paste capabilities to a widget. You walk through adding pasteboard handlers to a widget and calling the handlers with pasteboard events.

❑ Chapter 10, "Adding Drag and Drop to the Widget," shows you how to add drag-and-drop functionality to the widget.

❑ Chapter 11, "Access Keys," discusses limiting your widget's access to information from the filesystem, the command line, plugins, and the Internet through access keys. You also learn about widget security.

❑ Chapter 12, "Using Plugins and Applets," shows you how to use Internet plugins and Java applets in a widget.

❑ Chapter 13, "Easy Envelopes," walks you through the Easy Envelopes widget internals to show you how it works. This widget demonstrates the use of the full access key.

❑ Chapter 14, "SecureCopy Widget," creates a widget interface for the scp utilities in BSD. This widget demonstrates the use of the network and system access keys.

❑ Chapter 15, "Amazon Album Art," shows you how the Amazon Album Art widget gets album information from iTunes and retrieves the artwork from Amazon. This widget demonstrates the use of the `AllowFileAccessOutsideOfWidget`, `AllowSystem`, and `AllowNetworkAccess` keys and shows how AppleScripts can be used in a widget

❑ Chapter 16, "Timbuktu Quick Connect," shows you how the Timbuktu Quick Connect widget can control Timbuktu. This widget demonstrates the use of the `AllowSystem` access key and AppleScript.

❑ Chapter 17, "iPhoto Mini," shows you how the iPhoto Mini widget can display your photos without launching iPhoto. This widget demonstrates the use of the `AllowFileAccessOutsideOfWidget` and `BackwardsCompatibleClassLookup` access keys.

❑ Chapter 18, "iTunes Connection Monitor," shows how the widget is able to display the users connected to your iTunes library and which songs they are playing. This widget demonstrates the use of the `AllowSystem` access key.

❑ Chapter 19, "More Widgets," shows how the More Widgets widget retrieves and parses the XML feed from the Dashboard Downloads website. This widget demonstrates the use of the `AllowNetworkAccess` and `BackwardsCompatibleClassLookup` access keys.

Additional information is gathered into the appendixes at the end of the book. Appendix C discusses distribution channels and how to get your widget ready for delivery. As mentioned earlier, Appendix A contains the answers to all of the chapter exercises. WebKit information is covered throughout the book. Appendix B contains pointers to additional sources of Dashboard programming information on the Web.

What You Need to Use This Book

Dashboard is part of the Macintosh OS X 10.4, or Tiger, release. To follow the examples in this book, you must have Tiger installed on your Macintosh. You may also want to install Apple's Xcode developer tools environment.

The Xcode developer tools can be downloaded from `http://developer.apple.com`. Xcode provides an integrated developer environment (IDE) for your widget programming. Example widgets, documentation, and tech notes are also included with the Xcode installation. If you don't want to incur the overhead of Xcode, you can use your favorite text editor and browser. These options are discussed in greater detail in Chapter 3, "Widget Development Environment."

Conventions

To make it easy to follow the instructions and examples in the text, this book follows a number of conventions.

> **Boxes like this one hold important, not-to-be forgotten information that is directly relevant to the surrounding text.**

Tips, hints, tricks, and asides to the current discussion are offset and placed in italics like this.

As for styles used in the text

❑ URLs and code within the text are shown in a monofont typeface, like this: `currentContent.style.display`.

❑ Code is presented in two different ways:

```
In code examples, new and important code is highlighted with a gray background.
```

```
The gray highlighting is not used for code that is less important in the present
context or has been shown before.
```

On the Website

Typing in the code from the examples in this book may help you learn, but you if prefer to download the source code files that accompany the book, you will find them at `www.wrox.com`. You can locate the book on the Wrox website by entering the title of the book or ISBN number in the Search Titles box and then clicking the Download Code link.

Because many books have similar titles, you may find it easiest to search by ISBN; this book's ISBN is 0-471-77825-7 (changing to 978-0-471-77825-7 as the new industry-wide 13-digit ISBN numbering system is phased in by January 2007).

After you have downloaded the code to your Macintosh, you can decompress it by double-clicking on the file. The Finder supports uncompressing ZIP files, and it will unzip the file to a folder with the same name.

Errata

We make every effort to ensure that there are no errors in the text or in the code. However, no one is perfect, and mistakes do occur. If you find an error in one of our books, such as a spelling mistake or faulty piece of code, we would be very grateful for your feedback. By sending in errata you may save other readers hours of frustration and at the same time you will be helping us provide even higher quality information.

To find the errata page for this book, go to www.wrox.com and locate the title using the search box or one of the title lists. Then, on the book details page, click the Book Errata link. On this page you can view all errata that have been submitted for this book and posted by Wrox editors. A complete book list including links to each book's errata is also available at www.wrox.com/misc-pages/booklist.shtml.

If you don't spot "your" error on the Book Errata page, go to www.wrox.com/contact/techsupport .shtml and complete the form there to send us the error you have found. We'll check the information and, if appropriate, post a message to the book's errata page and fix the problem in subsequent editions of the book.

p2p.wrox.com

For author and peer discussion, join the P2P forums at http://p2p.wrox.com. The forums are a web-based system for you to post messages relating to Wrox books and related technologies and interact with other readers and technology users. The forums offer a subscription feature to email you topics of interest of your choosing when new posts are made. Wrox authors, editors, other industry experts, and your fellow readers are present on these forums.

There are several different forums here that will help you not only as you read this book, but also as you develop your applications. To join the forums, just follow these steps:

1. Go to http://p2p.wrox.com and click the Register link.
2. Read the terms of use and click Agree.
3. Complete the required information to join as well as any optional information you wish to provide and click Submit.
4. You will receive an email with information describing how to verify your account and complete the joining process.

   You can read messages in the forums without joining P2P but in order to post your own messages, you must join.

Once you join, you can post new messages and respond to messages other users post. You can read messages at any time on the Web. If you would like to have new messages from a particular forum emailed to you, click the Subscribe to this Forum icon by the forum name in the forum listing.

For more information about how to use the Wrox P2P, be sure to read the P2P FAQs for answers to questions about how the forum software works as well as many common questions specific to P2P and Wrox books. To read the FAQs, click the FAQ link on any P2P page.

Part I

An Introduction
to Widgets

Tiger, Dashboard, and Widgets

If you have had a chance to play with Dashboard widgets, you know how useful they are. Although widgets cover applications when they're active, most of the time this won't negatively affect your work. For example, if you are checking the temperature, you really don't need to leave the thermometer open after you know how hot or cold it is. Widgets also support copy and paste, so if you look up information on the Web, you can close Dashboard and paste it into your report. Even though they can't be used simultaneously, applications and widgets work well together.

In this chapter, you learn about Dashboard in Tiger. You also find out everything you need to know about working with widgets. You find out about security issues with widgets and how Apple has modified widget installation to make them more secure.

By the end of this chapter, you will know:

- ❑   How to manage widgets
- ❑   How to install widgets
- ❑   How to reload widgets

OS X Tiger

Tiger is the fourth big cat in the OS X parade. If you can't immediately remember the name before Panther and Jaguar, you shouldn't debit your Macintosh geek points. The 10.0 and 10.1 — yes, there are actually five — releases had codenames, but they must not have passed the coolness test because they weren't used widely outside of Apple. As with those previous releases of OS X, Tiger adds a number of features and tweaks to an already loaded operating system. Apple's technical briefs describe over two hundred features, and the regular listing of feature tips on its website suggests as many.

As with those previous systems, Tiger has a few new features that stand out from all the others and three features have improved usability in common. Those three are Spotlight, Automator, and Dashboard. Spotlight makes it easier to find information and files you've lost on your hard drive. Spotlight creates and regularly updates an index of the files on your Macintosh, so searching in Spotlight looks at the content of the files as well as the names of the files. Automator makes it easier to create workflows that make using your Macintosh more . . . automatic. For example, you can automate the process of selecting a directory, opening each of the files in BBEdit, and changing the tabs in the files to the appropriate number of spaces. Dashboard brings the information of the Web, as well as information from your Macintosh and your network, to your fingertips. Another thing these three features have in common is that they can be extended. You can create Automator actions, Spotlight plugins, and Dashboard widgets and share them with others. But unlike the other two, widgets feel like small applications.

Dashboard and Widgets

Dashboard is an overlay that zooms into place Exposé-like, floating the widgets above your applications, whenever you press a keyboard shortcut or click the Dashboard icon in the Dock. Dashboard does not affect any of your open applications, and its transparency allows you to see your applications below.

Widgets run inside of Dashboard and provide you with immediate access to information that you might otherwise have to load an additional application or two to get. Just as Dashboard's gauge icon implies, widgets give you an instant way to check the health of your system or track information you need. Widgets may be small web pages, but Dashboard is faster than waiting on your browser to load.

F12 is the key assigned to open Dashboard by default, but this assignment can be changed in the Keyboard and Mouse panel in System Preferences. To close Dashboard, press F12 again or click in the Dashboard outside of a widget.

> *On older PowerBooks, some of the function keys do double duty, and F12 is one of them. Pressing it ejects the CD or DVD in the PowerBook's optical drive (F1 through F6 also have predefined, hardware-related functions). You can use F12 to invoke Dashboard on these PowerBooks by holding down the function (fn) key when you press F12.*

In Figure 1-1, you'll notice that you can see the Finder's desktop beneath Dashboard's widgets. Tiger ships with a suite of 14 Dashboard widgets, and you can see 5 of them in the screenshot: Calendar, World Clock, Calculator, Weather, and the Widget widget, in counter-clockwise order. Notice that the cursor is pointing to an *i* in the lower-right corner of the Weather widget. Any widget with preferences displays an *i* when you are over it. Clicking the *i* flips the widget over so you can change its preferences (Figure 1-2).

Clicking the plus sign (+) button in the lower-left portion of the screen in Figure 1-1 displays the Widget Bar at the bottom of the window. You can also display the Widget Bar by pressing Command-+ while Dashboard is open (Figure 1-3).

The Widget Bar, which has the metal grill look of a G5, runs along the bottom of Dashboard. In the Widget Bar you can see all of the widgets that are installed on your Macintosh in the root-level /Library/Widgets/ folder and your users-level /Library/Widgets/ folder. The 14 widgets that ship with Tiger are installed in the /Library/Widgets/ folder at the root level of your hard disk and everyone who has an account on your Macintosh can see them when they log in. Any widget that you install is placed in the /Users/<your account>/Library/Widgets/ folder. Others users that have accounts on your Macintosh cannot see your widgets unless you copy them to their Widgets folder.

Figure 1-1

Figure 1-2

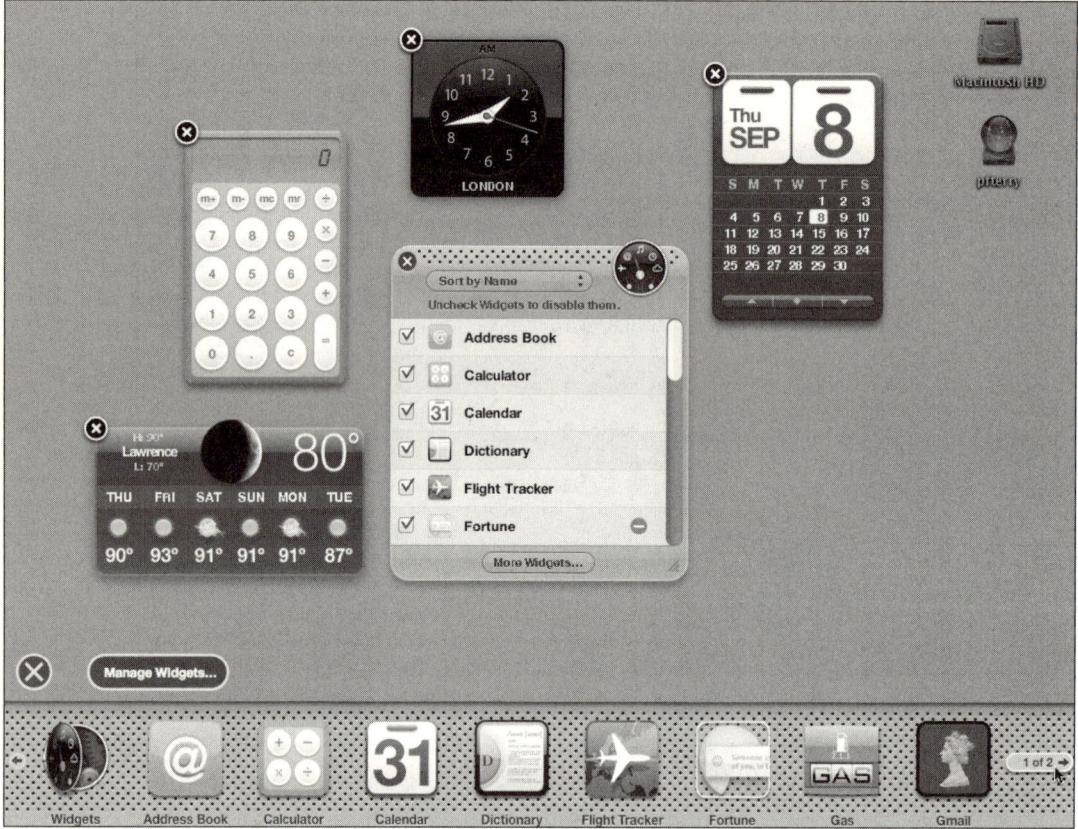

Figure 1-3

OS X has four filesystem domains: User, Local, Network, System. These domains
control access to resources on your Macintosh. The User domain contains resources
specific to the user who is logged in to the system. The System domain contains
resources that are required by the system to run. Users cannot add to, remove, or
change items in this domain. Each domain has its own Library folder and the contents of one Library folder can override another. If you modify the Weather widget
and place a copy of it in your Widgets folder, for instance, it will be used instead of
the copy in the System's Widgets folder.

*Though you can copy a widget into the System's Widgets folder, it isn't advisable because any update of
the operating system may overwrite the widgets you place there.*

The small arrows on the left and right sides of the Widget Bar allow you to see the next page of widgets. When you move the cursor over the arrow, it shows you how many more pages of widgets you have, like the "1 of 2" on the right side of the Widget Bar. You can scroll from one page of widgets to the other by typing Command-Left Arrow or Command-Right Arrow.

You can add a widget to Dashboard by dragging it from the Widget Bar into the Dashboard area. A ripple effect, like dropping a leaf on a pond, lets you know that the widget has been added (Figure 1-4). If you want to remove a widget from Dashboard, click the Close box in the upper-left corner of the widget that you want to remove, and the widget disappears into the Close box.

You can close a widget without opening the widget by holding down the Option key whenever you move your cursor over it. This displays the Close box for the widget.

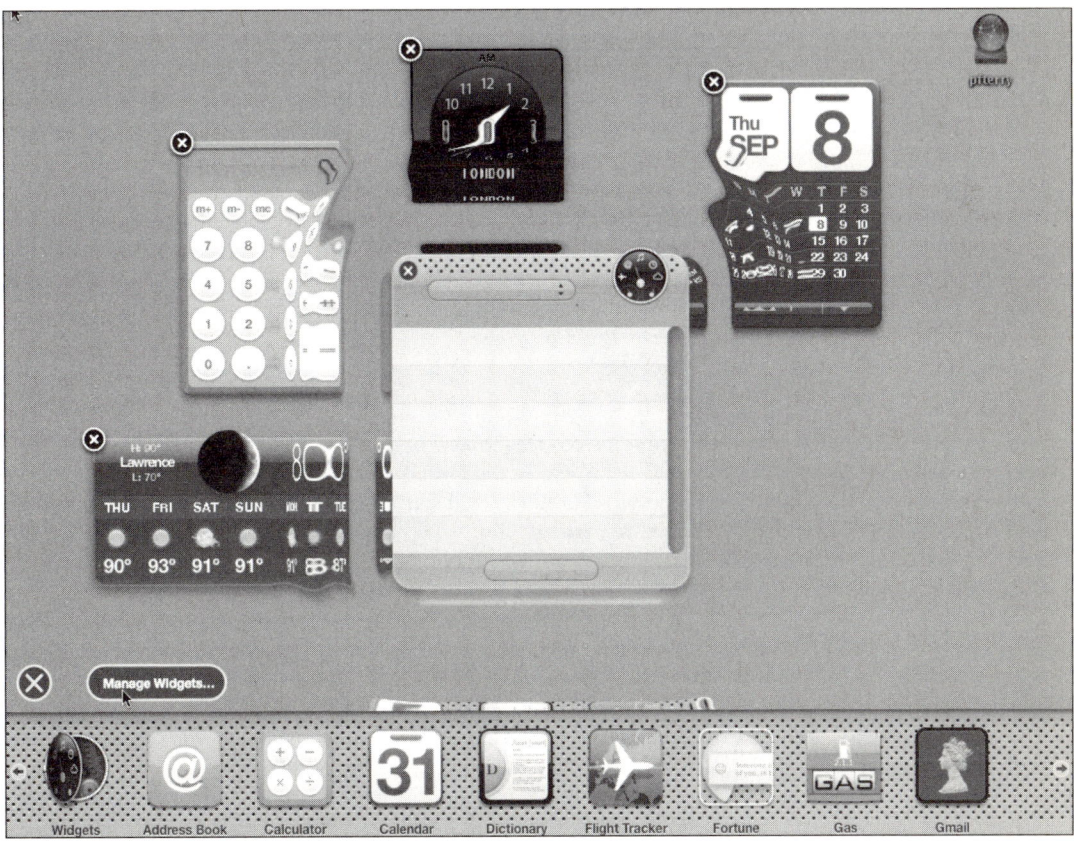

Figure 1-4

Managing Dashboard's Widgets

In the Tiger 10.4.2 release, Apple introduced the Widgets widget. The Widgets widget provides a compact interface for managing widgets (Figure 1-5). You open the Widgets widget by clicking the Manage Widgets button after you have opened the Widget Bar. Widgets provides you with a scrolling list of the widgets installed in your account and the System. This widget allows you to sort, hide, remove, and find additional widgets. The Sort menu at the top of the widget lets you sort installed widgets by name or by date.

Figure 1-5

You can hide a widget without removing it from Dashboard by unchecking the checkbox next to the widget's name in the scrolling list. Doing this leaves the widget installed, but it is no longer displayed in the Widget Bar, which reduces the amount of horizontal scrolling that you have to do when you are adding widgets to Dashboard. One way to manage your widgets, for instance, is to uncheck all of the widgets that you want to keep installed, but don't use very often. The widgets that you use regularly but don't add to Dashboard are in the Widget Bar, ready for you to add quickly.

If you want to remove or uninstall a widget, you click the red minus sign next to its name in the Widgets widget. Dashboard will confirm that you want to trash the widget (Figure 1-6).

The minus also helps you distinguish between the widgets that you've installed from those included with Tiger because the latter are not followed by a minus sign in a red circle.

> **You will not see a red minus next to the widgets installed in the System's /Library/ Widgets/ folder. This is primarily because you don't have modification privileges to that folder as a standard user, but even if you log in as root, a red minus does not appear next to these widgets.**

Figure 1-6

Clicking the More Widgets button at the bottom of the Widgets widget launches Safari, if it isn't already running, and takes you to Apple's Dashboard Widgets website (`http://www.apple.com/downloads/dashboard/`).

Installing Widgets

So how do you get additional widgets installed? In the Tiger 10.4.2 release, Apple changed widget installation procedures to respond to concerns about security. When Tiger was first released, widgets were automatically installed after they were downloaded. In addition to explaining the problem, Stephan Meyers created a page on his website (`http://stephan.com/widgets/zaptastic/`) that would automatically install a benign Zaptastic widget when you visited it. If you visit that page now, you'll see how Apple has improved the installation security by preventing automatic installation and adding confirmation dialogs.

Installing Local Widgets

If you want to install a widget that you are developing, you have two options. You can open your /Library/Widgets/ folder and drag the widget directly into the folder. After you do this, you must open Dashboard and drag it from the Widget Bar onto Dashboard.

You will probably spend lots of time in your /Library/Widgets folder as you develop widgets, but another approach is to use the Finder's built-in mechanism for installing widgets. Before you run through this example, you should have Apple's Xcode development environment installed because you will use one of the example widgets supplied with it.

Try It Out   **Install a Local Widget**

   1.   Open the /Developer/Examples/Dashboard/Sample Widgets/ folder.

2.   Double-click the Hello World widget (Hello World.wdgt). The Widget Installer prompts you to make certain that you want to install the widget (Figure 1-7).

Figure 1-7

3.   Click Install. Dashboard opens and prompts you to keep or delete the widget (Figure 1-8).

Figure 1-8

4.   Click Delete to remove the Widget without installing it in Dashboard, or click Keep to add it to Dashboard.

How It Works

The Widget Installer is part of the Tiger 10.4.2 revision and was included to address security concerns. The Widget Installer prevents the automatic installation of widgets so a malware widget can't be installed without your knowledge. If a web page tries to install a widget, as the Zaptastica page at Stephan Meyers's website does, you will know immediately and be able to cancel the installation.

If you decide to install the widget, the Widget Installer adds it to your Widgets folder and opens Dashboard with the widget in a box. The widget is fully functional, and you can try it out before you decide if you want to keep it. If you decide that you don't want to keep the widget and click the Delete button, the widget is moved to the Trash.

Because the Hello World.wdgt has been moved to your Widgets folder, you will not have a copy in the Sample Widgets folder. You will need to keep this in mind when you are developing widgets and always keep a copy in your development area.

Downloading and Installing

Typically, users are going to download widgets from Apple's Dashboard website or from another website. When they do this, Safari interacts with the Widget Installer to install the widget in Dashboard after it has been downloaded.

When you download a widget, Safari notices that it is an application and confirms that you want to continue downloading (Figure 1-9).

This allows you to cancel the download if the file isn't what you thought it was.

> Widgets may be web pages, but they are bundled and executable and, as a result, are considered applications.

Clicking the Download button continues the download and decompresses the file. You are asked if you want to install the widget after downloading it (Figure 1-10).

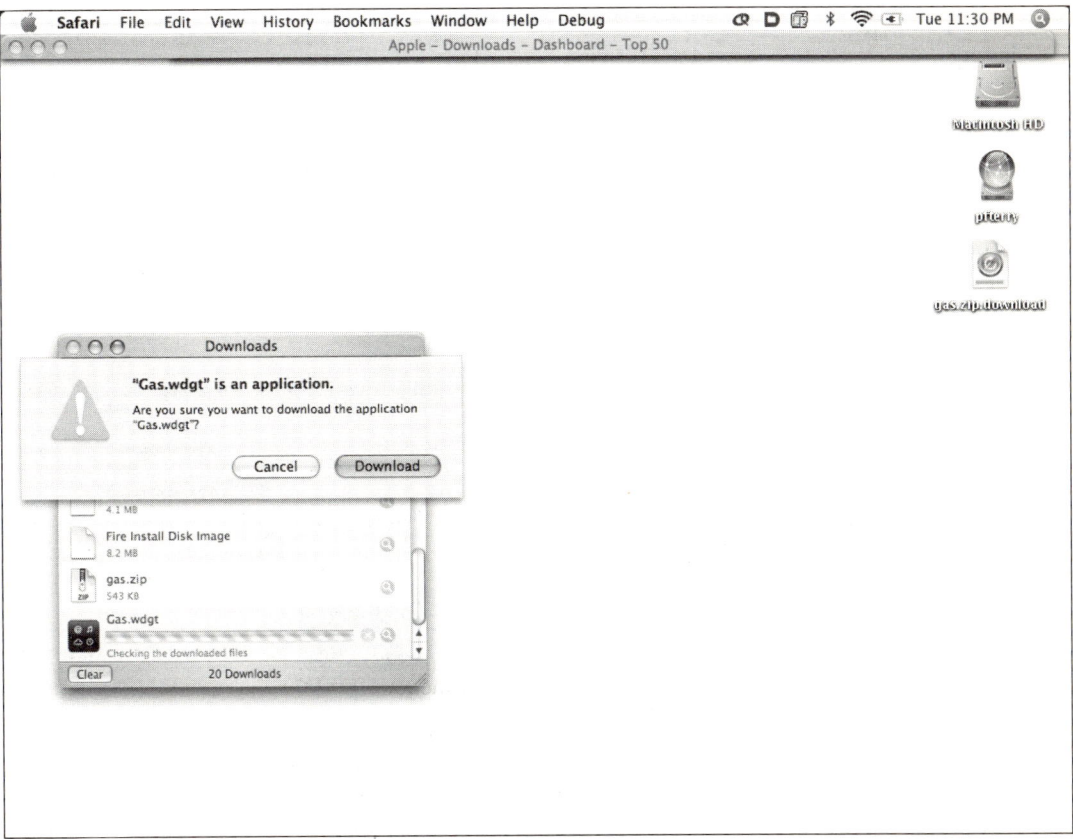

Figure 1-9

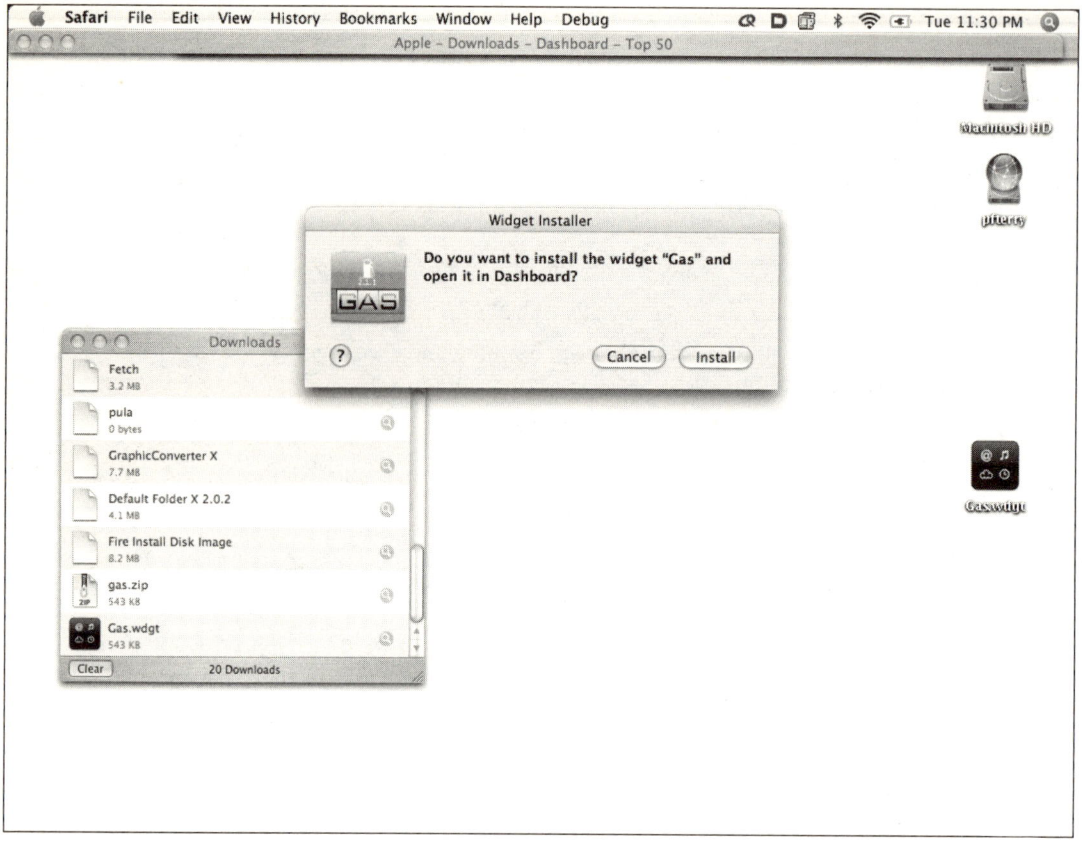

Figure 1-10

Notice that Gas.wdgt is downloaded to your downloads folder. If you use the Desktop as your down-loads folder, it will show up as in Figure 1-10.

As you saw in the Try It Out section, if you click the Install button, the widget is copied to the Widgets folder in your Library folder and Dashboard opens with the widget in a box and the option to keep or delete it (Figure 1-11).

Figure 1-11

If you aren't using Safari, you will probably have to double-click the widget to open the Widget Installer.

Reloading Widgets

Because widgets are essentially web pages, they behave the same way web pages do in browsers. If you make a change to a widget while you are developing it, you will have to reload the widget. You reload a widget in the same way you reload a page in Safari — you press Command-R. Select a widget and then press Command-R, the widget will spin (Figure 1-12) to let you know that it has reloaded.

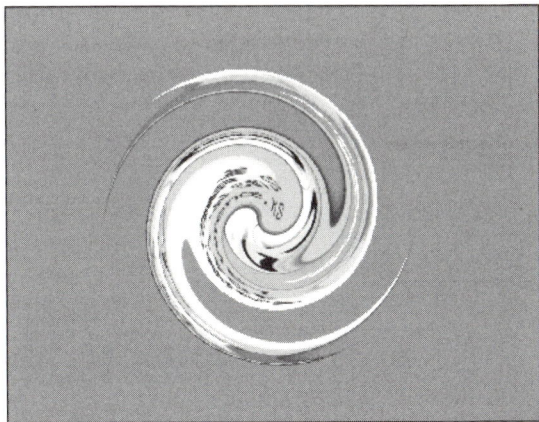

Figure 1-12

You have to reload a widget for the same reason that you have to reload a page in Safari. Safari maintains a cache to make pages that you visit regularly load faster. Dashboard also maintains a cache.

What Widgets Are Not

Now that we know what widgets are, a word or two is in order about what widgets are not. Widgets are not applications that run in Dashboard. In other words, you should not plan to write a large, multifunction application as a widget. A word processor would not make good widget. A good widget should be small, focused in purpose.

Perhaps the best thing to do is to think of a real-world widget. That simple device typically does one thing very, very well and is better than anything else at what it does. The epitome of a widget for me is a paint scraper. You can find several varieties, but they all have one thing in common: a standard flat blade perfectly mounted to slide along glass under a layer of paint.

A Dashboard widget should functionally mimic that real world widget. Rather than create a database application to run as a widget, create your database in MySQL or Postgresql and create a widget interface to your database. The database itself runs in its own memory space as a process so you don't have the overhead of a GUI, and your widget provides at-your-fingertips access to the data so you can query or create records. At least one web browser widget has been written for Dashboard. Ignoring the recursive ness, this is a good example of what not to do. Though widgets are essentially web pages running under Dashboard, they still use memory, as we will see in Chapter 7. The larger and more complex the widget, the greater the impact it will have on memory. Widgets should be thought of as a delivery mechanism for data.

A widget can be a very elegant solution to normally intractable problem, and the best thing about widgets is that they are easy to write. So let's get started!

Summary

Dashboard widgets zoom into place with the touch of a keystroke and provide access to information on your computer, your network, and the Internet. Because widgets are based on familiar web technologies, they are easy to create. Over a thousand widgets have already been uploaded to Apple's Dashboard website with more coming in every day — everything from Asteroid Run to Wikipedia. Because they run inside of Dashboard, you can create widgets that look more like applications than web pages because you aren't limited to a rectangular browser window.

In this chapter, you learned to:

❑   Manage widgets to reduce scrolling

❑   Install widgets using the Widget Installer

❑   Reload widgets whenever you make changes

In Chapter 2, you look inside one of Apple's example widgets to see how it is created from different source and image files. You also look at how to bundle the files to make an executable widget and how to install the widget to test it.

Before you move on to Chapter 2, you may want to work through the exercises below to check your understanding of the concepts in this chapter. The answers to the exercises are in Appendix A.

Exercises

1.   What were the code names of OS X 10.0 and 10.1?

2.   Why do you have to keep a copy of your widget in your development area?

3.   What's a Unixy way to describe the location of your Widget folder, not the System's Widget folder?

The Basics of Widgetry

In Chapter 1, you learned about Dashboard and Dashboard widgets as well as how the Widget Installer works. Now you look under the hood and see how widgets are assembled before moving on to writing a widget. In this chapter, you examine the individual components of some Tiger widgets to see how they are made as well as learn how to put together an example widget.

When you look under the hood of these widgets — where you can easily see the source code and how widgets are constructed — you can learn how to access the filesystem and files, how to use Core Image, how to pull information from the Internet, and how to perform calculations.

By the end of this chapter, you will know:

❑   What a widget is composed of

❑   How to create an Info.plist file

❑   How to bundle your widget

What a Widget Is Composed Of

Widgets are based on a set of standard web technologies that you may already know. A widget is based on HTML pages and HTML provides the structure for the widget.

Just as any good web page contains graphics, a widget has graphic elements to give it a user interface. These are Portable Network Graphics (PNG) files. A widget has a graphic file for the icon that is displayed in the Widget Bar. It has at least one graphic file for its user interface. If the widget has preferences, it may have a graphic file for the back of the widget. If a widget has a very complicated interface, it may have a number of graphic files. You can see this by looking at the contents of the Weather widget. To do this:

1.   Open the /Library/Widgets/ directory on your system.

2. Find the Weather widget and Control-click it. A contextual pop-up menu appears (Figure 2-1).

Figure 2-1

If you have a mouse with multiple buttons, you can typically right-click an item to display the contextual menu.

3. Select Show Package Contents from the menu. A new Finder window opens with the contents of the widget (Figure 2-2).

Figure 2-2

> **On OS X, applications are usually bundles and you can see the contents of the application with the Show Package Contents command.**

At the root level of the widget directory, you see a Default.png file and an Icon.png file. The Icon.png is the icon that appears in the Widget Bar at the bottom of Dashboard. The Default.png file contains the Weather widget interface that you see whenever you add it to Dashboard. Most widgets have these two PNG files. In the Weather widget, there's also an Images folder.

4. Open the Images folder. When you look around in the folder, you see a weather_backside.png file. Open this file in Preview and notice that it is the image you see whenever you flip the Weather widget over to change the preferences. The Weather widget is one of the more graphically interesting widgets. Notice that it has separate image files for the top, middle, and bottom of the widget for either night or day. Whenever you are checking the weather at night, the interface changes to match the time of day. If you look in the Minis folder, you find the different weather icons for clouds, rain, snow, and other weather conditions that appear above the temperature in the widget. Look in the Icons folder to find the images that appear in the top middle of the Weather widget. For instance, the moon appears at the top of the widget at night and the sun, during the day.

In addition to HTML and PNG files, widgets all have Cascading Style Sheets (CSS). These CSS files provide the design for the widget. Granted widgets are usually just one web page, but the presentation elements that CSS brings to web pages still apply. Finally, JavaScript provides the widget's functionality. Any widget with preferences contains some basic JavaScript to control flipping the widget over.

Besides these standards, a widget has an XML property list, like most OS X applications, which provides Dashboard with information about the widget. Let's look at each one of these components in more detail to see how they fit together.

HTML, CSS, and JavaScript

To get a better sense of how all of these pieces work together, you should assemble a widget. If you have installed the Xcode developer tools, you will find example widgets in the /Developer/Examples/Dashboard/Sample Code/folder. Copy the Contents folder from the Fortune folder to your Documents folder where you can modify it. You may want to rename it Fortune.

Organizing your development files is a matter of personal preference. However you decide to organize your files, you should be consistent — it makes things easier to find — and you should back them up regularly — trying to recreate code is a bear.

Open the folder you copied and see that the Fortune widget has the CSS, HTML, JavaScript, Default .png, and Icon.png files (Figure 2-3). The HTML, CSS, and JavaScript files aren't required to have the same names or have the same name as the widget, but it does make it easier to keep track of the files as you are developing a widget.

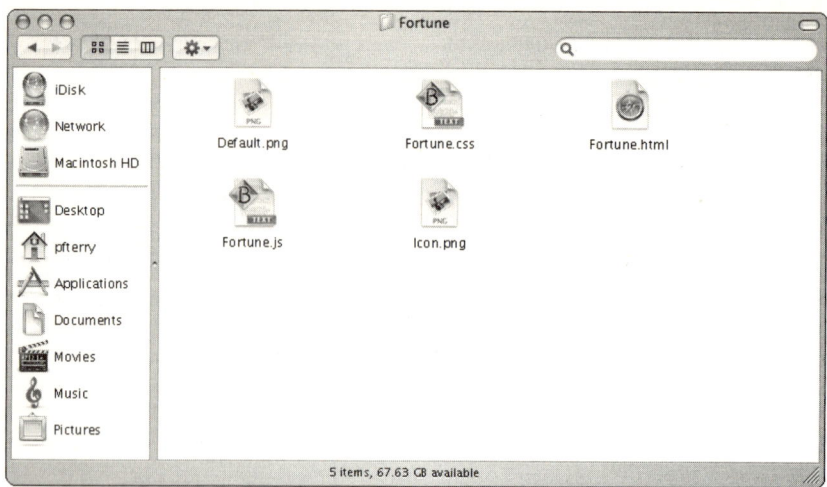

Figure 2-3

HTML

Open Fortune.html file in your favorite text editor so you can look at the source.

If you use Text Edit, you'll need to launch Text Edit, select Open from the File menu, and then click the Ignore Rich Text Commands before you select Fortune.html. Otherwise, you will see rendered HTML and not the HTML source.

You'll see the following HTML file:

```
<!--

Copyright © 2005, Apple Computer, Inc.  All rights reserved.
NOTE:  Use of this source code is subject to the terms of the Software
License Agreement for Mac OS X, which accompanies the code.  Your use
of this source code signifies your agreement to such license terms and
conditions.  Except as expressly granted in the Software License Agreement
for Mac OS X, no other copyright, patent, or other intellectual property
license or right is granted, either expressly or by implication, by Apple.

-->

<html>
<head>

<!-- The CSS file for this widget -->
<style type="text/css">
  @import "Fortune.css";
```

```
</style>

<!-- The JavaScript for this widget -->
<script type='text/javascript' src='Fortune.js' charset='utf-8'/>

</head>
<body onclick="next()"> <!-- If a click occurs anywhere on this widget, go to the
next fortune -->
  <img src="Default.png">                    <!-- The fortune cookie/paper image -->
  <div id="quote">Click here to obtain a fortune.</div>  <!-- Basic placeholder
text -->

</body>
</html>
```

Notice that the Fortune.html file has the typical source structure of any web page. The top portion of the file is Apple's copyright information inside of a comment block set off by `<!--` and `-->`. If you glance down the rest of the file, you'll see comments marking other sections. The file also begins and ends with HTML tags and it contains head and body sections. The links to the CSS and JavaScript files are included in the head section. For the CSS file, the style is given `type=text/css` and the Fortune.css file is included using an import directive. The head section also contains the link to the Fortune.js file. You look at the CSS and JavaScript files more closely in the following sections.

The body section of the Fortune.html file contains an action for clicking in the widget, a link to the image file, and a placeholder for the fortune text that appears in the Fortune widget. The onclick command in the body of the file takes you to the next fortune whenever you click anywhere within the widget. The Default.png is linked to the widget through an `<img src="">` tag. Because the image file has the name Default.png and it is linked through the Fortune.html file, it is used as the interface for the widget. The `div id="quote"` is the placeholder for the fortune that is inserted whenever you click the widget, and the default phrase "Click here to obtain a fortune." is inserted inside the `div` tags.

CSS

Open the Fortune.css file to see the style sheet for the widget. Like the Cascading Style Sheet for any web page, Fortune.css controls the look and placement of text in your widget. For the Fortune widget, the Cascading Style Sheet places the text in a very specific location. If you're familiar with Cascading Style Sheets, you'll see all of the familiar elements in the file.

The Apple copyright information is included at the top of the file in CSS-style comments, which are similar to C/C++ comments. The file also contains the selectors for the body and the quote of the HTML file. The declaration block for the body selector contains only the default margin setting of 0.

```
/*

Copyright © 2005, Apple Computer, Inc.  All rights reserved.
NOTE:  Use of this source code is subject to the terms of the Software
License Agreement for Mac OS X, which accompanies the code.  Your use
of this source code signifies your agreement to such license terms and
```

```
conditions.  Except as expressly granted in the Software License Agreement
for Mac OS X, no other copyright, patent, or other intellectual property
license or right is granted, either expressly or by implication, by Apple.

*/

body {
  margin: 0;
}

#quote {
  font: 10px "Lucida Grande" ;
  font-weight: bold;
  color: gray;
  text-shadow: white 0px 1px 0px;
  position: absolute;
  top: 111px;
  left: 75px;
  width: 165px;
  opacity: 1.0;
}
```

All of the formatting for the quote that is going to appear in the widget and the placeholder text is contained in the quote selector. The font and style for the font is set in the first four elements: 10pt. Lucida
Grande, bold style, gray color, with a white text shadow that has a 1 pixel vertical offset. The next four
elements set the text position on the widget. With an absolute position, the top, left, and width settings
place the text inside of the fortune paper (Figure 2-4). The top position is given in pixels and is the distance from the top of the fortune cookie to the top of the fortune paper. The left setting is the distance in
pixels from the left side of the fortune cookie to the right side of the smiley face on the fortune cookie
paper with a few pixels offset. The width setting places the fortune inside the fortune paper between the
two smiley faces. The last element determines the opacity of the text: in this case, the default setting of
100 percent.

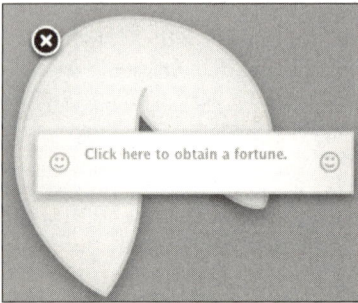

Figure 2-4

Though Cascading Style Sheets aren't the subject of this book, seeing the relationship between the
Default.png image file and the CSS file helps you understand how the widget is constructed.

JavaScript

Open the Fortune.js file to see the JavaScript code for the Fortune widget. You can see that it is divided into two sections: the Fortune-specific code that drives the widget and the animation code. Using a plugin, the widget retrieves a fortune. Once it has the fortune, the script uses the animation in the animation portion of the script to replace the existing fortune. If there is a problem with the widget plugin, the JavaScript sends an alert to the console. The second half of the JavaScript provides the animation for the switch from the old to new fortune. The script sets the start time for the animation, the duration of the animation, and the beginning and final opacity.

```
/*

Copyright © 2005, Apple Computer, Inc.  All rights reserved.
NOTE:  Use of this source code is subject to the terms of the Software
License Agreement for Mac OS X, which accompanies the code.  Your use
of this source code signifies your agreement to such license terms and
conditions.  Except as expressly granted in the Software License Agreement
for Mac OS X, no other copyright, patent, or other intellectual property
license or right is granted, either expressly or by implication, by Apple.

*/

/**************************/
// Fortune-specific code
// This code drives the Fortune widget
/**************************/

// swap
//
// Swaps out the current fortune for a new one.  Uses the Obj-C/JavaScript widget
// plugin to get the new fortune.
function swap() {
  if (FortunePlugin) {
    FortunePlugin.logMessage("calling getFortune...");        send a message to
console via the widget plugin
    var line = FortunePlugin.getFortune();          // get a fortune via the
widget plugin
    FortunePlugin.logMessage("getFortune returned \"" + line + "\"");
    document.getElementById("quote").innerHTML = line;        // drop in the new
fortune
  }
  else {
    alert("Widget plugin not loaded.");
  }
}

// next
//
// Performs the transition from the current fortune to the next one.
function next()
```

```
{
  hideContent();          // fades out the current fortune
  setTimeout("swap();",500);     // swaps in the new fortune
  setTimeout("showContent();",550);  // fades in the new fortune
}

/*************************/
// Animation code
// Handles the fades in and out
/*************************/

var animation = {duration:0, starttime:0, to:1.0, now:1.0, from:0.0,
firstElement:null, timer:null};

function showContent()
{

    if (animation.timer != null)      / reset the animation timer value, in case a
value was left behind
    {
      clearInterval (animation.timer);
      animation.timer  = null;
    }

    var starttime = (new Date).getTime() - 13;   // set it back one frame

    animation.duration = 500;      / animation time, in ms
    animation.starttime = starttime;     / specify the start time
    animation.firstElement = document.getElementById ('quote');      / specify the
element to fade
    animation.timer = setInterval ("animate();", 13);             / set the
animation function
    animation.from = animation.now;    / beginning opacity (not ness. 0)
    animation.to = 1.0;         / final opacity
    animate();          // begin animation

}

function hideContent()
{
    if (animation.timer != null)
    {
      clearInterval (animation.timer);
      animation.timer  = null;
    }

    var starttime = (new Date).getTime() - 13;

    animation.duration = 500;
    animation.starttime = starttime;
    animation.firstElement = document.getElementById ('quote');
    animation.timer = setInterval ("animate();", 13);
    animation.from = animation.now;
    animation.to = 0.0;
```

```
            animate();

}

function animate()
{
  var T;
  var ease;
  var time = (new Date).getTime();


  T = limit_3(time-animation.starttime, 0, animation.duration);

  if (T >= animation.duration)
  {
    clearInterval (animation.timer);
    animation.timer = null;
    animation.now = animation.to;
  }
  else
  {
    ease = 0.5 - (0.5 * Math.cos(Math.PI * T / animation.duration));
    animation.now = computeNextFloat (animation.from, animation.to, ease);
  }

  animation.firstElement.style.opacity = animation.now;
}


// these functions are utilities used by animate()

function limit_3 (a, b, c)
{
    return a < b ? b : (a > c ? c : a);
}

function computeNextFloat (from, to, ease)
{
    return from + (to - from) * ease;
}
```

Property Lists

If duct tape holds the universe together, property lists are the OS X equivalent. The property list is a Unicode text file written in the Extensible Markup Language (XML). Property lists on OS X are used to store information for just about everything. If you look inside the Preferences folder of the Library for your account, you can see property list files (with the .plist extension), named in reverse domain fashion, for the applications that you've installed. Property lists in applications or widgets store information about the bundles and their contents. The Info.plist file inside of a widget's bundle contains information about the configuration of the widget that Dashboard uses whenever the widget is activated. Among other things, the property list provides the name, the main HTML file, the location of the close box, and the size of the widget. Each one of these items is specified by using a widget property key.

If you look at the Info.plist file for the Weather widget shown in Figure 2-5, you'll see the property key names in the left column and the property value in the right column. For instance, the CFBundleName and CFBundleDisplayName are the name of the widget and have the value Weather. CFBundleDisplayName can't be the same as another widget or the Widget Installer tries to replace the widget with the same name. The property key MainHTML is the filename of the Weather widget's HTML file and is given the value Weather.html.

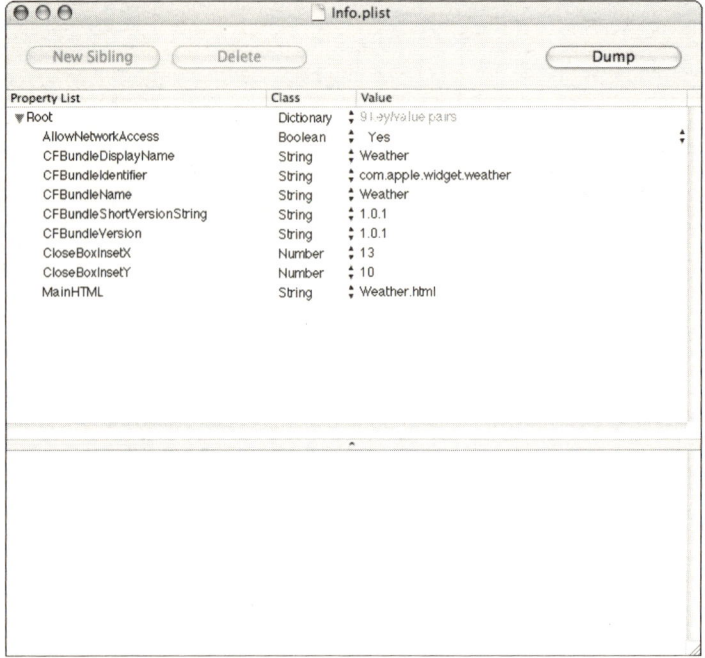

Figure 2-5

Widget Properties

If you look at the property lists of Apple's widgets or widgets from the Dashboard Downloads website, you'll see a number of different properties. The widget property keys that you will use most often are listed in the table below along with the type of property, whether it is optional or required, and a brief description. You can also find a list of the properties on Apple's Developer website (http://developer.apple.com/) in the Runtime Configuration Guidelines doc.

Key	Type	Use	Description
AllowFileAccess OutsideOfWidget	Boolean	Optional	Specifies if the widget can access the filesystem outside of the widget. Access is limited by the user's permissions.
AllowFullAccess	Boolean	Optional	Specifies if the widget can access the filesystem, Web Kit, and standard browser plugins, Java applets, network resources, and the command-line utilities.

Key	Type	Use	Description
AllowInternet Plugins	Boolean	Optional	Specifies if the widget can access Web Kit and standard browser plugins, such as QuickTime.
AllowJava	Boolean	Optional	Specifies if the widget can access Java applets.
AllowNetwork are Access	Boolean	Optional	Specifies if the widget can access any resources that not file-based, including those through the network.
AllowSystem	Boolean	Optional	Specifies if the widget can access command-line utilities using the widget script object.
AllowMultiple Instances	Boolean	Optional	Tells Dashboard that it is okay to have more than one copy of the widget open.
Backwards Compatible ClassLookup	Boolean	Optional	Tells Dashboard to use the copy of AppleClasses in the widget for 10.4 to 10.4.2 systems.
CloseBoxInsetX	Number	Optional	Specifies the offset for the location of the widget close box on the x-axis. Positive values move the close box toward the right of the widget. The number must be between 0 and 100.
CloseBoxInsetY	Number	Optional	Specifies the offset for the location of the widget close box on the y-axis. Positive values move toward the bottom of the widget. The number must be between 0 and 100.
Font	Dictionary	Optional	This key contains an array of strings. Each string is the name of a font included within the widget bundle. The font files must be located at the root of the widget.
Height	Number	Optional	This key contains a number indicating the height of the widget, measured in pixels.
MainHTML	String	Required	This key contains a string with the relative path to the widget's main HTML file. This file is the implementation file of the widget. It will not load without this key set. Remember that the path to the file is case sensitive.
Plugin	String	Optional	This key contains a string with the name of the custom plugin used by the widget. Plugins must be located inside of the widget bundle. Fortune's SimplePlugin, which you look at later, is an example of a widget plugin.
Width	Number	Optional	This key contains a number indicating the width of the widget, measured in pixels.
CFBundle Identifier	String	Required	This key contains a string that uniquely identifies the widget in reverse domain format. If this is absent, the widget won't run.

Table continued on following page

Key	Type	Use	Description
CFBundleName	String	Required	This key contains a string with the name of your widget. This string must match the name of the widget bundle on disk without the .wdgt file extension.
CFBundleDisplay Name	String	Required	This key contains the name of the widget that is displayed in the Widget Bar and the Finder.
CFBundleVersion	String	Required	This key contains the build version number of the widget.
CFBundleShort VersionString	String	Optional	This key contains the formal version number of the widget.

You'll notice when you compare the items in the preceding table with the Info.plist of the Weather widget in Figure 2-5 that the latter does not contain the optional height and width keys. When these two keys are omitted, Dashboard automatically sizes the widget based on the height and width of the Default.png image.

Also note the CFBundleShortVersionString key in the Weather widget Info.plist. Though it is the same as the CFBundleVersion in this table, the CFBundleShortVersionString normally represents a formal version number that doesn't change with every build. The CFBundleVersion is the number that would change with every build.

These properties are discussed in more detail as they are used in the examples for the remaining chapters. Chapter 11 is devoted to a discussion of the Access keys that give your widget access to information in the filesystem, on the network, and on the Internet.

Creating Property Lists

Because a property list is just an XML file, you can edit it with any text editor. While you could use a word processor for editing your code—I have a friend who used to write all of his C code with WordStar, the word processor—most word processors leave formatting cruft in their files, so you are better off using an editor that defaults to text format.

You may also want to pick a text editor that can save your file in Unicode, or at least UTF-8, format. Some text editors, like BBEdit, can save in the various Unicode formats and are ideal for editing XML and HTML markup files. Some text editors, and BBEdit is one of these, will color the syntax, making the XML a little easier to read (Figure 2-6).

If you are not familiar with XML syntax, or if you would rather use an XML-specific editor, you can find a number of third-party tools. One of the utilities included with Xcode is the Property List Editor, which you can find in /Developer/Applications/Utilities/. The Property List Editor provides you with a hierarchical representation of the XML file (Figure 2-7).

When you create the property list for your widget, you need to include the required keys and then any of the optional keys that your widget needs. If you are editing your property list in a text editor, you need to put the XML header at the top of the file.

```
<?xml version="1.0" encoding="UTF-8"?>
<!DOCTYPE plist PUBLIC "-//Apple Computer//DTD PLIST 1.0//EN"
"http://www.apple.com/DTDs/PropertyList-1.0.dtd">
<plist version="1.0">
```

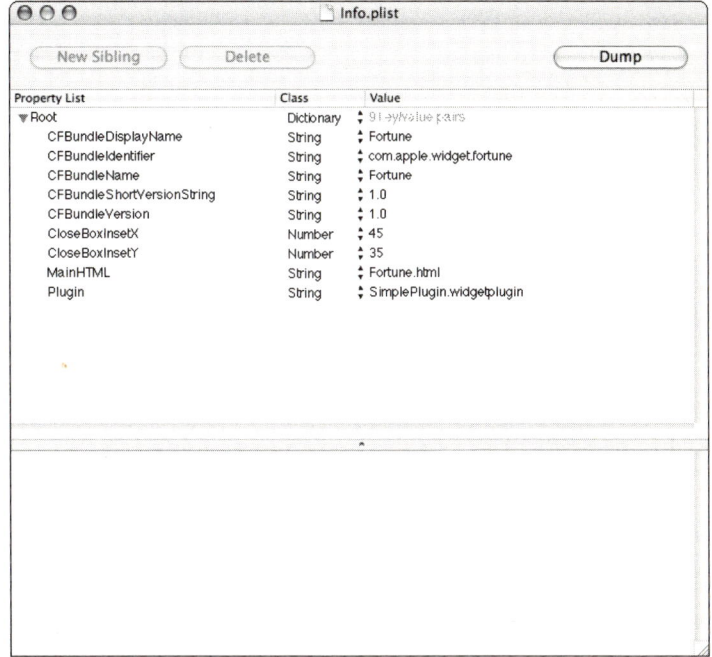

Figure 2-6

Figure 2-7

Begin with a root element and give it the class Dictionary. Dictionary is one of the collection types and it contains the array of child properties that you add below it. Then you begin to add the required property keys, their types, and their values under the root. Once you have the required keys in your property list, you can add the optional keys that your widget requires. If you are creating a widget that requires network access, for instance, and you don't include the appropriate property key, your widget won't be able to get to the network until the key is added to the property list.

Try It Out   **Creating the Info.plist for the Fortune Widget**

Now that you know about the Info.plist file and understand the property keys that appear in the file, you can create an Info.plist file for the Fortune widget. Unless you are familiar with XML and want to create the file in a text editor, use the Property List Editor included with Xcode (/Developer/Applications/Utilities/Property List Editor).

1.   Run the Property List Editor. When it starts up, it automatically opens a blank property list.

2.   Click the New Root button at the top of the window. The Root item is created and assigned the type "Dictionary."

3.   Click the triangle next to Root to show the rest of the list as you create it.

4.   Click the New Child button at the top of the window and a new item is added under Root (Figure 2-8). Enter CFBundleDisplayName as the property name and "Fortune" for the value.

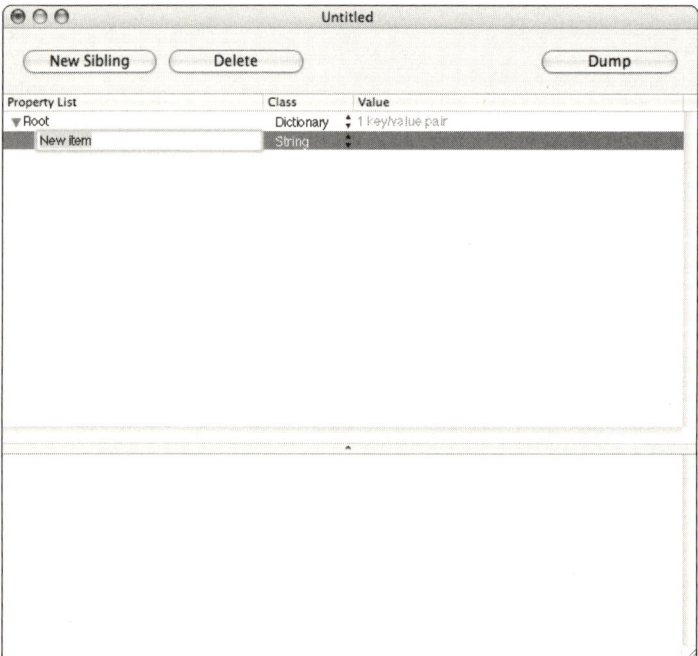

Figure 2-8

5. Notice that the button at the top of the window has changed from New Child to New Sibling because the CFBundleDisplayName property is selected. Click the New Sibling button and enter CFBundleIdentifier as the property name and "com.apple.widget.fortune" as the value.

6. Click the New Sibling button and enter **CFBundleName** as the property name and **Fortune** as the value.

7. Click the New Sibling button and enter **CFBundleVersion** as the property name and **1.0** as the value.

8. Click the New Sibling button and enter **CloseBoxInsetX** as the property name. Click the arrows next to the Class column for this property and select Number from the pop-up menu (Figure 2-9). You'll see that a zero is placed in the Value field. Enter **45** for the property value.

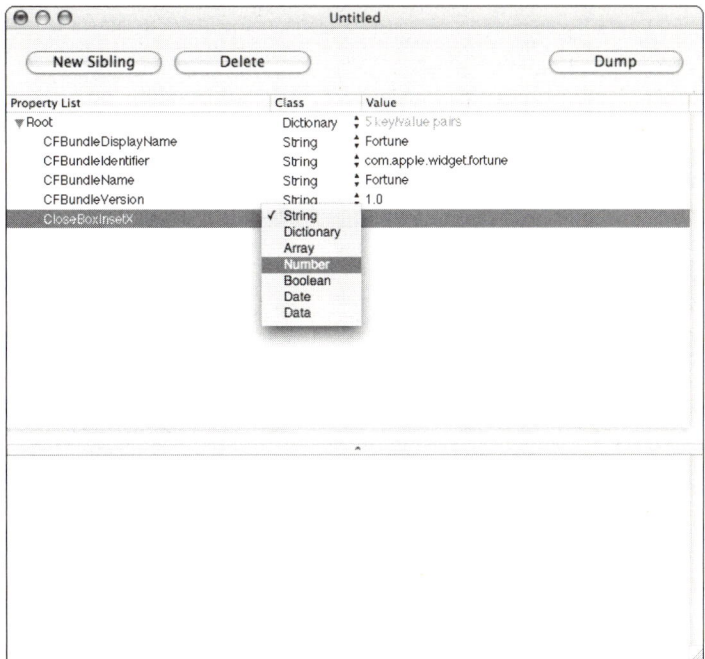

Figure 2-9

9. Click the New Sibling button and enter CloseBoxInsetY for the property name. Click the arrows next to the Class column for this property and select Number from the pop-up menu. Enter **35** as the property value.

10. Click the New Sibling button and enter MainHTML for the property name and enter **Fortune.html** as the property value.

11. Click the New Sibling button to enter the last property for the Info.plist file. Enter **Plugin** as the property name and enter **SamplePlugin.widgetplugin** as the value. This is the plugin that the JavaScript calls to get the new quote.

Case Matters: Because OS X is at base BSD — a Unix-variant operating system — upper- and lower-case matter in filenames. Enter fortune.html or samplePlugin.widgetPlugin for the last two steps and your widget won't work.

How It Works

Each of the properties in the Info.plist file links the files within the widget, provides Dashboard information about how to display the widget, or supplies the Finder with information about the widget. CFDisplayName tells Dashboard what name to place beneath the widget in the Widget Bar. MainHTML tells Dashboard what the widget's HTML file is. The Plugin property tells Dashboard the name of the plugin that the widget needs. CFBundleName and CFBundleVersion tell the Finder what name to use, if the Hide extension checkbox is selected, and what version information to show when you get information about the widget.

The CloseBoxInsetX and CloseBoxInsetY properties tell Dashboard where to place the close box in relation to the widget's image. Dashboard displays a close box for each widget when you display the Widget Bar. It takes the values from the widget's Info.plist file to move the close box closer to the right side of the widget along the x-axis and closer to the bottom of the widget along the y-axis. If the values aren't correct, the close box will hover in space next to the widget (Figure 2-10).

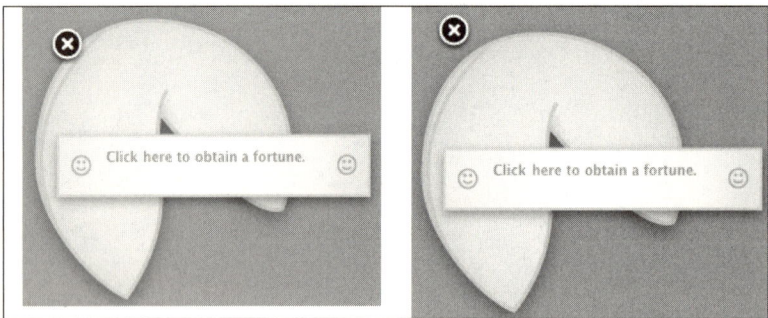

Figure 2-10

Icons and Images

As you've seen in the preceding sections, a widget's interface comes from its image files. Each widget must have two image files: the default image and an icon. Both image files must be in Portable Network Graphics (PNG) format. They must be called Icon.png and Default.png, and they both must have initial capital letters.

The Icon.png file is used for the widget's icon in the Widget Bar in Dashboard and also in the Widget widget when you install it. The Default.png file is the image that the user sees. In Figure 2-10, for example, the Default.png image is the fortune cookie. As you saw when you examined the Weather widget previously, the Default.png file was a rectangle with areas on it to contain the temperature and weather graphics for each day of the week. Some widgets have preferences, and they have an additional image for the back side of the widget—more about those in a later chapter.

How to Bundle Your Widget

Taking apart a widget is almost like dissecting a magic trick. The trick isn't quite as magical as when you saw it for the first time without knowing its mechanics, but you can better appreciate the skill of the magician and the art of the trick. After you dissect a widget, it won't seem as magical, but you understand how all of the pieces fit together. There is still, however, a little magic left for us to explore.

Try It Out   **Bundling the Fortune Widget**

Earlier in this chapter, you copied the Fortune folder from the Dashboard Examples folder. You've been working with this widget in this chapter, so you should be ready to bundle it.

1. Make certain that your Fortune widget folder has the Default.png, Fortune.css, Fortune.html, Fortune.js, and Icon.png files in it and that they are all spelled and capitalized correctly.

2. If you haven't already, place into this folder the Info.plist file that you created earlier.

3. Close the folder and add the .wdgt extension to the end of the folder's name. The Finder asks you if you want to change the folder's name (Figure 2-11).

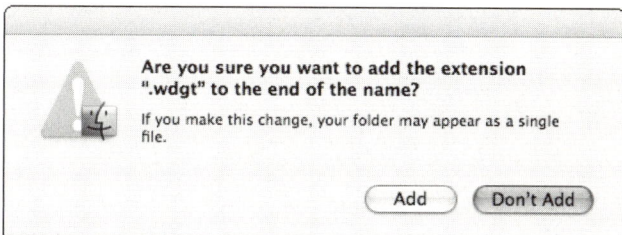

Are you sure you want to add the extension ".wdgt" to the end of the name?

If you make this change, your folder may appear as a single file.

Add   Don't Add

Figure 2-11

4. Click Add to change the name of the folder. You'll see the folder magically take the generic widget icon.

5. You can tweak the widget to make it look more like an application. Control-click the widget and select Get Info from the contextual menu to open the file information window (Figure 2-12).

6. Click the Hide extension checkbox below the name and extension text box. In the Finder, you'll see the extension disappear.

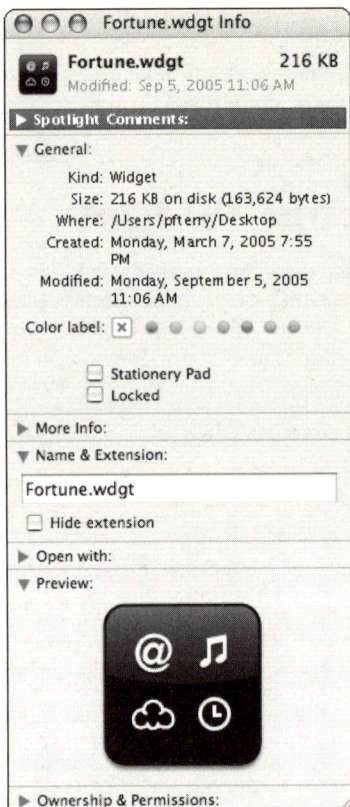

Figure 2-12

How It Works

On Mac OS X, a bundle is a way to package software. The extension appended to the folder tells Finder what kind of bundle it is. If you Get Info on an application in OS X, you'll probably find that the folder name ends with .app and the Hide Extension checkbox is selected. The extension tells the Finder what the bundle is, but the contents and the structure determine how and if the bundled object works. For instance, if you leave the Info.plist file out of the Fortune directory and add .wdgt to the end of the directory name, it looks like a widget in the Finder. If you double-click it, however, the Widget Installer doesn't recognize it as a widget (Figure 2-13), because the properties file that it needs is absent.

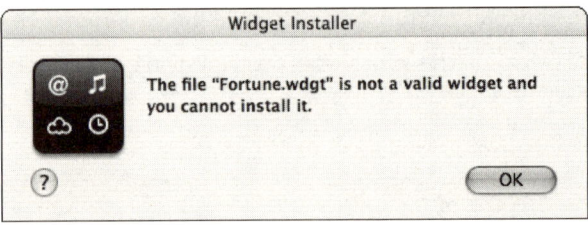

Figure 2-13

A bundle may contain image files, headers, libraries, and executables. Application bundles contain everything that the application needs to run, which may be image files, resources, and executables. Often an application bundle contains the application's documentation. If you show the package contents of an application, you'll see that it is organized a little differently than a widget. All of its files are inside of a Contents folder instead of being at the root level of the application folder. When you look inside of the Contents folder, you'll see that applications have some items in common with widgets. For example, they have Info.plist and version.plist files.

If you double-click the Fortune widget at this point, the Widget Installer installs it in your widgets directory and you are able to see it and add it to Dashboard. However, when you click inside the Fortune cookie, you will not get a new fortune because the plugin is missing. You fix that in Chapter 3.

Summary

Like most Unix systems, OS X is a text-based system. It may look and feel like the comfortable Classic that you've used or seen, but that magic is provided by the use of bundles and property lists. When you double-click an application, it behaves like apps do in Classic, but you aren't double-clicking a binary as you do in Classic. Now you know that it just an appropriately named folder with a structure and property list specific to the kind of bundle it is.

In this chapter, you learned:

- ❑   What a widget is composed of
- ❑   How to create an Info.plist file
- ❑   How to bundle your widget

In Chapter 3, you look at the different development environment options available. Before you turn to Chapter 3, however, you may want to run through these exercises. The answers to the exercises are in Appendix A.

Exercises

1.   How would you measure the area for placing text in your widget?

2.   Which one of Apple's widgets has an Allairports.js file?

3.   If you are organizing the images for your widget inside of a folder, how do you point to them in your HTML, CSS, and JavaScript files?

Widget Development Environment

In Chapter 2, you looked under the hood of widgets to see how they are assembled. You looked at the individual components of some of the widgets to learn how the components work together and how to put together an example widget. This chapter introduces you to the tools you need to create and assemble widgets. While a full-blown development environment is not required, picking the right tools can make creating and debugging easier. You'll take a brief look at third-party debugging tools, but their use will be fully addressed in Chapter 5.

By the end of this chapter, you will know:

- ❏ Programming tools available for developing widgets
- ❏ How to compile a plugin
- ❏ How to use a debugging tool

An Editor and a Browser

Not only are widgets easy to develop, you don't need a fancy development environment. You can use any text editor to create your widget, and you should pick the one that you like to use the most. You may not need a development environment, but you will need an editor that you're comfortable using. Like any coding project, developing a widget follows a regular cycle. If you have developed web pages, you're already familiar with this cycle: Make changes, switch to your browser and reload the page, switch back to your editor and make additional tweaks and changes, and repeat as necessary. Whatever tools you use to develop your widget, they should make the process as smooth and fluid as possible. We'll look at different editors and tools in this chapter.

Among all of the features that development environments provide, one set of features is more important than it is usually given credit for: organization features. In some fashion, most integrated development environments or IDEs, help you organize your files during the development process by keeping them together or keeping track of multiple versions of files. If you aren't using an IDE to develop your widget and your text editor doesn't have any organizational tools built in, you should have a plan or methodology for managing and versioning your files. Maintaining previous versions of your source files becomes even more important as you reach the testing and debugging stage.

You could develop a widget by scattering the files on your desktop, but—if you are like a number of Mac users and me—your OS X desktop is probably littered with every kind of file imaginable: the application you downloaded yesterday, files you need to work on now, and digital pictures from your summer trip. Because the source code, the JavaScript, HTML, and CSS files that make up your widget, eventually need to be in the same folder, you should start by dropping them all in a folder that will become your widget, much as you did with the Fortune widget in Chapter 2. You could place that folder on your desktop, but you may want to create a folder in your home folder called Projects and drop each one of the individual widget folders in it. You can add the Project folder to the sidebar of Finder windows to make it easier to get to your widgets. This organization also works well with Xcode if you are creating plugins for your widgets.

TextEdit and Safari

If you don't want the overhead of an integrated development environment, you can develop your widget with TextEdit. It doesn't give you many fancy text manipulation options or syntax coloring, but TextEdit ships with OS X, has a small memory footprint, and loads quickly. If seeing JavaScript source code and HTML tags and attributes in different colors makes editing easier, you may want to look at some of the other text editors that are available. BBEdit is a popular commercial editor and, like some shareware editors including skEdit, is tuned for website development. If you prefer to go the free route, you can get a copy of TextWrangler from Bare Bones Software or get Aqua Emacs. Both of these editors provide syntax coloring and are primarily developed for text files and programming.

In addition to an editor, you'll need a way to test your widget as you are developing it. You have a couple of options. You can test your widget in Dashboard or in Safari. Dashboard may seem like the obvious place to test your widget, but it has some drawbacks as a testing environment. For starters, you will have to be far enough along in the development that you can install it. This means that in addition to the other source files, your widget will require an Info.plist, a Default.png, and an Icon.png file.

Another issue with testing in Dashboard is that keeping multiple versions of your widget is problematic. You can edit the widget files after it is installed in Dashboard, but you will need to manually make copies of the different versions in case you want to back out of a change that you've made. On the other hand, you can develop your widget outside of Dashboard and install it after you've made changes.

When you install another copy of a widget that you already have installed and open, the Widget Installer warns you that the open copies of the widget will be closed (Figure 3-1). This effectively reloads your widget, so it saves you a step.

Another problem with testing in Dashboard is that you may have to wait for a few moments while Dashboard loads. Whenever you have installed a widget that gets updates from the Internet, Dashboard pauses while those widgets update. When you consider the time it takes to copy and rename the widget before you install and then wait on Dashboard to load, the time for each revision of your widget during development can begin to add up.

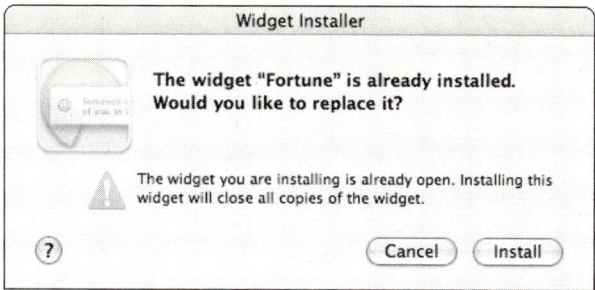

Figure 3-1

You could save yourself some time and begin testing sooner if you test your widget in Safari. You can begin the iterative process with the widget with only the CSS, HTML, and Default.png files. If you open the main HTML file in Safari (Figure 3-2), it displays the same way it does in Dashboard. The widget may not perform in exactly the same way it would under Dashboard, but during the change-test–change-test iterative cycle, you can leave Safari open in the background, then switch to it and reload your widget after you make changes.

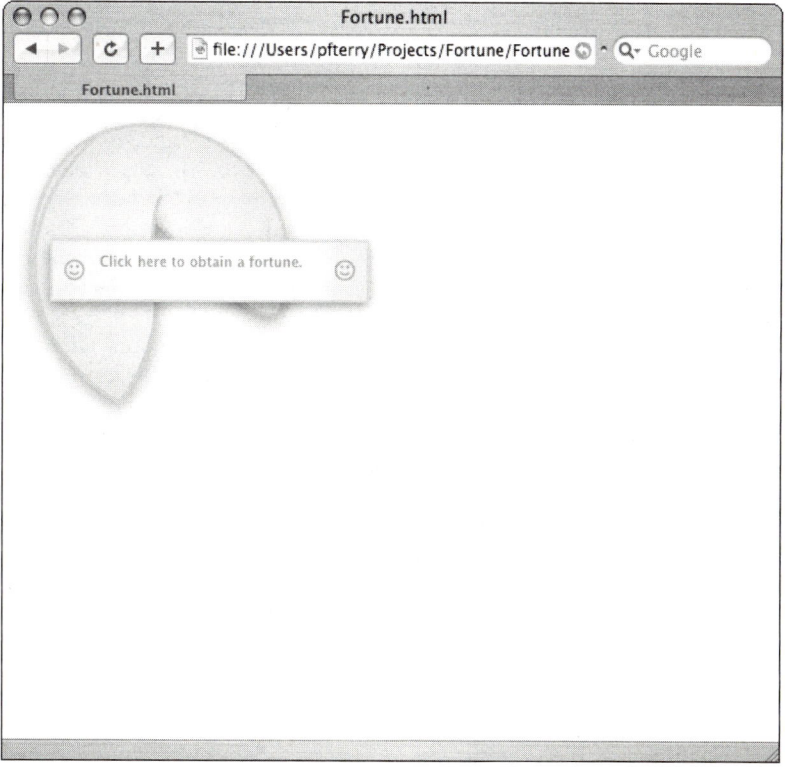

Figure 3-2

Though Safari may let you test most of the functionality of your widget, it won't work for every function. The widget object in JavaScript isn't available in Safari and so any functions that require the widget object will not run in Safari. For instance, your widget won't be able to accomplish any of the following tasks:

❑ Access the user preferences system.

❑ Flip the widget over to access its preferences.

❑ Respond to Dashboard activation events.

❑ Open other applications.

❑ Execute shell scripts or command-line tools.

If your widget relies on any of these functions, you'll need to install it in Dashboard or enable the Dashboard developer mode, which is discussed later in this chapter.

BBEdit

Text editors are almost as numerous as the different features that attract people to them, and everyone has his favorite. One of the most common religious wars on the net (next to what's the best operating system or what's the best programming language) is what the best editor is.

BBEdit is a favorite among the programming and website development crowd on the Mac. It has been around since the early 1990s and has a number of text features that make it great as a code editor. Its Find command supports regular expressions. It can search across files and has function navigation. It also has source code syntax coloring — this includes HTML, CSS, XML, and JavaScript — and support for shell and Perl scripts, and CVS — the Concurrent Versions System. Additionally, BBEdit has a great set of features for web developers. It is able to open and save a page on your web server using FTP or SFTP. It has a Markup menu item that allows you to insert HTML tags into your file by making a menu selection, and it supports previewing the HTML file that you are working directly in a browser.

All of those things make BBEdit a good choice for your widget editor, but one feature in particular makes using BBEdit a brain-dead simple choice: editing hidden files. On a Unix system, hidden files are those that you can't see or don't have permissions to edit. On OS X, hidden files are those down in your Library and the system Library directories where widgets live. If you use the Open Hidden command in BBEdit (Figure 3-3), you are able to open the files inside the Weather widget installed in your System's /Library/Widgets/ directory. If you used the Open command and pointed at the contents of this widget with BBEdit, the files would be grayed out — indicating that you don't have permission to open them. Typically, you must copy the files in these directories to a directory where you have write permissions and then copy them back into the original directory overwriting the original after providing your authentication.

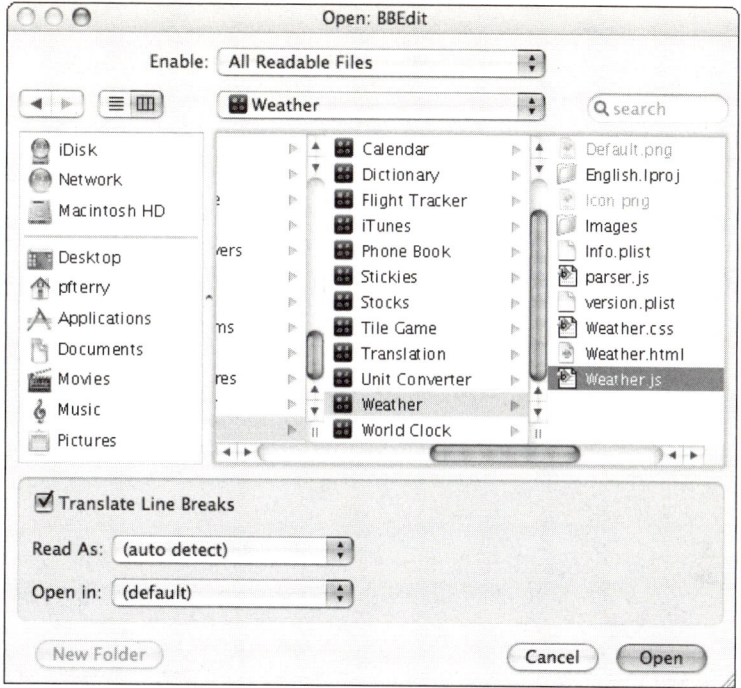

Figure 3-3

More important than being able to open files in the Library directories, you can also save your changes by authenticating. This can really make a difference if you have installed your widget and you need to tweak it. Rather than having to drag the widget out of the Library directory to edit it as you would in TextEdit, you can leave the widget down in the Library directory and open with BBEdit.

Using an Integrated Development Environment

While most of the discussion so far has been about using basic tools for creating widgets, you can also use, and may need, more specialized tools, particularly if you are creating plugins. An Integrated Development Environment (IDE) is a suite of specialized development tools. Most IDEs include a source code editor, a compiler or an interpreter, a debugger, GUI tools, and build automation tools or utilities. You may not need a full-blown IDE to create widgets, but some tools are available if you want to use them. The first third-party IDE for widgets is Widgetarium from Gandreas Software. The granddaddy of IDEs for OS X is Apple's Xcode development environment, which has been around since the beginning of OS X and is regularly updated.

Widgetarium

Widgetarium is specifically for creating Dashboard widgets (Figure 3-4). Like most IDEs, it allows you to create and edit the source files as well as the GUI elements — the PNG files — for your widget. It provides organization for your files and a built-in editor with syntax coloring, code completion, and searching with regular expression support. Besides keeping your files organized, it can install the widget or create a ZIP file of it that you can email to your friends or upload.

Widgetarium also emulates Dashboard so you can run your widget with full support, including the widget object, during development. This means that you don't have to play tricks with Dashboard to load a new version of your widget as you are making changes. It can also redirect the widget to run in Dashboard or a web browser.

Other tools include a Document Object Model (DOM) inspector that allows you to examine the model hierarchy and the node properties and values. You can edit the values, and type in JavaScript that will be executed in the context of your widget. Additionally, Widgetarium has a Console Log so you can watch for errors as your widget is running and see any alerts you have set in your JavaScript. Widgetarium can also open Xcode's Dashboard documents, if you have Xcode installed.

In addition to the development and emulation tools built into Widgetarium, it also has a source level JavaScript debugger that allows you to set break points and step through the JavaScript.

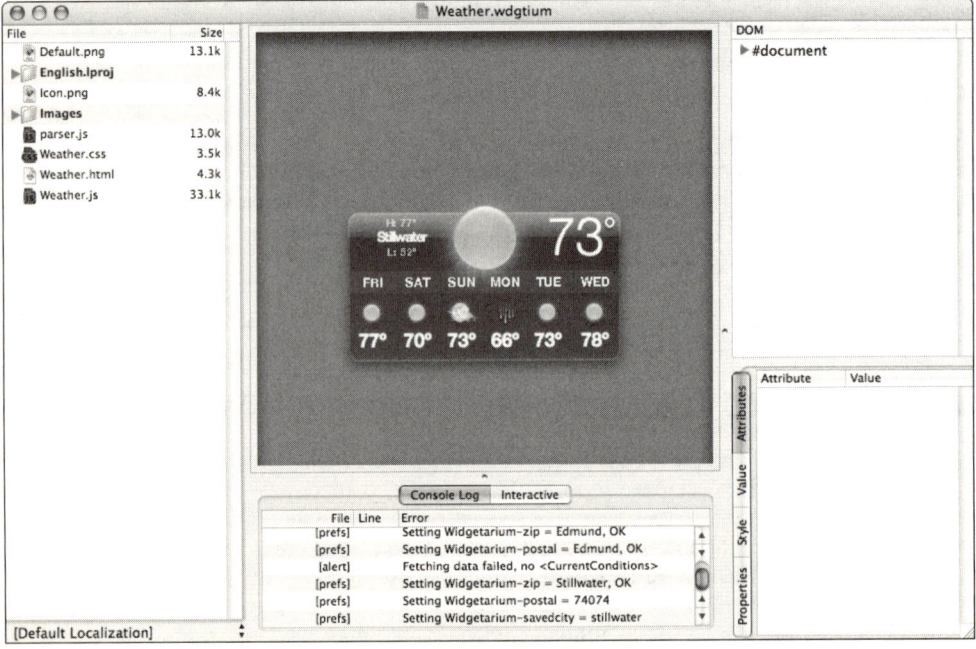

Figure 3-4

Xcode

Apple's Xcode environment is like most development environments; it has an editor, a compiler (gcc), a debugger (gdb), Interface Builder for the creation of a GUI, and a collection of build tools and utilities. gcc and gdb are both open source tools that Apple has wrapped with the Xcode package. Whenever you compile a program in Xcode, it calls gcc. Whenever you step through the debugger in Xcode, it is using gdb. In addition to providing all of the tools that you need to create, build, and debug applications, it also contains all of the documentation that is available on Apple's Developer site.

While Xcode may seem like overkill for creating your widget because you don't have to compile it, Xcode is what you'll need if you want to create a plugin for your widget, or if you want to make use of a plugin that you have the source code for. Let's run Xcode and compile the plugin for the Fortune widget.

Starting Xcode

The first time you run Xcode, an assistant walks you through the initial configuration options. After the welcome window, the second window you see is for building files (Figure 3-5). For example, you can choose to put your compiled plugin and the intermediate files that are created during the build process in the project directory, or you can specify different directories in the text boxes. Putting them in the build directory keeps all of the files together.

Figure 3-5

The last window you see during the initial configuration (Figure 3-6) allows you to specify whether the window states in your projects are saved. In other words, this setting remembers which files you opened and the size and location of their windows. This setting allows you to pick up where you left off quicker.

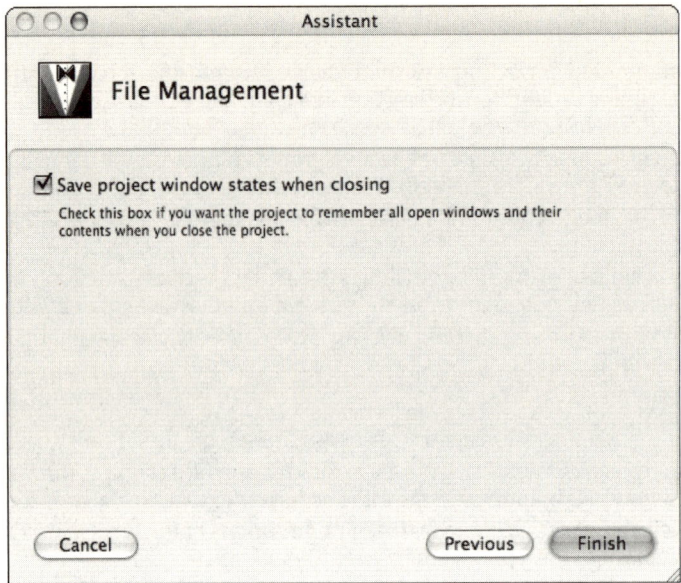

Figure 3-6

Now that you have the Xcode preferences set, you can build the SimplePlugin.

Building a Plugin

When you look in the Fortune folder inside of /Developer/Examples/Dashboard/Sample Code/ Fortune/, you will find a SimplePlugin folder. Copy that folder to your projects directory so you can compile it.

If you want your widget to work on Intel-based Macs as well as PowerPC-based Macs, you will need to compile your plugin as a Universal Binary.

1. In Xcode, select Open from the File menu and navigate to the SimplePlugin folder that you just copied into your projects folder. Select the SimplePlugin.xcode file and click the Open button. If you are running Xcode 2.2, you will see a warning dialog (Figure 3-7).

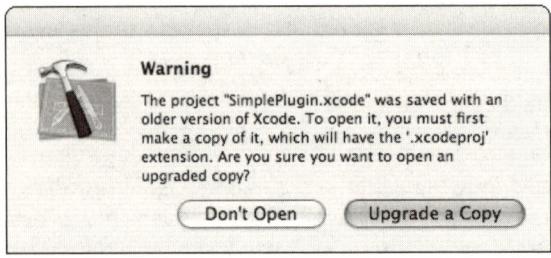

Figure 3-7

If you don't see this warning, you should upgrade your copy of Xcode before you continue.

2. Click the Upgrade a Copy button and Xcode prompts you to save the file with the same name in the SimplePlugin folder (Figure 3-8).

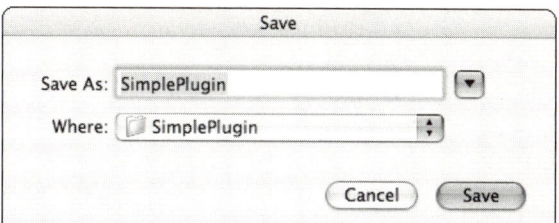

Figure 3-8

3. Click OK. This creates a copy of the project file with the .xcodeproj extension (Figure 3-9).

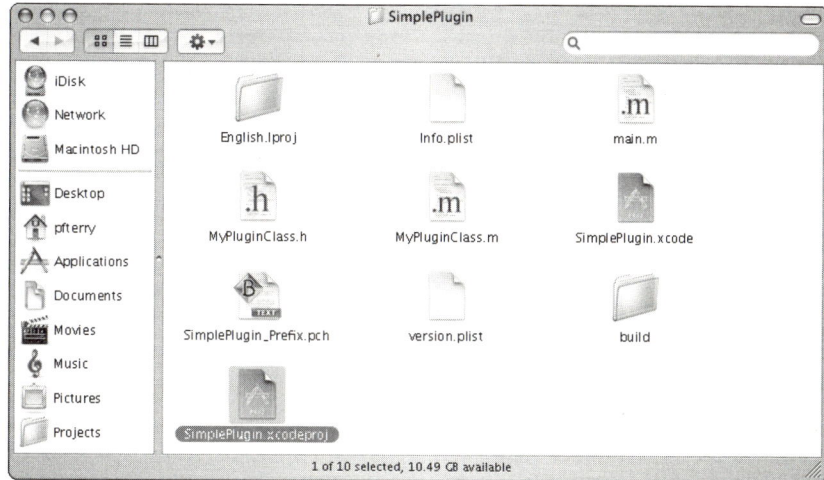

Figure 3-9

The Xcode project window for the SimplePlugin opens (Figure 3-10).

Whenever you create a project in Xcode, you are asked to select the kind of project that you are creating. In the case of this SimplePlugin, I selected a Cocoa Bundle and Xcode automatically added the AppKit, Cocoa, and Foundation frameworks to the project, and I added the WebKit framework. These frameworks are resources that must be compiled with the plugin for it to work. You can also see that Xcode created the Info.plist file for the bundle.

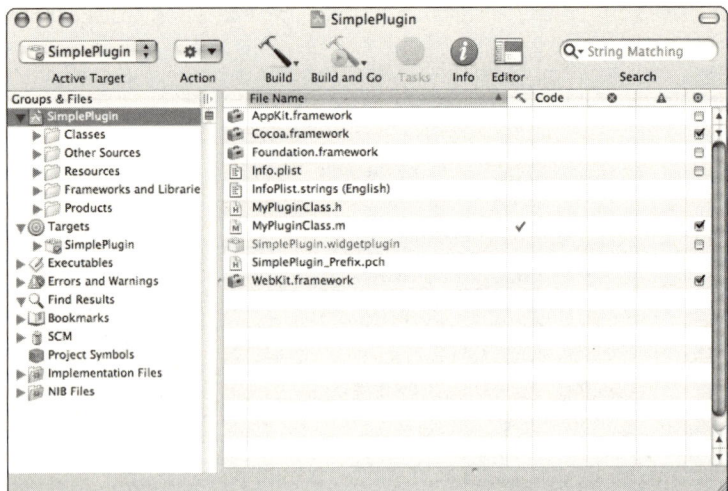

Figure 3-10

Among the Files listed on the right side of the project window, you can see that the SimplePlugin.wid-getplugin is red. This indicates that the plugin hasn't been built yet. If you expand the Targets hierarchy in the Groups & Files list on the left side of the project window, you can see that SimplePlugin is the target for the build. Along the top of the project window are the buttons for actions and utilities. Clicking the Build button compiles and links the different resources and source files to create the plugin. The Info button displays path, name, and target information about the selected file. The Editor button opens the selected file in an editor window.

Now that you have the SimplePlugin ready to compile, let's try out the build process in Xcode to see how it works.

Try It Out   **Compiling a Plugin**

The following example uses Xcode 2.2. The build path referred to in Step 4 will be slightly different in earlier versions.

1. Click the Build button at the top of the window. As the build is running, information about the process is displayed in the status area at the bottom of the project window.

2. After the build is finished, a successful build is reported in the status area (Figure 3-11). If there are any errors, that information appears in the status area.

3. Click the SimplePlugin target in the Groups & Files area to see the contents of the SimplePlugin bundle.

4. Open the Build folder in your SimplePlugin folder and to see two folders: Development and SimplePlugin.build. Open the Development folder and to find the SimplePlugin.widgetplugin folder. This is the plugin that you just built (Figure 3-12).

5. In a separate window, show the contents of the Fortune widget in your /Library/Widgets/ folder and copy the SimplePlugin.widgetplugin into the root level of the Fortune widget.

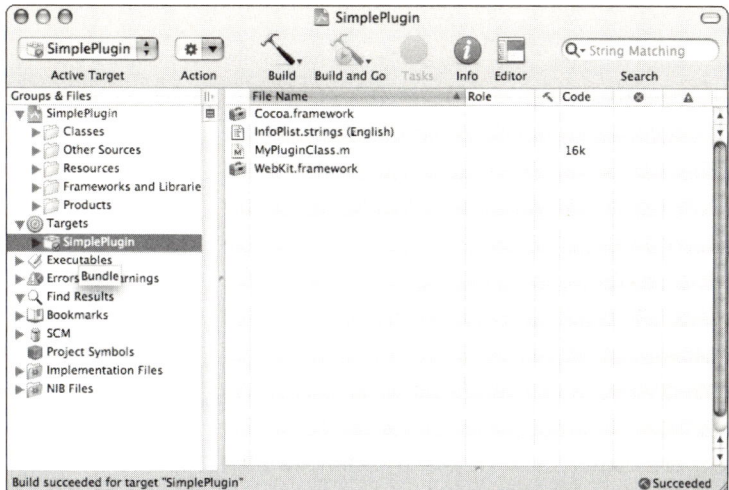

Figure 3-11

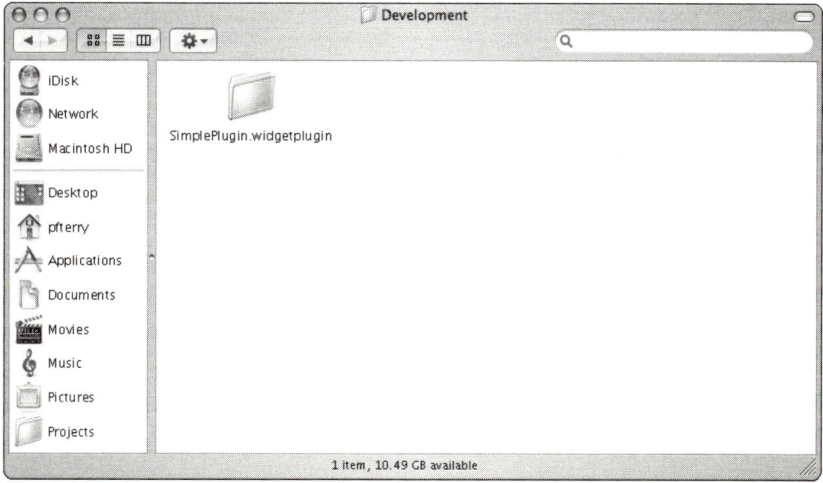

Figure 3-12

How It Works

The widget plugin must be at the root level of the widget bundle with a .widgetplugin filename extension and the filename must match the Plugin key (the shaded area) in the Fortune widget's Info.plist file. The plugin is linked into the widget through the Info.plist file.

```
<?xml version="1.0" encoding="UTF-8"?>
<!DOCTYPE plist PUBLIC "-//Apple Computer//DTD PLIST 1.0//EN"
"http://www.apple.com/DTDs/PropertyList-1.0.dtd">
<plist version="1.0">
```

```
<dict>
  <key>CFBundleDisplayName</key>
  <string>Fortune</string>
  <key>CFBundleIdentifier</key>
  <string>com.apple.widget.fortune</string>
  <key>CFBundleName</key>
  <string>Fortune</string>
  <key>CFBundleShortVersionString</key>
  <string>1.0</string>
  <key>CFBundleVersion</key>
  <string>1.0</string>
  <key>CloseBoxInsetX</key>
  <integer>45</integer>
  <key>CloseBoxInsetY</key>
  <integer>35</integer>
  <key>MainHTML</key>
  <string>Fortune.html</string>
  <key>Plugin</key>
  <string>SimplePlugin.widgetplugin</string>
</dict>
</plist>
```

This key tells Dashboard the name of the plugin, but the JavaScript makes the call to the plugin. The swap function in the Fortune.js file swaps the fortune.

```
function swap() {
  if (FortunePlugin) {
    FortunePlugin.logMessage("calling getFortune...");         // send a message
to console via the widget plugin
    var line = FortunePlugin.getFortune();                     // get a fortune via the
widget plugin
    FortunePlugin.logMessage("getFortune returned \"" + line + "\"");
    document.getElementById("quote").innerHTML = line;         // drop in the new
fortune
  }
  else {
    alert("Widget plugin not loaded.");
  }
}
```

The fortunes that get displayed in the widget are in the plugin. If you look in the MyPluginClass.m file in Xcode, you'll see the fortunes under the NSString quotes.

```
/*********************************************/
// The number of quotes and the quotes themselves; they are randomly chosen
// below and fed back to the Fortune widget
/*********************************************/

enum {
  NUM_QUOTES = 8
};

static NSString *quotes[NUM_QUOTES] = {
```

```
        @"You will be awarded some great honor.",           /cpw
        @"You are soon going to change your present line of work.",     //cpw
        @"You will have gold pieces by the bushel.",            //cpw
        @"You will be fortunate in the opportunities presented to you.",  //cpw
        @"Someone is speaking well of you.",            //Melina
        @"Be direct, usually one can accomplish more that way.",     //Melina
        @"You need not worry about your future.",           //Toni
        @"Generosity and perfection are your everlasting goals.",     //Katherine
    };
```

The placeholder for the fortune appears in the body of the Fortune.html file.

```
<body onclick="next()"> <!-- If a click occurs anywhere on this widget, go to the
next fortune -->

    <img src="Default.png">        <!-- The fortune cookie/paper image -->
  <div id="quote">Click here to obtain a fortune.</div>  s<!-- Basic placeholder
text -->

</body>
```

The placeholder text Click here to obtain a fortune is replaced by the JavaScript from the plugin whenever you click in the widget.

Enabling Dashboard Developer Mode

In addition to using Safari as the development environment, you can also run Dashboard in developer mode so that the widget is always available while you are making changes to it. The advantage of this is that you do not have to activate Dashboard and wait while widgets update. For example, if you have a widget that gets information from the system or an Internet site, you have to wait while the widget refreshes before you can refresh your widget to see the changes you've made. If the widget is always available, you have only to set the focus to the widget by clicking it and then press Command-R to reload it.

To use this technique, you have to enable Dashboard development mode and then drag the widget to the desktop so it is available. To do this, open Terminal and type:

```
defaults write com.apple.dashboard devmode YES
```

followed by a Return. To activate debugging mode after you have executed this command, you must log out and log back in. Once you have logged back in, activate Dashboard by pressing F12 — or the assigned key — and begin dragging the widget. Press F12 again and let go of the mouse button. Dashboard closes and the widget opens.

This is equivalent to having a small Safari window that floats above all of your applications open all of the time. You won't be able to minimize the window and it will not be available in the Dock or the Application Switcher when you cycle through applications. You will be able, however, to use the reload command to refresh the widget.

To move the widget back to Dashboard, begin dragging the widget and press F12. Dashboard activates and when you release the mouse button, the widget will be back inside of Dashboard.

If you don't want to log out and back in to activate developer mode, you can also activate it by killing and restarting the Dock. Do this through the Activity Monitor. Select the Dock in Activity Monitor and click the Quit Process button at the top of the window (Figure 3-13).

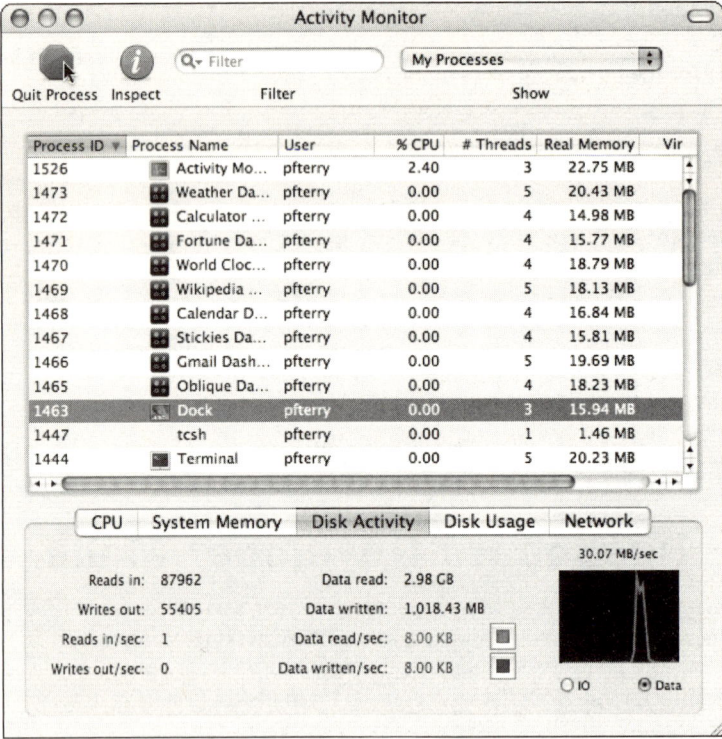

Figure 3-13

You can turn the developer mode off by executing the command again replacing the YES with NO.

```
defaults write com.apple.dashboard devmode NO
```

Leaving developer mode enabled will not have any impact on OS X, but you may want to disable the ability to run widgets outside of Dashboard and return Dashboard to its normal state once you have finished developing your widget.

Debugging Tools

Debugging tools are important for finding elusive problems during development. Debugging can be as simple as following error messages in the Console.log to stepping through the source code and examining the variables to locate problems. Being able to see error messages as you are working helps you identify problems. Usually the error messages tell you what the problem is so that you can fix it in your code. Stepping through the code is slower, but allows you to watch everything that happens in your widget. However, you don't have to purchase a debugger to be able to find and fix problems in your code.

Using Safari as Your Debugger

If you are using Safari as your development environment, you can enable the Debug menu in Safari and use it as your debugger. The Debug menu is a hidden feature that you have to enable to use. You can enable the menu using Terminal by entering the following code and pressing return.

```
defaults write com.apple.safari IncludeDebugMenu 1
```

The next time you open Safari, you will see a Debug menu. You can disable the menu with the same command replacing the 1 with a 0.

```
defaults write com.apple.safari IncludeDebugMenu 0
```

You can also enable the Debug menu without touching Terminal by using an application from Marcel Bresink Software-Systeme called TinkerTool (Figure 3-14). Dr. Bresink's TinkerTool allows you to tweak hidden options in some programs and the operating system. For instance, you can turn on two headed arrows in your scroll bars. TinkerTool has a Safari pane that allows you to change some of the hidden options in the application.

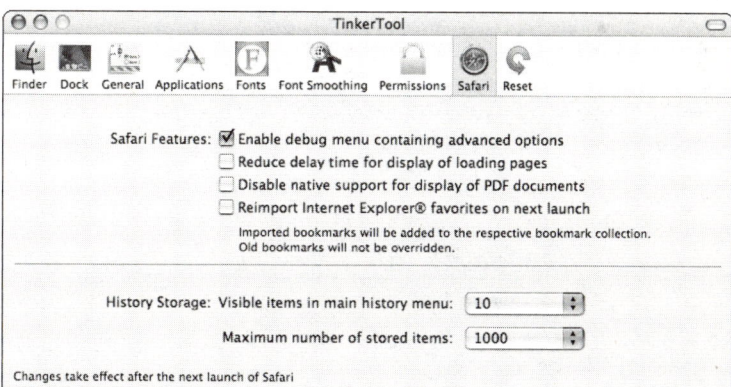

Figure 3-14

When you restart Safari, the Debug menu appears as the last item on the menu bar (Figure 3-15). Select Log JavaScript Exceptions to log as much information as possible about JavaScript errors generated by running your widget in Safari. Select Show JavaScript Console to display the console where you can watch the errors as you test your widget. You'll also notice that you can view the DOM tree from the Debug menu in Safari.

Once you have the JavaScript Console open, you can watch for JavaScript errors. The status bar in the Safari page will also tell you about some errors. For instance, missing file errors will be flagged in the status bar along with information about the error.

Figure 3-15

Third-Party Debugging Tools

Widgetarium's debugger is probably the best and most direct tool for debugging JavaScript in a widget. You can set breakpoints in the JavaScript file and run the widget until you reach the breakpoint and then examine the values of the variables (Figure 3-16).

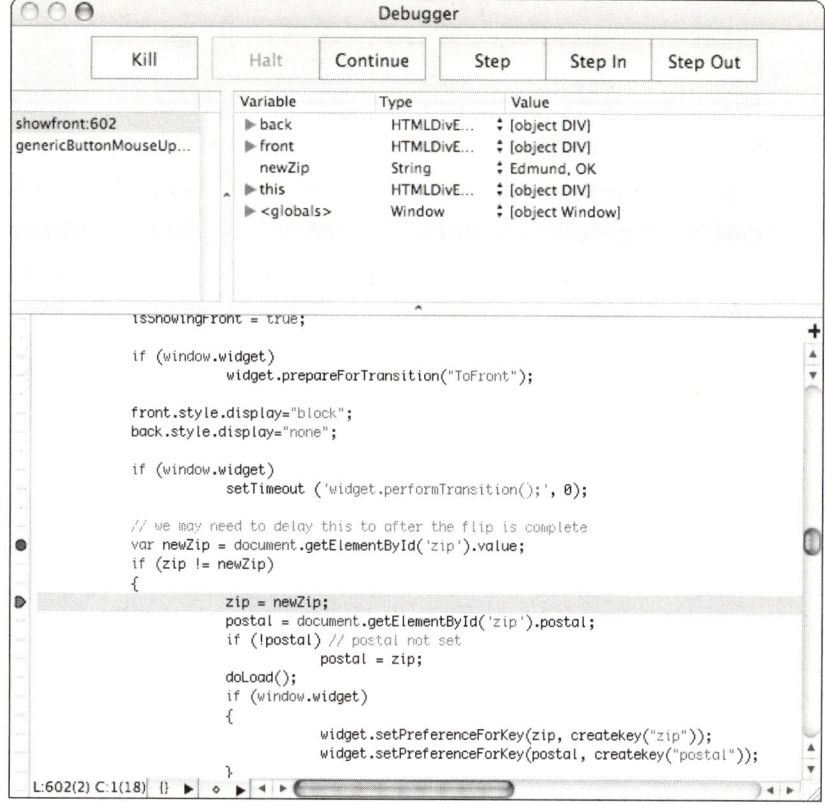

Figure 3-16

From the break point you can step through the code — stepping into, out of, and over calls — or run to the next break point or until complete. Widgetarium also allows you to set trace points in your JavaScript.

Try It Out   Debugging Error Messages

Now that you know a little about the debugging tools that you have at your disposal, let's use one of them to see how an error would appear. To set this up, show the package contents of the installed Fortune widget and remove the SimplePlugin.widgetplugin folder that you installed earlier. If you have the Fortune widget loaded in Dashboard, you will also need to remove it and add it again.

1. Show the JavaScript console by selecting it from Safari's Debug menu. Position the console so you can see it and the Safari window at the same time.

2. Open the Fortune.html file in Safari. With the plugin removed, you should see only the "Click here to obtain a fortune" placeholder text.

3. Click the fortune cookie in the Safari window.

4. Look in the console window and you'll see the error message about the missing plugin (Figure 3-17).

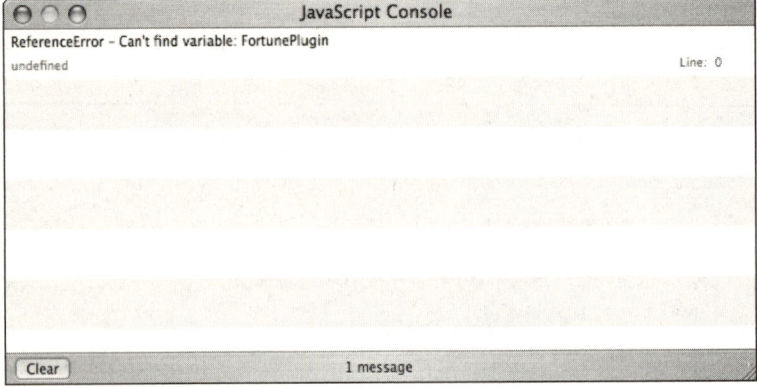

Figure 3-17

How It Works

The JavaScript Console gets any JavaScript errors that are generated in Safari. But these error messages also find their way into the OS X console.log (Figure 3-18). You can see these by opening the Console application in the Utility folder in the Applications folder.

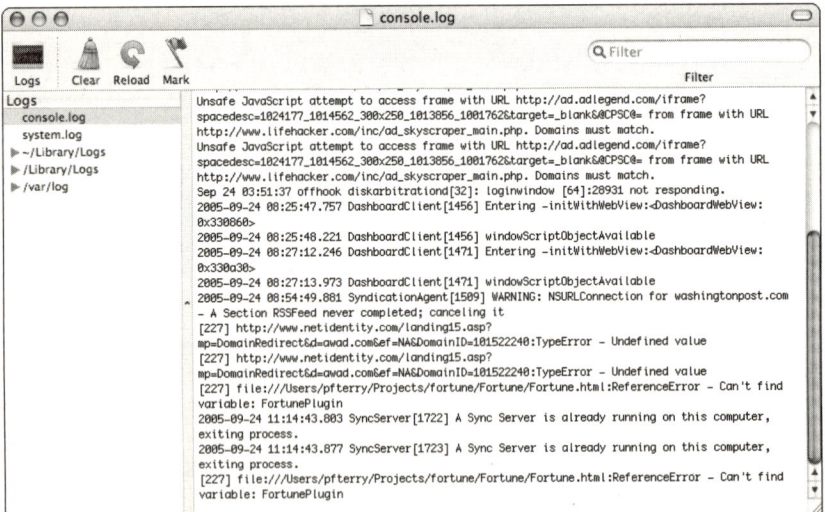

Figure 3-18

To see the console.log, you may need to click the Logs button at the top of the window and select the console.log in the list on the left. The line at the bottom of the window is the error you see in the JavaScript console.

```
[227] file:///Users/pfterry/Projects/fortune/Fortune/Fortune.html:ReferenceError -
Can't find variable: FortunePlugin
```

The line in console.log gives you the file that generated the error. If you look in the Fortune.html file, you'll see the link to the JavaScript file.

```
<!-- The JavaScript for this widget -->
<script type='text/javascript' src='Fortune.js' charset='utf-8'/>
```

As you saw earlier, the JavaScript is supposed to get the fortune from the plugin and place it in the widget.

As you can see, the system's console.log file contains more information about the error than the JavaScript console, so you may prefer to use it when you are trying to track down difficult problems. The downside of using the console.log is that you see information from all of the processes running on your machine. If you have enough screen real estate, you can use Tynsoe's GeekTool preference pane to display the console.log file in your desktop to reduce the number of windows that you have open and allow you to check for problems with a glance at your desktop.

Summary

You could purchase third-party tools for your widget development, but you don't have to. Most of the tools that you need are freely available and ship with OS X. Third-party tools can speed your development cycles because they directly support widget development and may have features that work around system limitations.

In this chapter, you learned:

❏ What the available programming tools are for developing widgets

❏ How to compile a plugin

❏ How to use a debugging tool

In Chapter 4, you create your first widget. Before you turn to Chapter 4, you may want to run through these exercises to review what you've learned in this chapter.

Exercises

1. How do you allow the Fortune widget to use the SimplePlugin?

2. Will the SimplePlugin display the next fortune if you are testing the Fortune widget in Safari?

3. How can you edit a widget installed in the /Macintosh HD/Library/Widgets/ folder?

Creating a Widget

In Chapter 3 you looked at the different tools available for developing Dashboard widgets and learned that you could use any text editor to create your source files and that you could use Safari for testing your widget. You also learned some strategies for testing your widget during development and how to compile a plugin. In this chapter, you create a widget from scratch, building it from the HTML and CSS through the JavaScript functionality.

By the end of this chapter, you will know:

❑ How to begin developing a basic widget

❑ How to use HTML and cascading styles sheets to give shape to the widget

❑ How to incorporate JavaScript into your widget

HTML Beginnings

In the previous chapters you spent some time looking at the way widgets have been assembled, now let's use what you've learned to create a widget from scratch.

You can develop a widget from any website that you visit on a regular basis or routine tasks that can be accessed through the filesystem or performed by script. Or to put it more succinctly, anything you can do in a browser can be developed into a widget.

I check the weather maps for my region of the country at least twice a day. If storms are moving into the area, I may check them once an hour. I can reduce my trips to the browser by creating a widget that displays the maps I always check. Let's call it WeatherMaps.

Beginning the Project

Everyone starts a project from a different point. If you are working with a team of programmers developing a large and complex program for the marketplace, you typically begin with specifications and use case interviews and diagrams. Widgets lend themselves to a much smaller scope.

You don't need a specifications document, but you may want to decide on the functionality of your widget before you begin hacking HTML and JavaScript. This need not be complicated; just a listing of features that you want in the widget and how you want them to behave will suffice. This will change, of course, as you develop your widget and you spend time using it.

The real advantage of developing a list of features (or formal specifications or use case scenarios, for that matter) is that you start thinking about how to organize the development. I know I want this widget to accomplish the following tasks:

❑   It should get the current radar.

❑   It should get the current temps map.

❑   It should get the overnight temps map.

❑   It should get tomorrow's temps map.

I may decide that this is the only way to view weather maps and add a few more to the list. When I look at the map, I'll see that it is pretty large for my PowerBook screen, so showing multiple maps at once is probably not an option (Figure 4-1).

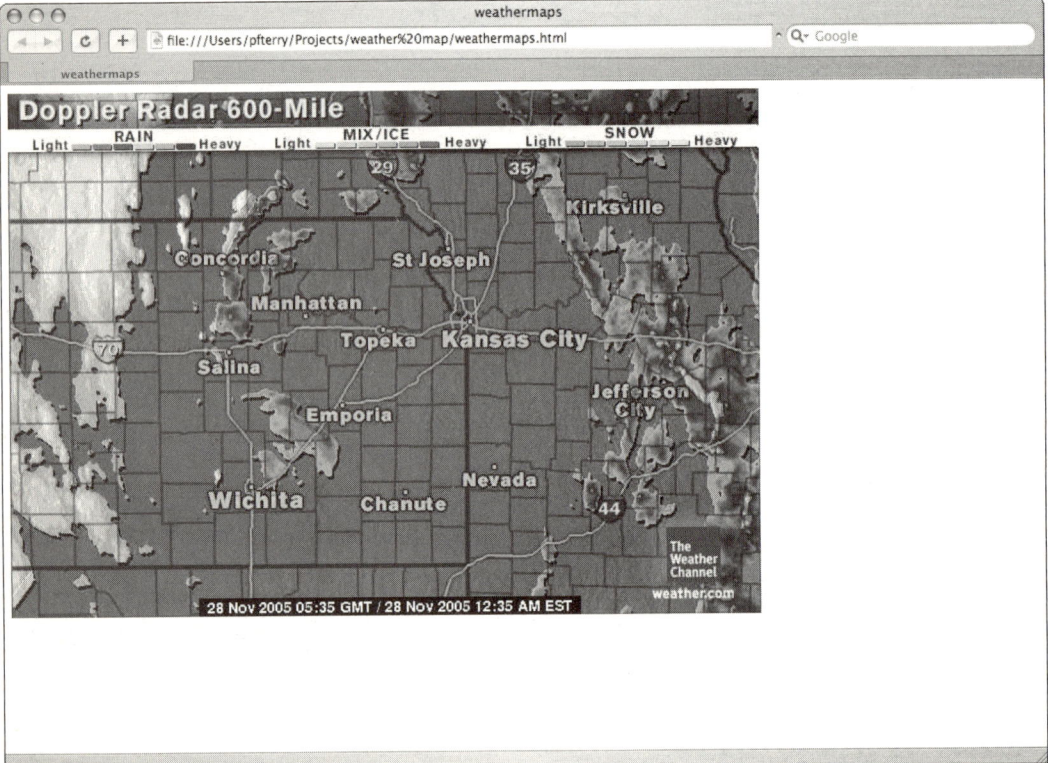

Figure 4-1

The size of the map probably won't even allow enough space for the other widgets I normally keep open. The size of the maps also makes using them on the typical widget backgrounds not an option. As I check the maps that I want to display, I also notice that they are two different sizes. Whatever I use as a background for the current weather map will leave a noticeable gap when I display the current temperature maps. The following questions become design considerations as I'm working on the widget:

❑ Can the current weather map be resized so it is the same size as the current temps and overnight temperature maps?

❑ If all of the maps won't fit on the screen at the same time, how can switching among them be made easier?

❑ What can I use as a widget background?

❑ If the widget is going to be shared, how can others set the maps they want to view?

You may be able to think of several or a dozen additional things to consider, but you get the idea. By making a list of the features you want your widget to have and then thinking about their uses, you will be able to come up with a list of items to consider as the widget takes shape. You can keep the list on paper or in a text editor file, but keep it nearby while you are developing the widget so you can review and add to it.

Begin with HTML

Because Dashboard widgets are essentially web pages, the best place to begin is with the HTML that you will use to retrieve the maps.

```
<!DOCTYPE html PUBLIC "-//W3C//DTD XHTML 1.0 Strict//EN"
        "http://www.w3.org/TR/xhtml1/DTD/xhtml1-strict.dtd">
<html xmlns="http://www.w3.org/1999/xhtml">
<head>
  <title>WeatherMaps</title>
  </head>
<body>
<img src="http://image.weather.com/web/radar/us_mkc_closeradar_large_usen.jpg">
<!--
http://image.weather.com/web/radar/us_mkc_closeradar_medium_usen.jpg
http://image.weather.com/images/maps/current/cen_curtemp_720x486.jpg
http://image.weather.com/images/maps/forecast/map_lotmpf_night1_3usc_enus_600x405.jpg
http://image.weather.com/images/maps/forecast/map_hitmpf_day2_3usc_enus_600x405.jpg
-->
</body>
</html>
```

This is a bit of straightforward HTML wrapped around the radar map. This widget allows you to check the current radar map without loading all of the ads and content on the web page that you aren't interested in at the moment. You can find the URL of the radar map by right-clicking it and selecting the Open Image in New Window or Open Image in New Tab options. When you do this, the map loads in a separate page with the URL of the map itself in the location window.

You can gather the URLs of the other maps that you want to retrieve and include them in a comment at the bottom of the page. This makes it easier for you to check the sizes of the other maps as you begin to develop your widget.

The link to this radar map and the temperature maps discussed later in this chapter were obtained by Control-clicking the map at weather.com's website. You may want to insert maps for your region or part of the world.

If you look back to your list of design considerations, you'll see that the size of the maps is the first thing you're thinking about. HTML has a way of resizing images as they are loaded that may work for your widget. You do this by setting the height and width of the image in the source line like so:

```
<img src="http://image.weather.com/web/radar/us_mkc_closeradar_large_usen.jpg"
width="432" height="290">
```

Setting the height and width of the image in the source line results in a weather map that is a size more conducive to display on screen (Figure 4-2).

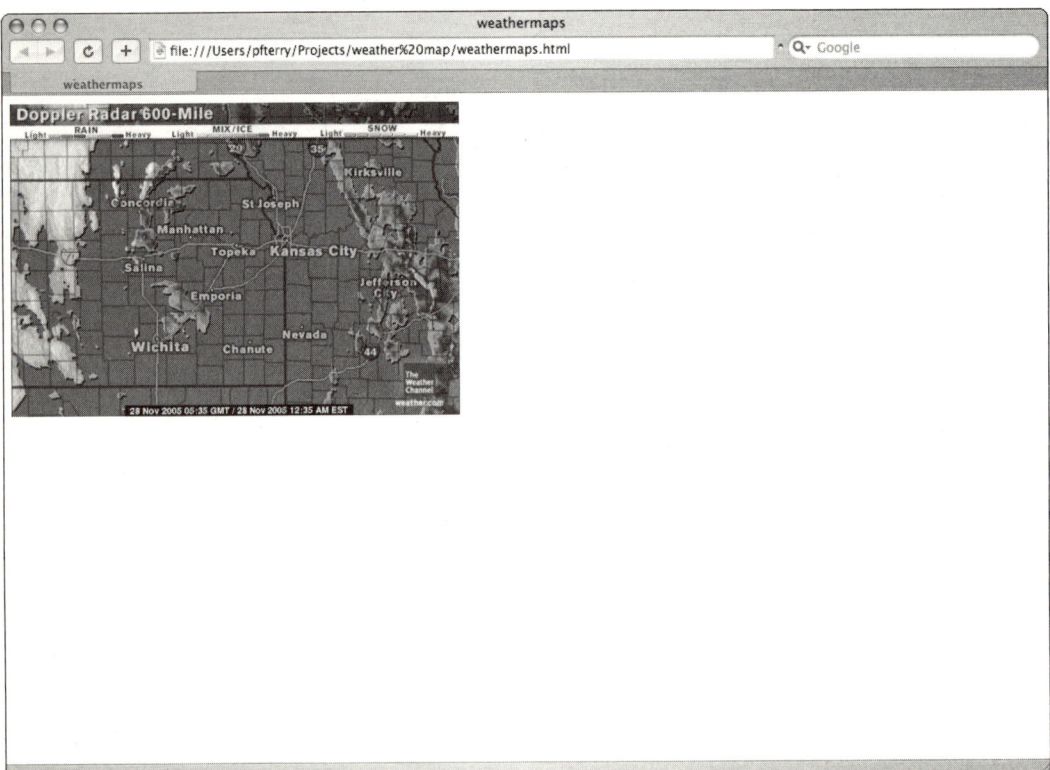

Figure 4-2

Setting the height and width of the image in the source line solves two design considerations at once: the large size of the maps and making the maps the same size. The trick is to display the resized maps with the same proportions as the original ones. If you just type in any numbers, you could have an elongated mess. You can try trial and error until the maps look right, but you can't automate that process very well in the future if the map sizes change. You can start with the current temps map because it tells you the image size is 720×486 in the name of the map. Multiply these numbers by .60 to reduce the size of the maps by 60 percent. This calculation returns an image size of 432×290, which — as you can see in Figure 4-2 — is proportional.

As a test that all of the images look good with their new sizes, you can move all of the commented URLs into the body of the HTML so they are all displayed together in the web page. Once you are satisfied that the maps are the same size and can be swapped without leaving any space around them, you can work on putting together the remaining portions of the widget.

You now have the basic HTML document that you can use for your widget. You are ready to create a background that will serve as the user interface as you add more functionality.

Adding a Background

If you look at the backgrounds of different widgets, you'll see that they can be very elaborate or quite simple. As you noticed in Chapter 2, the Weather widget has a simple background, and the weather information comes from the graphics representing day and night and the different weather conditions placed on top of it. The Stocks widget is also based on a simple rectangle with the information provided through the share price and charts.

Because one of the design considerations is how to switch among the different maps, you know that you may want to add controls along the top or bottom of the widget. For the moment, however, you'll just need to create a background on which to display your maps.

You can create your background image in any graphics application that you prefer. The only requirement is that the application should be able to save your background as a PNG file. Graphics Converter, a shareware graphics application, can save files in this format. If you have a copy of Widgetarium, it can export your background image as PNG and will even name it Default.png. In Widgetarium, you can open the Panel Maker window and enter the width and height values of your background as well as the style and color of the background (Figure 4-3).

When you have your background the size and color that you want, you can save it using the Export Graphic command. If you do this inside of a Widgetarium project, saving the background is done for you automatically and the back side and icon images are created for you at the same time.

When you assemble all of the pieces in your widget directory, Dashboard automatically picks up the PNG file named Default.png that is in the widget directory. If you want to test the background image in Safari with your maps before you install the widget in Dashboard, you need to add the Default.png to your HTML file.

```
<!DOCTYPE html PUBLIC "-//W3C//DTD XHTML 1.0 Strict//EN"
        "http://www.w3.org/TR/xhtml1/DTD/xhtml1-strict.dtd">
<html xmlns="http://www.w3.org/1999/xhtml">
```

```
<head>
  <title>weathermaps</title>  </head>
<body>
<img src="Default.png">
<img src="http://image.weather.com/web/radar/us_mkc_closeradar_large_usen.jpg"
width="432" height="290">

<!--
http://image.weather.com/web/radar/us_mkc_closeradar_medium_usen.jpg
http://image.weather.com/images/maps/current/cen_curtemp_720x486.jpg
http://image.weather.com/images/maps/forecast/map_lotmpf_night1_3usc_enus_600x405.j
pg
http://image.weather.com/images/maps/forecast/map_hitmpf_day2_3usc_enus_600x405.jpg
-->
</body>
</html>
```

When you have done this, you can open your widget's HTML file in Safari to preview what it will look like. Though the map isn't overlaid on your background, you can see that the map will fit inside of the background image you've created for the widget (Figure 4-4).

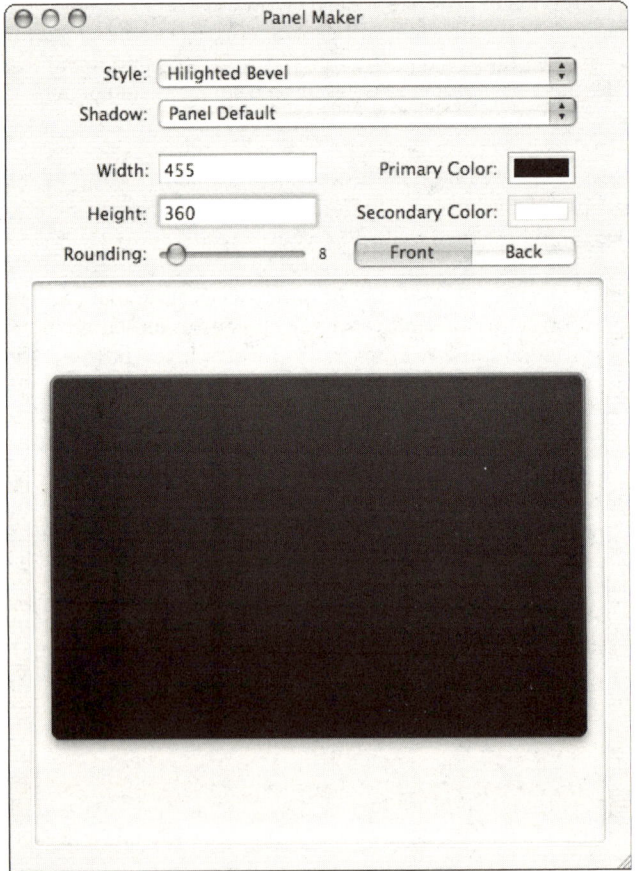

Figure 4-3

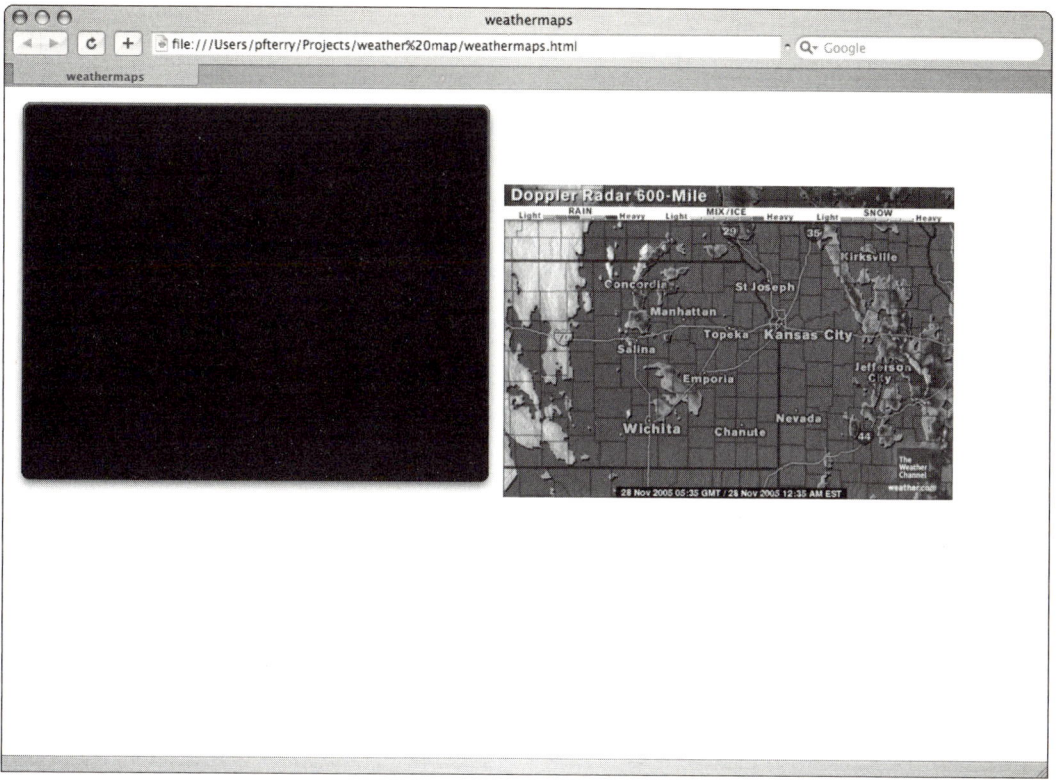

Figure 4-4

Now that you have the basic HTML for your widget and the Default.png created, you will need to create a Cascading Style Sheet for it in order to place the maps on top of your background and position them accurately.

Creating Widget Structure with CSS

If you have worked with Cascading Style Sheets, you know that they are a painless way to apply style attributes to all of the elements in your HTML pages without the niggling problem of touching the tag for each individual element. More important, Cascading Style Sheets give you precise layout control of your HTML pages in ways that HTML tables never allowed you to. For Dashboard widgets, this means that you are able to mix text and graphics in a way that gives your widget the polished and professional look of a commercial application.

If you test your Cascading Style Sheet in Safari while you are working out alignment issues, you will make your widget's transition to Dashboard easier.

You can create a very basic CSS file to align the weather maps with the background. The Cascading Style Sheet needs only to contain a section for the body of the page, the location of the map, and the location of the background image.

```
/*
pfterry, weathermaps, 2005
*/

body {
   margin: 0;
}

#mapImage {
   position: absolute;
   top: 55px;
   left: 16px;
}

.backgroundImage {
   position: absolute;
   top: 0px;
   left: 0px;
}
```

In this CSS, the body rule is the first item and is a margin property with a value of 0. The next rule is the style used for the map image and it is named #mapImage. The hash sign before the name indicates that it is an ID selector and will be applied only to the element in your HTML page that has an ID selector with the same value.

```
<img id="mapImage"
src="http://image.weather.com/web/radar/us_mkc_closeradar_large_usen.jpg"
width="432" height="290">
```

You can also see that the mapImage rule has position, top, and left properties, and their values.

ID selectors should be used only once in your HTML file to make applying the style easy and so the Javascript getElementByID() *function will work.*

The style used for the background is called .backgroundImage. The period before the name indicates that it is a class selector. Like the ID selector, the .backgroundImage style will be applied only to the HTML element with the value backgroundImage.

When the style sheet is applied to the widget, the body has no margins. Because the maps and any buttons or links will be placed on the background image, the image has an absolute position of 0 pixels from the top and 0 pixels from the left. All of the other items in the widget will be offset from the top and left edges of the background. The position of the map image, for instance, is 55 pixels from the top of the background and 16 pixels from the left.

To test the CSS file, you must save it with the same name as the HTML file and .css as the extension. You will need to make two modifications to the weathermaps.html file to incorporate the Cascading Style Sheet into the widget. First, the lines

```
<style type="text/css">
   @import "weathermaps.css";
</style>
```

are added above the body and below the head in weathermaps.html. When the base HTML page of the widget loads, the weathermaps.css file is imported and used as the style sheet. Second, you need to give the image the ID selector `id="mapImage"` to place the map on the background image via JavaScript and CSS.

```
<!DOCTYPE html PUBLIC "-//W3C//DTD XHTML 1.0 Strict//EN"
          "http://www.w3.org/TR/xhtml1/DTD/xhtml1-strict.dtd">
<html xmlns="http://www.w3.org/1999/xhtml">
<head>
  <title>weathermaps</title>
</head>
<style type="text/css">
  @import "weathermaps.css";
</style>
<body>
<img src="Default.png">

<img id="mapImage"
src="http://image.weather.com/web/radar/us_mkc_closeradar_large_usen.jpg"
width="432" height="290">

<!--
http://image.weather.com/web/radar/us_mkc_closeradar_medium_usen.jpg
http://image.weather.com/images/maps/current/cen_curtemp_720x486.jpg
http://image.weather.com/images/maps/forecast/map_lotmpf_night1_3usc_enus_600x405.j
pg
http://image.weather.com/images/maps/forecast/map_hitmpf_day2_3usc_enus_600x405.jpg
-->
</body>
</html>
```

Figure 4-5 shows the result of placing the map at the bottom of the widget background and leaving space at the top for buttons or links to switch among the other maps.

At this point you could bundle your pages and create the widget, but you still have more work to do to add the links to load the other maps. You probably want to continue working in Safari while you add the remainder of the functionality to the widget.

<div> Regions

As you can see from the use of IDs in the weathermaps.html, you can use selectors in the CSS file to control placement in your widget as well as manipulate the content using JavaScript. You can also use <div> tags to create divisions for content in your widget. The <div> tag allows you to add logical divisions to your HTML page. It creates a division for the map, and you can use the ID selector with the <div> tag as the location to place the other maps as the user cycles through them.

By giving the <div> tag an ID, you are able to use that selector to change that portion of your widget with the style sheet. In this case, the position of the map on the background is determined by the #mapImage ID selector of the Cascading Style Sheet.

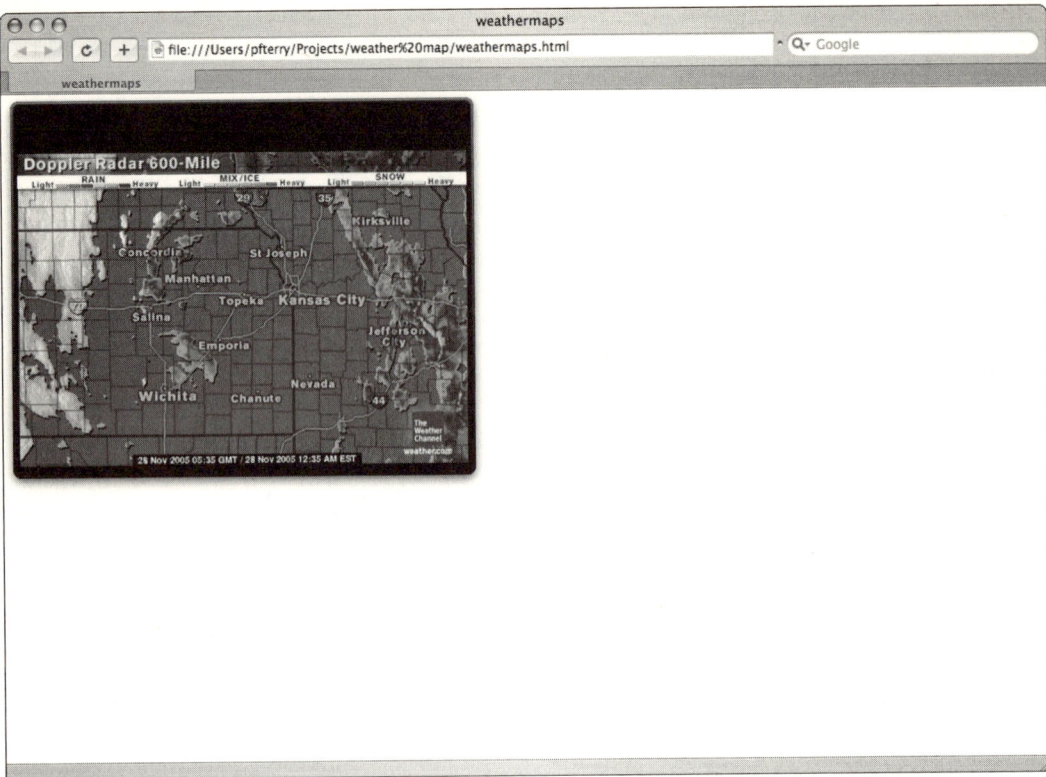

Figure 4-5

By extension, you can see that you can create multiple divisions in your widget and give them each a different style via the <div> tag. For instance, you can add buttons or links for the three additional maps that you want to display in the widget: current temps, overnight temps, and tomorrow's temps. You could add buttons above the map (Figure 4-5), but buttons take extra space. If you added the names of the maps above the current map, they will take less space than buttons and provide the same functionality.

Because you want to position the map names and you may want to use JavaScript to reference them, you need to use the <div> tag again. For instance, you can add a <div> tag with an ID selector for each one of the maps that you plan to display in your widget.

```
<!DOCTYPE html PUBLIC "-//W3C//DTD XHTML 1.0 Strict//EN"
        "http://www.w3.org/TR/xhtml1/DTD/xhtml1-strict.dtd">
<html xmlns="http://www.w3.org/1999/xhtml">
<head>
  <title>weathermaps</title>
</head>
<style type="text/css">
  @import "weathermaps.css";
</style>
```

```
<body>
<img src="Default.png">

<div id="radar">Radar</div>
<div id="curTemp">Current Temps</div>
<div id="nightTemp">Overnight Temps</div>
<div id="tomorrowHigh">Tomorrow's Highs</div>

<img id="mapImage"
src="http://image.weather.com/web/radar/us_mkc_closeradar_large_usen.jpg"
width="432" height="290">

<!--
http://image.weather.com/web/radar/us_mkc_closeradar_medium_usen.jpg
http://image.weather.com/images/maps/current/cen_curtemp_720x486.jpg
http://image.weather.com/images/maps/forecast/map_lotmpf_night1_3usc_enus_600x405.j
pg
http://image.weather.com/images/maps/forecast/map_hitmpf_day2_3usc_enus_600x405.jpg
-->
</body>
</html>
```

For each map that you plan to display in the widget, you have added an ID selector and included its name: Radar, Current Temps, Overnight Temps, and Tomorrow's Highs.

Try It Out   Positioning Text Using CSS

Now that you see how to use the Cascading Style Sheet to position text and graphics on your widget background, you can modify the weathermaps.css file for the four map names in the weathermaps.html file.

1. Open the weathermaps.css file and place the cursor above the #mapImage line and press Return.

2. Add a rule for the radar map assigning a font, font size, weight, and color. Your rule and its declaration should look something like this.

```
#radar {
  font: 10px "Lucida Grande";
  font-weight: bold;
  color: white;
}
```

3. Place the cursor after the font color and press Return. Enter absolute for position, and enter the offset of 20 pixels from the top and 20 pixels from the left side of the widget for your text. The remainder of the #radar rule should look like this.

```
position: absolute;
top: 20px;
  left: 20px;
```

4. If you haven't already, open weathermaps.html in Safari and press Command-R to reload your widget. You'll see the map name Radar at the top of the widget window (Figure 4-6). When your widget is finished, this will take you back to the radar map that you see whenever the widget loads after you have looked at the temperature maps.

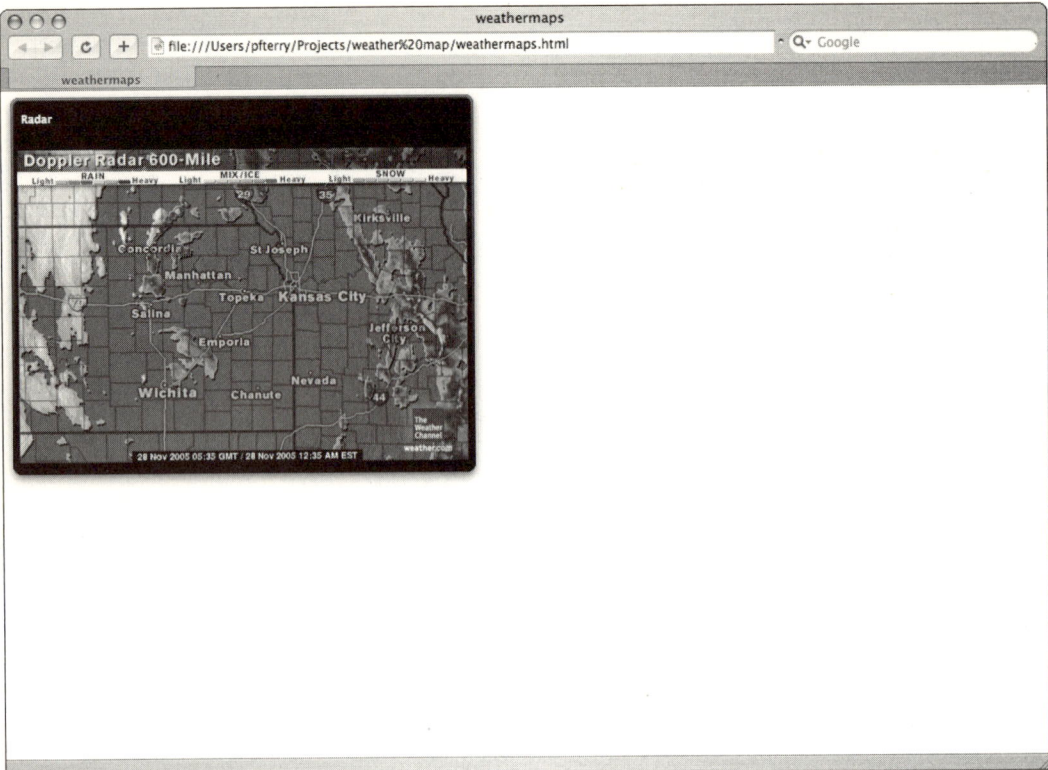

Figure 4-6

5.   Under the radar rule, add rules for the Current Temps, Overnight Temps, and Tomorrow's Highs maps. As you add each rule, you will need to adjust the Left offset value to move the next map name to the right.

When you have finished your edits, the weathermaps.css file should look like this.

```
/*
pfterry, WeatherMaps, 2005
*/

body {
  margin: 0;
}

#radar {
  font: 10px "Lucida Grande";
  font-weight: bold;
  color: white;
```

```
      position: absolute;
      top: 20px;
      left: 20px;
   }

   #curTemp {
      font: 10px "Lucida Grande";
      font-weight: bold;
      color: white;
      position: absolute;
      top: 20px;
      left: 75px;
   }

   #nightTemp {
      font: 10px "Lucida Grande";
      font-weight: bold;
      color: white;
      position: absolute;
      top: 20px;
      left: 170px;
   }

   #tomorrowHigh {
      font: 10px "Lucida Grande";
      font-weight: bold;
      color: white;
      position: absolute;
      top: 20px;
      left: 280px;
   }

   #mapImage {
      font: 20px "Lucida Grande";
      font-weight: bold;
      text-align: center;
      color: white;
      position: absolute;
      top: 55px;
      left: 16px;
   }

   .backgroundImage {
      position: absolute;
      top: 0px;
      left: 0px;
   }
```

Once you save your changes and reload the HTML file, you'll see the names of the maps listed along the top of your widget (Figure 4-7).

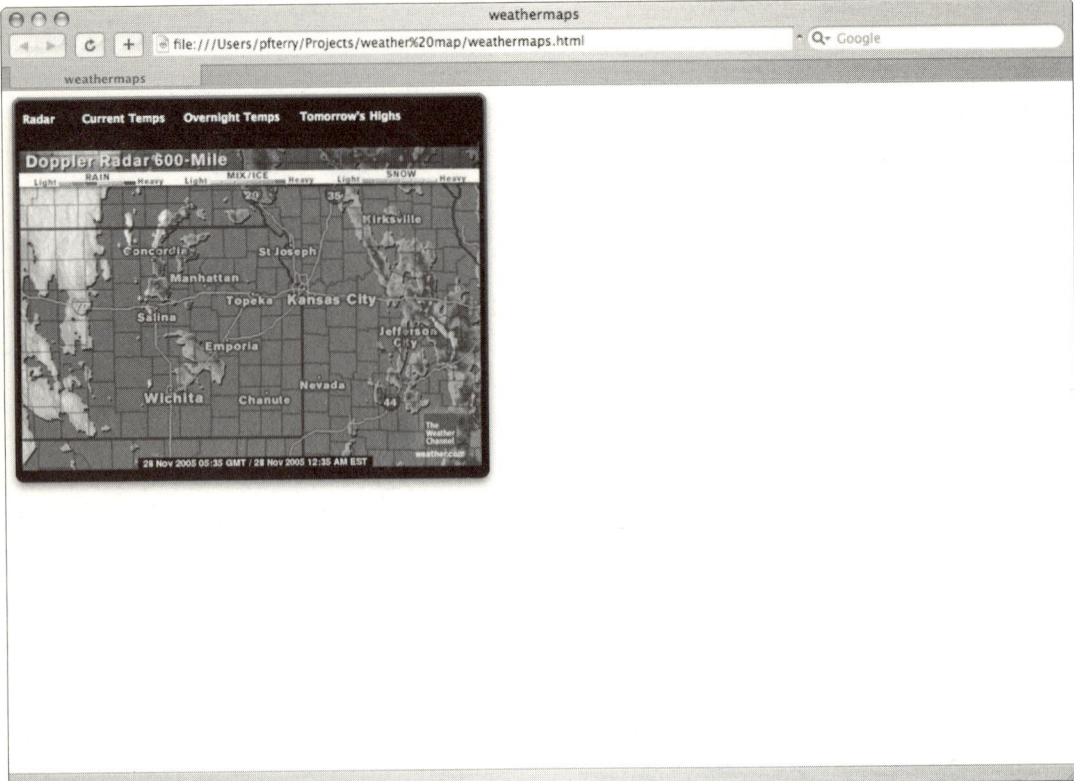

Figure 4-7

How It Works

In a Cascading Style Sheet, each rule has two parts: the selector and the declaration. The declaration contains the properties and values of the style. In a typical rule, the selector and declaration matches a standard HTML element. In this rule, for instance,

```
h1 {font: 18px Verdana; color: grey}
```

Head 1 is the selector. It determines what the rule is applied to. The rule contains two declaration blocks between the curly braces — font and color, with their two values — separated by a semicolon. The rule can be written as a line, or it can be written like the ID selectors in your weathermaps.css file.

```
#radar {
    font: 10px "Lucida Grande";
    font-weight: bold;
    color: white;
    position: absolute;
```

```
    top: 20px;
    left: 20px;
}
```

In the rule above, `radar` is the selector the declaration will be applied to. In this case, however, it is an ID selector instead of a standard HTML element. Placing each declaration block on a separate line makes the rule easier to read. When Dashboard displays the widget, the rule in the CSS is applied to the `radar` ID selector when it is found in weathermaps.html.

```
<div id="radar" onclick='replaceMap("radar")'>Radar</div>
```

The division marker identifies the portion of the HTML file the CSS rule is applied to.

Doing the Work with JavaScript

Now that you have the basis for the widget, you can add the functionality of switching between the different temperature maps. You could just add the links to the maps as HREF tags in the weathermaps.html file, but that would give the map names the unmistakable look of a link on a web page. Because you are trying to create a widget that has the illusion of being an application rather than point to the widget's web origins, you should use JavaScript to load the maps as you click the map names.

When you are developing a JavaScript to power your widget it is sometimes easier to begin inside of the HTML file. This is especially useful if you are using Safari and a text editor as your development environment. Keeping the JavaScript inside the HTML file means that you have to make your changes in one file only. When you have finished developing the script, you can move it into a separate file. If you are developing a complex JavaScript, however, you may want to separate HTML from CSS from JavaScript sooner to take advantage of a modular approach. In the end, the choice is a matter of personal preference and development style. For the purposes of this discussion, the JavaScript begins its life inside of the main HTML file.

If you think about the functionality that you are trying to achieve, you want the map to change each time you click one of the map names at the top of the widget. To accomplish this, you need a function that can take the result of a mouse click in the widget, associate that result with a map URL, and insert the correct map.

The simple JavaScript function would determine the correct map to insert by testing the result of the mouse click. Whenever you click in your widget, the name of the map is passed back to the `replaceMap(mapLink)` function as the mapLink value. The correct URL is then determined by comparing that value to the four possible values in a series of if . . . else if conditions.

```
function replaceMap(mapLink)
{

if (mapLink == "radar") {
```

```
var theImage = (src='http://image.weather.com/web/radar/us_mkc_closeradar_large_
usen.jpg');

} else if (mapLink == "curTemp") {

var theImage = (src='http://image.weather.com/images/maps/current/cen_curtemp_
720x486.jpg');

} else if (mapLink == "nightTemp") {

var theImage = (src='http://image.weather.com/images/maps/forecast/map_lotmpf_
night1_3usc_enus_600x405.jpg');

} else if (mapLink == "tomorrowHigh") {

var theImage = (src='http://image.weather.com/images/maps/forecast/map_hitmpf_day2_
3usc_enus_600x405.jpg');
}

document.getElementById("mapImage").src = theImage;

}
```

For example, if your onclick returns the value nightTemp in the mapLink variable, the JavaScript compares that in each else . . . if condition. When it makes the comparison, it sets the variable theImage to the source URL and then executes the next statement in the JavaScript, which sets the mapImage <div> in the widget with the new map URL. It does this using the getElementByID() function.

This is what the JavaScript looks like incorporated into the weathermaps.html file.

```
<!DOCTYPE html PUBLIC "-//W3C//DTD XHTML 1.0 Strict//EN"
        "http://www.w3.org/TR/xhtml1/DTD/xhtml1-strict.dtd">
<html xmlns="http://www.w3.org/1999/xhtml">
<head>
  <title>WeatherMaps</title>

  <script type="text/javascript">
  // simple script to switch between the different maps

  function replaceMap(mapLink) {
    if (mapLink == "radar") {
      var theImage =
(src='http://image.weather.com/web/radar/us_mkc_closeradar_large_usen.jpg');
    } else if (mapLink == "curTemp") {
      var theImage =
(src='http://image.weather.com/images/maps/current/cen_curtemp_720x486.jpg');
    } else if (mapLink == "nightTemp") {
      var theImage =
(src='http://image.weather.com/images/maps/forecast/map_lotmpf_night1_3usc_enus_600
x405.jpg');
    } else if (mapLink == "tomorrowHigh") {
      var theImage = (src='http://image.weather.com/images/maps/forecast/map_
hitmpf_day2_3usc_enus_600x405.jpg');
```

```
    }
    document.getElementById("mapImage").src = theImage;
  }
  </script>
  <meta name="generator" content="BBEdit 8.2" />
</head>
<style type="text/css">
  @import "weathermaps.css";
</style>
<body>
<img src="Default.png">



<div id="radar" onclick='replaceMap("radar")'>Radar</div>
<div id="curTemp" onclick='replaceMap("curTemp")'>Current Temps</div>
<div id="nightTemp" onclick='replaceMap("nightTemp")'>Overnight Temps</div>
<div id="tomorrowHigh" onclick='replaceMap("tomorrowHigh")'>Tomorrow's Highs</div>

<img id="mapImage" src="http://image.weather.com/web/radar/us_mkc_closeradar_
large_usen.jpg" width="432" height="290">

<!--
http://image.weather.com/web/radar/us_mkc_closeradar_medium_usen.jpg
http://image.weather.com/images/maps/current/cen_curtemp_720x486.jpg
http://image.weather.com/images/maps/forecast/map_lotmpf_night1_3usc_enus_600x405.
jpg
http://image.weather.com/images/maps/forecast/map_hitmpf_day2_3usc_enus_600x405.jpg

-->
</body>
</html>
```

Notice that the JavaScript is set apart in the HTML file with the `<script type="text/javascript">`
tag at the beginning of the script. In the old days of browser incompatibilities, this tag hid the JavaScript
from browsers that could not execute it. You don't have to worry about Dashboard not recognizing
JavaScript; the tag tells Dashboard what language the script is written in and then executes it.

You can also see the mechanism that links the map names to the appropriate map URLs in the HTML
file. Each ID selector contains an onclick event that calls the `replaceMap` function and passes it the ID
name as the mapLink. Once you have the JavaScript added to your HTML file, you can reload your widget in Safari and test the functionality of swapping between the maps.

After you have tested the JavaScript in your widget, move the JavaScript out to its own file. It should
look like this.

```
// pfterry, WeatherMaps, 2005
// a simple script to switch between the different maps in the WeatherMaps widget

function replaceMap(mapLink)
{

if (mapLink == "radar") {
```

```
var theImage = (src='http://image.weather.com/web/radar/us_mkc_closeradar_
large_usen.jpg');

} else if (mapLink == "curTemp") {

var theImage = (src='http://image.weather.com/images/maps/current/cen_curtemp_
720x486.jpg');

} else if (mapLink == "nightTemp") {

var theImage = (src='http://image.weather.com/images/maps/forecast/map_lotmpf_
night1_3usc_enus_600x405.jpg');

} else if (mapLink == "tomorrowHigh") {

var theImage = (src='http://image.weather.com/images/maps/forecast/map_hitmpf_
day2_3usc_enus_600x405.jpg');
}

document.getElementById("mapImage").src = theImage;
}
```

The reference `<script type="text/javascript">` in the weathermaps.html file now changes. It points to the file that you've moved the JavaScript to:

```
<script type="text/javascript" src='weathermaps.js' charset='utf-8'/>
```

The `charset='utf-8'` at the end of the line specifies the character set of the JavaScript file that is being loaded.

> UTF-8 is the abbreviation for the 8-bit Unicode Transformation Format. Unicode is an industry standard that allows text and symbols from all languages to be represented and manipulated on computers as groups of bytes. It is backward compatible with good old ASCII. It is used here because it supports the widest range of languages.

Building the Widget

Now that you have your widget UI and all of the functionality implemented, you are ready to convert it and load it into Dashboard. As you saw in Chapter 2, bundling the widget is a simple process. You will need to create an icon and an Info.plist file. You can also add a version.plist file to the widget.

Try It Out   Finish Your Widget

You've already created an Info.plist file for the Fortune widget, and this process won't be any different.

1. Create an Info.plist file for the WeatherMaps widget. You can look at the previous one that you created, because it has a property that you need: AllowNetworkAccess. Your widget won't be able to retrieve the weather maps without network access. Your file should look something like this one:

```
<?xml version="1.0" encoding="UTF-8"?>
<!DOCTYPE plist PUBLIC "-//Apple Computer//DTD PLIST 1.0//EN"
"http://www.apple.com/DTDs/PropertyList-1.0.dtd">
<plist version="1.0">
<dict>
   <key>AllowNetworkAccess</key>
   <true/>
   <key>CFBundleDisplayName</key>
   <string>WeatherMaps</string>
   <key>CFBundleIdentifier</key>
   <string>com.apple.widget.weathermaps</string>
   <key>CFBundleName</key>
   <string>WeatherMaps</string>
   <key>CFBundleShortVersionString</key>
   <string>.04</string>
   <key>CFBundleVersion</key>
   <string>.04</string>
   <key>CloseBoxInsetX</key>
   <integer>12</integer>
   <key>CloseBoxInsetY</key>
   <integer>12</integer>
   <key>MainHTML</key>
   <string>weathermaps.html</string>
</dict>
</plist>
```

2. Save the Info.plist file in the WeatherMaps widget folder.

3. Create a version.plist file for your widget. Most widgets that you examine the contents of probably won't have a version.plist file. However, you can keep version information that will make it easier to track your modifications as you debug, improve, and add features to your widget. Here is a sample version.plist file.

```
<?xml version="1.0" encoding="UTF-8"?>
<!DOCTYPE plist PUBLIC "-//Apple Computer//DTD PLIST 1.0//EN"
"http://www.apple.com/DTDs/PropertyList-1.0.dtd">
<plist version="1.0">
<dict>
   <key>CFBundleShortVersionString</key>
   <string>.04</string>
   <key>CFBundleVersion</key>
   <string>.04</string>
   <key>ProjectName</key>
   <string>WidgetDev</string>
</dict>
</plist>
```

4. Save your version.plist file in your widget folder.

5. Now you are ready to create an icon for your widget. If you are adept with graphics programs and have a creative flair, this step should be fun. If you are graphically challenged, there is still hope. Widgetarium has an Icon Maker that will help you create an icon (Figure 4-8).

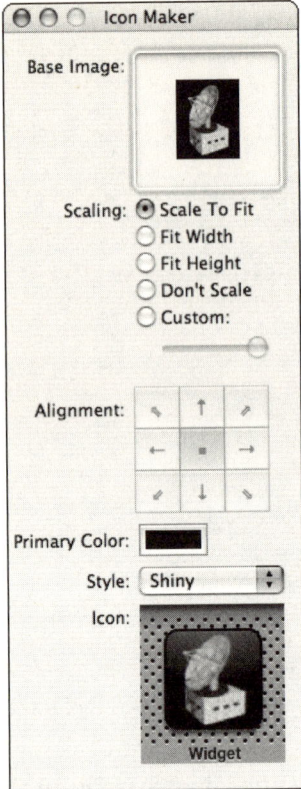

Figure 4-8

By selecting the color and style from the pop-up menus, you can create a professional looking icon quickly. As you make your changes, the icon is displayed on a Dashboard tray at the bottom so you can find the look you want and then export the icon to an Icon.png file.

6. Save your Icon.png file into your widget folder.

7. Make a copy of the WeatherMaps folder on the desktop.

8. Bundle your widget so you can install it in Dashboard.

9. Double-click the widget to install it in Dashboard. The widget installer asks you if you want to install the widget (Figure 4-9).

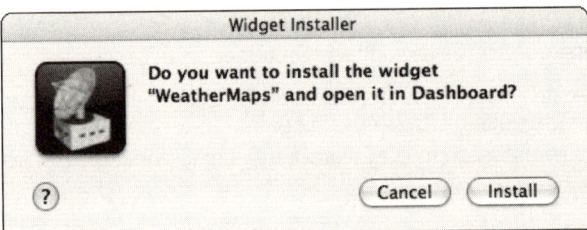

Figure 4-9

How It Works

As seen in Chapters 2 and 3, once you put all of the files in the widget bundle, you are able to install and run your widget. This is because you provided Dashboard with all of the information it needs to treat your collection of files as a widget and load it. Throughout the remainder of this book, we will concentrate on the different parts of the widget, but we need to remember that Dashboard performs the magic. It is the engine for running widgets. Dashboard is able to accomplish this magic because it makes use of Web Kit, the same engine that Safari uses for displaying web pages. In Chapter 3, you saw that both use Web Kit because you can run widgets inside of Safari. As you work through the following chapters, keep this common engine in mind.

Making Sure It Works

You probably don't have to be told to click each of the map names along the top of the WeatherMaps widget to make certain they work. Using your widget after you have built it is most of the fun. So the initial tests are a given. Before you hand your brand new widget off to your friends and begin fielding phone calls, however, you may want to run a few additional tests.

The simplest test is installing your widget on two or three different machines — preferably with different versions of Tiger — and running through the tests again. You want to test the widget on different machines to make certain that different configurations and software won't cause it to break. Installing your widget on different machines will tell you if you have installed something on your machine that is necessary for the widget to work. You should also create a pristine account on a machine with a basic Tiger installation to test the widget.

Finally, try to break it. When the widget gets into users' hands, they will unintentionally break your widget and not be able to explain what they were doing when they broke it. Try to beat them to the punch by testing all of the map links. We'll talk more about testing in Chapter 5.

Summary

Now that you have created a basic widget, you are ready to begin adding features and functionality to that foundation. You may want to add a feature that allows you to click one of the maps to go to the weather.com website and open the map. You may want your widget to update the radar image whenever you open Dashboard without having to reload the widget. You will definitely want to add preferences to the widget. You know that you don't want your users to have to edit your JavaScript file to change the maps that are loaded. You will need to provide an interface for this so they can make this kind of change without hacking your code.

In this chapter, you learned:

- ❏ How to begin developing a basic widget
- ❏ How to use HTML and Cascading Styles Sheets to give shape to the widget
- ❏ How to incorporate JavaScript into your widget

In Chapter 5, you'll see how to debug and test your WeatherMaps widget. Before you turn to Chapter 5, however, you may want to run through these exercises to review what you've learned.

Exercises

1. What is UTF-8?

2. Should ID selectors with the same value be used more than once in your widget?

3. In the other widgets you have looked at, what has the `<div>` tag been used for?

Debugging and Testing

In Chapter 4, you learned how to create a widget from scratch. In this chapter, you'll learn how to debug problems that arise as you are developing your widget. You'll also learn some basic principles for testing your widget before you release it. While these two activities aren't mutually exclusive, they come from very different points of view. Testing naturally flows from debugging and debugging is a natural result of testing, and both are necessary to release a bug-free widget.

By the end of this chapter, you will know:

- ❑ How to find problems in your widget using JavaScript alerts
- ❑ How to step through your widget with a debugger
- ❑ How to test your widget before you release it

First Steps

In Chapter 3, you looked at two methods of debugging problems in Safari: turning on the debug logging and enabling the JavaScript console. While you are in the initial stages of development and using Safari as part of your development environment, these can be effective for finding some problems. When you have installed your widget in Dashboard or if you are working on an event that Safari doesn't support, they obviously won't be very helpful.

When you have reached this point in your development, you have to resort to your wits, a handful of tricks using the tools at hand, and third-party applications to help you find the bugs in your widget. Let's start with your wits.

Debugging Tips

Given the ubiquity of computers in our society, our cars, and our toasters, it probably isn't necessary to define debugging — the removal of bugs from your code. You have probably encountered bugs in the software that you use. Now that you are developing widgets, you will find yourself on the other side of the software experience. You aren't the hapless user confronted with a bug when trying to finish a report; you are the programmer writing the bug into that report application. Granted, widgets aren't quite the same as commercial applications, but you should try to create a bug-free widget.

Apple has a tech note on debugging widgets that covers the basics of debugging as well as more advanced issues like using gdb — the GNU debugger — for debugging plugins. You can find the reference to the tech note in Appendix B. The note provides some specific places to look in your widget when you are having problems. But you can follow some more general principles for finding the source of errors in your code.

If you have experience with other programming languages, you may find debugging widgets to be a bit more problematic than a Visual Basic or Perl program due to the mix of languages and their interaction. For instance, a syntax error would normally keep a Visual Basic application or Perl script from compiling. Typically, however, a widget will load and may partially function with a syntax error. Plugins raise the level of difficulty.

When you are looking for a bug in your widget, you should start with a code review. Most bugs are very simple syntax mistakes that we all make. If the code review doesn't point out a syntax problem, you can focus on a logic review. If those don't work, you can step through the code using a debugger to find the source of the problem.

Syntax and Logic Errors

When you are trying to find a bug in your widget, look for simple errors first. You may think that if they are simple, you would have already caught them. But simple errors have a way of hiding in your blind spot. For instance, if you have misspelled a variable name in your `setMap()` function, that variable will not be updated by your `onShow()` function and your JavaScript will fail. You may even concentrate your debugging efforts in the `onShow()` function because that is where the script seems to fail, never realizing the problem is in another function. In fact, syntax errors can cascade through your widget and the error messages can have a way of misdirecting you. Remember that JavaScript variables are case sensitive, so `myFoo` is different from `MyFoo`.

Here are a few other general places to look for these types of errors:

❑   Have you checked your spelling?

In addition to variables, have you checked the spelling of your filenames? Have you checked the spelling of the settings in your Info.plist file? Do the function names in your HTML file match the function names in your JavaScript file?

❑   Are your quotes and braces balanced?

JavaScript uses the brace characters (`{` and `}`) for blocks of statements. If you are inserting if . . . else and else . . . if statements inside of your function, it is easy to leave out a brace. Failing to close a quotation mark in your HTML or JavaScript file can cause the remainder of the file to be misinterpreted.

❑   Have you set the right access keys in your Info.plist file?

If your widget can't run a shell command that should be able to run or it can't connect to the Internet, you may not have entered the AllowSystem or AllowNetwork keys in your Info.plist file and set them to true.

In addition to syntax errors, logic errors can creep into your widget's JavaScript during development. Logic errors occur when your widget runs but doesn't produce the result you intended. These can be the trickiest bugs to find.

❏ Have you reversed the parameters in the widget's properties?

You'll learn about the proper order of parameters in Chapter 6. Always pass the preference value first and the preference key second when writing preferences.

❏ Have you included the parameter that you are passing in a function?

If you have not included the parameter, your function will not execute. You should also check to make certain you are returning the value if you need to.

❏ Have you called the plugin from your JavaScript?

If you have included the plugin but haven't included a call to it in your JavaScript, your widget won't be able to display the information the plugin is delivering.

Widget Errors

Those are some of the quickest and least invasive things to check whenever you find a bug in your widget and you are having difficulty locating it. In addition to syntax and logic errors, some problems are inherently widget-based, as mentioned in earlier chapters of the book. They bear repeating here.

❏ Have you included all of the pieces of your widget?

If you haven't included a Default.png, main.html, or Info.plist file or you haven't included the CFBundleIdentifier, your widget won't load.

❏ Have you included the plugin?

You may remember this from Chapter 4. If the plugin isn't included, the widget may launch, but you won't get all of the functionality or you will be missing data.

Debugging Tricks

By employing a few tricks, you can make your debugging go faster.

Use a Helpful Editor

Using a text editor with syntax coloring should make it easier to identify syntax errors while you are still writing the code. It will definitely make your debugging go faster because you will be looking for the problems that it highlights. In the same vein, an editor that performs syntax checks of your code will also make your debugging sessions go quicker. While BBEdit can't check your JavaScript syntax, it can identify unbalanced quotes and braces. BBEdit can check your HTML syntax in addition to balancing tags and finding unbalanced quotes, parenthesis, braces, and brackets. Other text editors are available with varying sets of these features.

Simplify

Whenever possible, simplify what you are trying to debug. Strip away everything except the problem that you are working on. You may need to create a simple widget shell to test the code that you think is causing the problem. This technique won't always work because some bugs are a result of interactions between the parts of the whole.

Log Files

Another trick associated with the JavaScript Console in Safari is the console.log file. If you have run through your source code again looking for the problems using the hints list above and still haven't resolved your problem, you may want to open the Console application and look in the console.log file for clues. What you'll discover is that just about everything gets written to the console log (Figure 5-1).

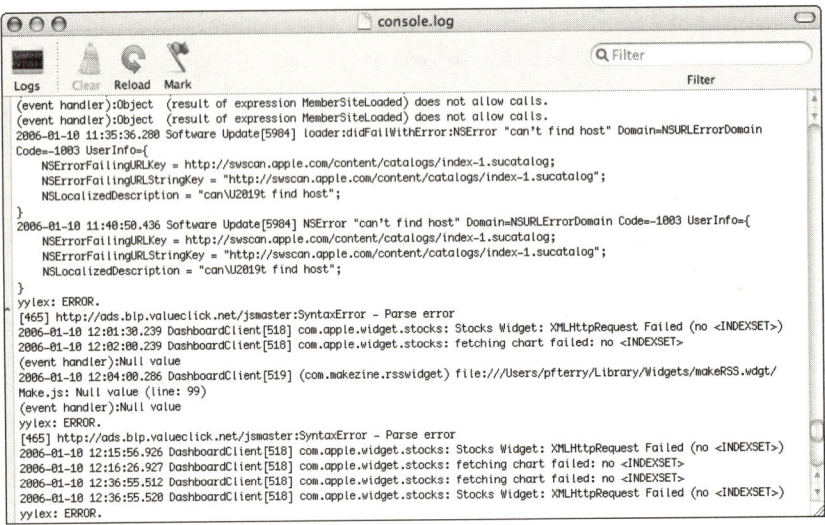

Figure 5-1

It may take a moment to weed through all of the different error messages, debug messages, and warnings in the log, but any problems that your widget is having will probably have been written to the console log. You only have to look in it for clues as to what the problem is.

In Figure 5-1, almost all of the error messages point to a loss of connectivity, and you can tell even more about what failed by reading the lines carefully. For instance, in the last few lines of the log you see that the Stocks widget (com.apple.widget.stocks) was not able to fetch the chart associated with the selected ticker symbol. (Part of that you know because you know how the widget works.) You can see that the PID number of the Stocks widget is 518 and that it is a Dashboard client. If you opened the Activity Monitor and filtered for the PID number 518, only the Stocks widget would show up in the window. You can also see where the failure occurred in the widget: the XMLHttpRequest object. You can also make a guess about the source of the problem based on the error in the Stocks widget and some of the other error messages. The "can't find host" error message from Software Update as well as the Null value from the MakeRSS widget suggest that the Macintosh lost its network connection.

Besides error messages from applications, the system, and widgets, you will also see debug and status messages in the console log from widgets. If you have the Wimic widget installed, for instance, you'll see status messages and debug messages written into the console log. Wimic writes status messages into the console log as it gets a comic, sets up the calendar, sets or unsets the timers, and provides status for setting variables, and setting the clock (Figure 5-2).

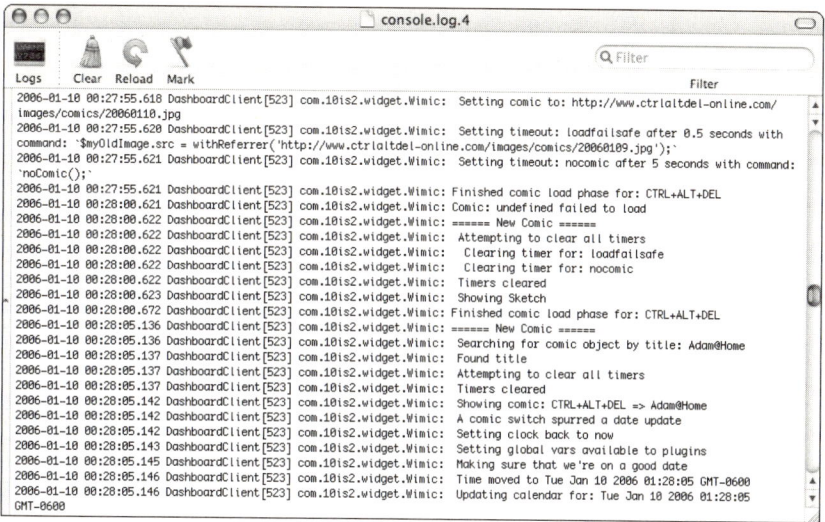

Figure 5-2

While the information you can get from this approach might be a bit excessive, you can see how simple it can be to use the console log to follow the status of your widget as it runs without the need for a debugger. You can't interact with the console.log file, but it is cheaper and lighter weight than a debugger.

Printing Debug Information with Alert Statements

In the days before sophisticated debuggers, one way to locate errors in your code was to insert a print statement. If, for instance, the program had a logic error and the wrong value was being returned, a print statement inserted at different points in the program would print the value of the variable. Whenever the questionable section of code was executed, the value would be printed to the terminal or nearby teletype machine.

Once you have installed your widget in Dashboard, you may find it difficult to isolate some bugs. You can use this same print statement strategy in JavaScript with the `alert()` function. You could insert `alert("Executing the radar menu function.")` within the function or portion of a function that you think isn't being executed. Or you could insert `alert(radMap)` when you are trying to determine if the variable has the right value or data.

| Try It Out | Debugging with Alert Statements |

Let's try the `alert()` function in the WeatherMaps widget to see how it can work.

1. Open the weathermaps.js file in your text editor.

2. Scroll down to the set of functions that set the preferences from the menu selection.

3. In the `radMap()` function, insert two alerts:

```
// Functions for selecting menu items and setting the preferences
// radarMenu function
function radMap() {
  var rMap = document.getElementById('radarMenu').value;
    alert("When the menu selection is made.");
    alert(rMap);

  if (rMap == '') {
    return;
  }

  widget.setPreferenceForKey(rMap,"radarMenu");
  replaceMap("radar");
}
```

4. Set similar functions in the `cTempMenu()` and other functions.

5. Save your changes.

6. Open the Console application and position the window where you can watch messages appear while you are working in your widget.

7. Reload your widget in Dashboard to pick up the changes.

8. Click the Info button to set the preferences and select a menu item for each function into which you inserted alerts. As you are selecting items, you should see the alerts inserted in the console log (Figure 5-3).

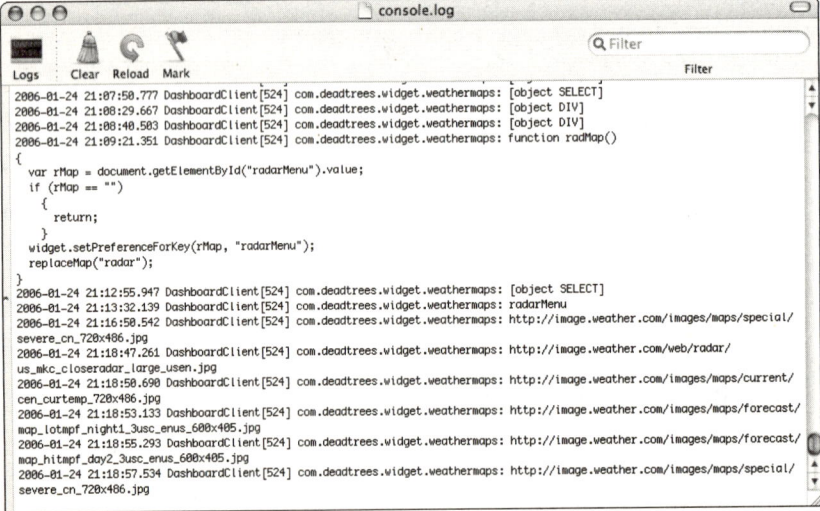

Figure 5-3

How It Works

Normally in a browser, as the `alert()` statement in your JavaScript is executed, a dialog box pops up on screen with the contents of the variable or the text statement displayed in it, and you would have to respond to the alert to send it away. When you are running your widget in Dashboard, JavaScript alerts are sent to the Console log. Having the alerts written to the log is less disruptive than responding to all of those modal dialog boxes as they are generated and gives you a printed record of your trip through your code.

Using a Debugger

Sometimes you have to bring out the big guns. If you don't see a logic problem as you are reading through the source code and can't isolate the problem with alert statements, you may have to resort to using a debugger to find the problem. A debugger allows you to step through your widget's code and examine the variables as they change while the widget is running. Stepping through your code in a debugger can be tedious, but you will have a better idea of how the data is flowing through your widget and how your widget functions at the variable level when you are done.

Debugging Tools

At this writing, Widgetarium (`http://projects.gandreas.com/widgetarium/`) is the only widget debugger available. From Gandraes Software, Widgetarium is more than just a debugger. An IDE for creating Dashboard widgets, it provides graphic tools for creating panels, a Dashboard emulator, syntax-aware editing for HTML, CSS, and JavaScript, a DOM inspector for widgets, and a JavaScript source-level debugger. It costs $29.00, but you can download the current version and use it in demo mode for one month.

Stepping Through a Widget

You can use Widgetarium to create your widget from the very beginning, but if you just want to take advantage of its debugging tools for an existing project, that is also easy to do. You can create a new empty project in Widgetarium and then add the files from an existing widget. If your widget has an images folder inside of it, you will need create a subfolder in the project and add the image files to that folder. Otherwise, you will have a number of broken links (Figure 5-4).

For purposes of demonstration, you can create an empty project and add the files from an Apple widget like the Ski Report. You'll notice in Figure 5-4 that Widgetarium has Dashboard emulation to speed up the debugging process. As the widget runs inside of Widgetarium, it appears on the transparent pane in the middle of the project window. A small version of the console log appears below the emulation window and a DOM inspector is to the right.

When you select the Debug command, the debugger window appears over the Project window (Figure 5-5). The buttons along the top of the Debugger window allow you to step through each line of JavaScript code and step into and out of functions. As you are stepping through the code, the relevant sections of your JavaScript appear in the bottom pane of the window and the top-left pane shows you the JavaScript filename. If you are stepping into functions, you may find yourself in the Apple JavaScript files that you have referenced. The variables and their values appear in the top-right pane.

If you click the disclosure triangle next to <globals>, you are able to see all of the global variables (Figure 5-6).

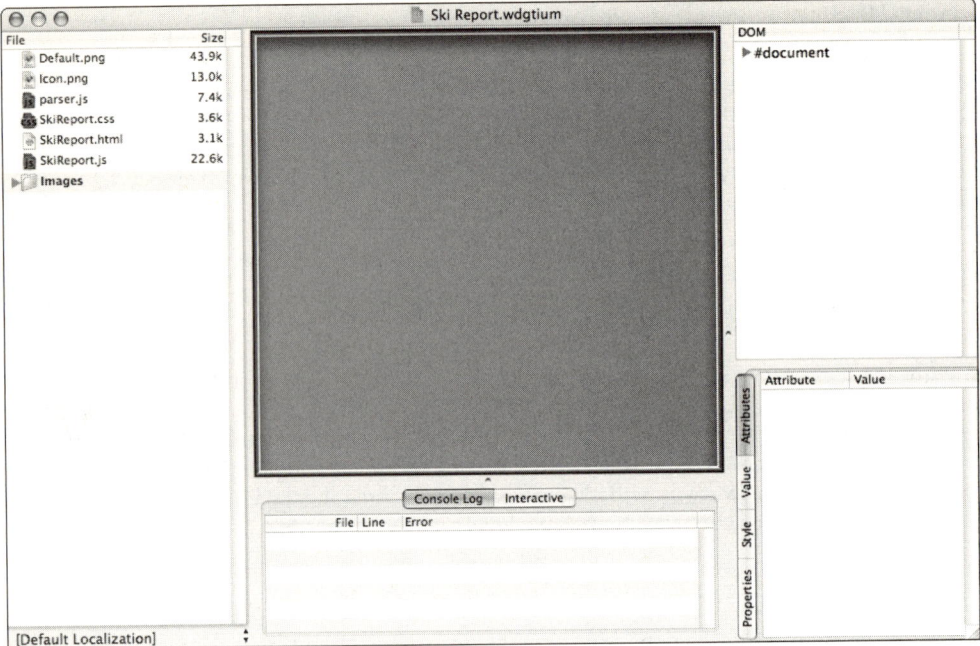

Figure 5-4

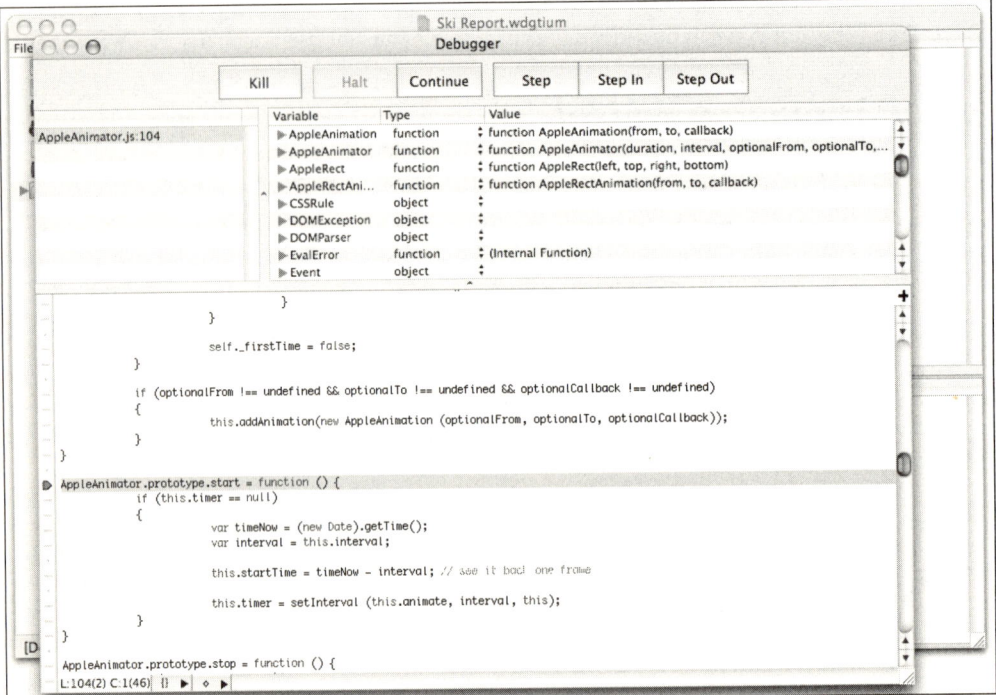

Figure 5-5

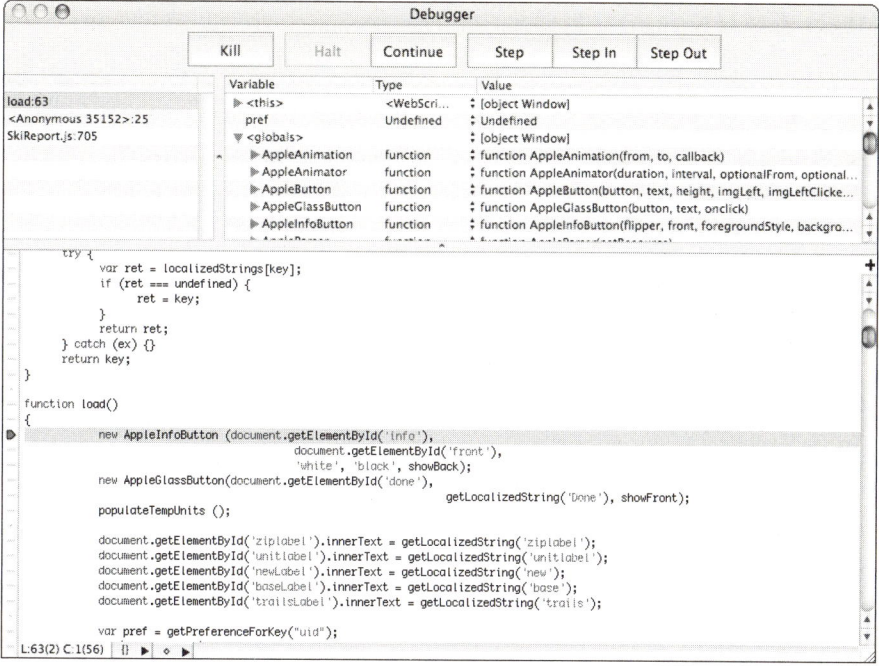

Figure 5-6

Once you have stepped through the JavaScript code to the point you are trying to examine, you can click the Continue button to continue loading and run the widget in the Dashboard emulator (Figure 5-7).

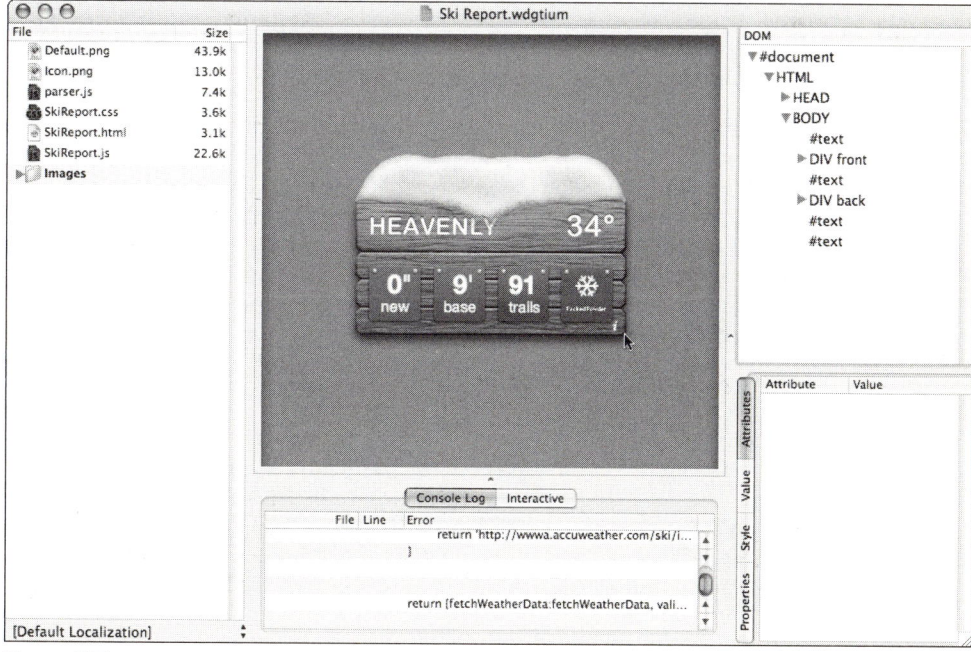

Figure 5-7

Testing Your Widget

First off, *you* shouldn't be testing your widget. Testing isn't the same as debugging. Debugging tries to determine why a feature or command doesn't work as expected or give the expected output. Testing tries to find functionality errors that you didn't anticipate while you were creating your widget. To put it another way, debugging is a programming exercise and testing is a postprogramming exercise.

But don't think you can just toss your widget over the wall to your testers; you should provide them with a little context for what they are testing. Write up release notes that tell your testers what they should concentrate their efforts on. Encourage them to ignore you and test everything. If you are sending your testers a bug fix version, you should let them know what bugs were found and what you have done to fix them.

Testing Tips

Testing is a discipline. At one time, software companies started new programmers in the testing group. The rationale was that if they learned how to test, they would be better programmers. Maybe. Here are three tips that will save you enormous amounts of time.

Don't Test Your Own Stuff

You have just spent a week creating your widget. You know every line of the code by heart. You've agonized over every pixel in the interface, how the preferences should be laid out, and the logic of your JavaScript. You can't test it, because you can't see the problems. Someone besides you needs to test what you've created because the problems will jump out at that person. Companies that follow an extreme programming model are using this principle in programming teams.

Always hand your creation over to another person or persons.

Break Your Widget

But *you* aren't testing the widget, right?

Testing starts from the point of looking for errors, not confirming the functionality. In other words, if your testing just runs through all of the functions of your widget, you aren't taking the right approach. Testing should try to break your widget. Your testers should try to enter characters where numbers are expected and vice versa. They should enter numbers in the wrong format. They should close the widget when it is in the middle of a task. They should unplug the network connection while the widget is updating. They should click everywhere. You will try to confirm that the widget does everything you intended; they may also do that. But they should also try all of the things that you never intended to make certain your widget can handle them.

Keep a Log

You should keep track of the results of testing. If you worked in a software house, this would be called a bug stack and be the single point of coordination between the quality assurance effort and the programming effort. You may not have a QA staff, but you probably have beta testers even if they are just your friends. You probably don't need to install Bugzilla, but you should keep track of what your friends find. If they are really good friends, they will provide you with as much information as possible about reproducing the bug they've found. Those steps should be captured in your log file.

As important as the bugs and the steps to reproduce them are, the changes that you make to fix the bug are just as important. As with the initial bug report, the more information that you include about how you fixed the bug, the better. If you capture this information in your log, generating the "what's been fixed" section in your widget's release notes is a piece of cake.

Finally, you should let your testers enter feature requests in your log. As you are finishing version 1.0 of your widget, you may have ideas for version 2.0. There is a better than average chance that your testers may have ideas for version 2.0 after an hour (or ten minutes) of testing. And those ideas may not be anything you have thought of. Make certain you capture them for the next version.

What Now?

Testing isn't entirely about finding and squashing bugs, though that is a big part of it. Testing can also point out design problems. For example, if you aren't validating the data a user is entering, you will find a problem when the user enters text and should have entered numeric values. You may also discover that your widget doesn't behave properly when it can't connect to the Internet. In these cases, the result of testing is to modify your code so that the user's entries are validated and he is alerted when he has entered text instead of numbers. Or you add error checking to your widget and alert the user when there is a network problem. The Stocks widget, for instance, lets you know when there's a problem (Figure 5-8).

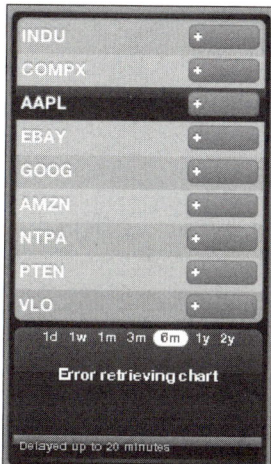

Figure 5-8

As much as you can, you should let the user know what is happening in a problem situation.

Fixing Bugs

Of course, you'll need to fix the bugs that testing uncovers. When you are in bug fix mode, you may be tempted to hack away at your widget until you fix the problem. A more effective approach is to identify the solution, make only the change to fix the bug, and then test your change by trying to reproduce the bug. Depending on the size of your testing and bug fix effort, you may want to keep track of the changes you make to your widget as you work on it. As part of keeping track, you may want to record why you made the change that you did, the expected result of the fix, and what the actual result of the fix is.

Much more could be said about the process of fixing bugs, but following these simple pointers will keep you on track and allow you to retrace your steps if you need to.

Summary

For most cases, these debugging and testing suggestions may be overkill for the kind of widget you are working on. You will have to gauge the complexity of your widget and then apply the right amount of testing and debugging effort. It isn't always possible to find all of the bugs — and some of them may be Dashboard bugs — but you should ask your friends and testers to look for the bugs, rather than allowing users to stumble upon bugs during everyday use.

In this chapter, you learned:

❑   How to find problems in your widget using JavaScript alerts

❑   How to step through your widget with a debugger

❑   How to test your widget before you release it

Exercises

1.   Why aren't JavaScript alert dialog boxes displayed on screen from alert statements in your widget?

2.   What is the PID number?

3.   What does a debugger allow you to do?

Part II

Providing User Interaction

Giving a Widget Preferences

In Chapter 4 you created a WeatherMaps widget from scratch using all of the knowledge that you'd gathered about widgets and how they are constructed from the previous chapters. You were able to incorporate JavaScript to switch between the weather maps that were displayed and add the links through the use of `<div>` tags in your HTML. You were able to use the CSS file to format and structure your widget. In this chapter, you will extend the functionality of your widget and make it more generalized for others to use.

By the end of this chapter, you will know:

- ❑ How to flip your widget to display the back side
- ❑ How to add preferences to your widget
- ❑ How to save and reload preferences

Adding Preferences to Your Widget

In WeatherMaps, you've created a widget for something you do every day—check the weather. It's based on the maps for your area and provides you with a quick way to check temperature and forecast without having to load a browser. If you hand it around to your local friends, it may contain the maps that they are interested in as well. If you send the WeatherMaps widget to your friend in San Antonio, Texas, however, it probably doesn't display the maps that she is interested in. You could include instructions for showing the contents of the widget package, opening the weathermaps.js file, and changing the URLs to maps that she is interested in, but the better approach is to give her an interface for changing those URLs.

If you have noticed the way preferences are set in the widgets that ship with Tiger, you have probably noticed that they are simple and yet collect all of the necessary information. All widgets with preferences have a small *i* that appears in the lower right hand corner of the widget whenever the arrow passes over the widget. When you place the arrow over the *i*, a circle appears around this info button, sometimes called a *rollie* (Figure 6-1).

Figure 6-1

Clicking the info button on the widget flips it over so you can change the preferences on the back side (Figure 6-2).

Figure 6-2

You'll notice that in addition to the info button on the front, the back side of widgets has logos or information about them. They also have a Done button so the user can save the changes that they have made. In keeping with the simple, one-function nature of any widget, your options are relatively few: location for your forecast, whether to display in Fahrenheit or Celsius, and whether to display daily low temperatures.

The Stock widget preferences are also simple (Figure 6-3). The text box at the top of the widget's back side lets you look up stock abbreviations and add them to the list. You can select a stock in the scrolling list and remove it from the listing and you can switch between showing stock changes as points or percentages.

Figure 6-3

In addition to these configured settings, you may have also noticed hidden settings for most widgets. For example, you can click the different stock symbols on the front of the Stock widget to display the performance graph for the company. You can also toggle between the point and percentage changes of the stock symbols without accessing the preferences by clicking the amount.

The Gmail Checker widget that you can download from `www.apple.com/downloads/dashboard` has one of the simplest widget interfaces (Figure 6-4). The widget checks your Google Gmail account and displays the number of new messages in your inbox. If you click the widget, it opens a browser to your Gmail account. The preferences are only your login name and password.

Figure 6-4

In the case of these three widgets, as well as many others, you are grabbing information from Internet websites and databases. Sometimes the owners of those websites provide you with guides about how to display their information on your website or they provide an XML feed of the information. Because a widget is just a very specialized web page, you can use those guides to simplify building your widget's interface to the website. In the case of XML feeds, you may be able to use them or extract what you need from them.

Sometimes you have to wade past several pages of information on a website as you build a query to get to the information you want to display in your widget. Because this can be difficult to do in the widget format and defeats the approach of making a widget as simple as possible, look for shortcuts. In Chapter 5, for instance, you saw how it's easier to collect the direct links to the maps on a website and use those in your widget. You may also be able to copy a database query from the location field of your browser and use it in your widget. If you are planning to distribute your widget, you will need to make it easy for the user to change the query or look at the information he wants to by allowing him to adjust the preferences.

How to Show Preferences

To add preferences to your widget, you need to create a back side panel, add the info and Done buttons, and then add a way to change the maps that are displayed in the widget. To add the info and Done buttons, you need to modify your widget's HTML, CSS, and JavaScript files to reference some of Apple's resources. Once you've added the basic functionality, you can add the preferences to your widget.

As you've seen from poking around in the contents of Apple's widgets and any of the thousand available from the Dashboard Download web page, a widget has a different background image for its back side than for its front. This makes it easy to distinguish and contrasts the front from the back so your users won't be confused about which side is the user interface.

Creating a Back Side Panel

Create the back side panel of the widget and make it the same size as the front panel. You can do this by using the front panel as a template for the size and changing the fill pattern or shade. If you create the panel in GraphicConverter, it has a micrometer tool for measuring the height and width of your images. You can also show the Position window — the window floating over the title bar — as you create the panel to get the size right (Figure 6-5).

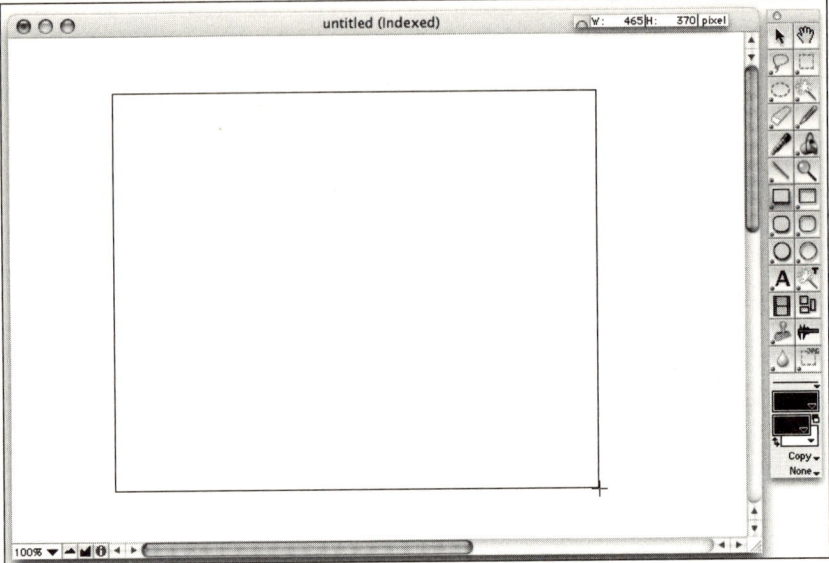

Figure 6-5

If you've lost the dimensions of the front panel, you can measure it in GraphicConverter or another graphics tool or you can open it in Preview and get the image size of the Default.png file (Figure 6-6).

Document Info	
Summary	Details	Keywords

File name:	Default.png
Document type:	Portable Network Graphics Image
File size:	5.8 KB
Image size:	465 x 370
Image DPI:	–
Color model:	RGB
ColorSync profile:	Color LCD

Figure 6-6

Widget Resources

You don't have to create all of your graphics from scratch when you are creating a widget. Apple has provided widget resources that you can use. For instance, Apple provides the info button graphics as well as scripts that you can use for widget animation. You can find these scripts and graphic files in /System/Library/WidgetResources (Figure 6-7).

Figure 6-7

In addition to the animation scripts, the AppleClasses folder contains JavaScripts for sliders and scrollbars if you are creating a widget with a scrolling area. The button and ibutton folders contain button graphics and a JavaScript for creating generic buttons. The AppleParser folder contains a JavaScript for fetching and parsing xml.

If you dip into any of Apple's widgets, you'll see references to these files and JavaScripts. You can see how they are used as you add a back side to your WeatherMaps widget.

Flipping a Widget

Once you have created the panel for the back side of the WeatherMaps widget, you'll need to make some changes to the widget source files to reference that PNG file and add the flipping capability.

The Widget's HTML File

You can start by making changes to the weathermaps.html file. Remember, as you found out in Chapter 3, that you won't be able to test the JavaScript for displaying the info button and flipping your widget in Safari. Among the widget actions that Safari doesn't support is access to the widget preferences. This will require you to install your widget after you make the changes to the files to test the functionality. If you are using BBEdit to edit the files, you can tweak them in place after you've installed the widget by using the Open Hidden command. You will have to remove the widget from Dashboard and add it again or reload the widget after your tweaks in order to see the changes you've made.

Try It Out **Modify the HTML File**

You can begin by making changes to the HTML file to add the JavaScripts. As you can see from the HTML listing below, the code has been slightly reorganized to make it easier to see the changes and read the file. All of the script references are moved into the HEAD section of the file.

1. Open the weather.html file in your text editor.

In addition to making the file easier to read, you should keep the contents of the widget front and back together in their own <div> tags. If you don't, the info and Done buttons won't display properly and sometimes may show up on the wrong side of the widget.

2. Add references in the HEAD section to the AppleButton, AppleInfoButton, and AppleAnimator JavaScripts in the AppleClasses folder. You can add these as full paths (`/System/Library/WidgetResources/AppleClasses/`) or as file URLs (`file:///System/Library/WidgetResources/AppleClasses/`).

If you are running OS X 10.4.2 or earlier, these files are not available. You will need to update to 10.4.3 or copy these files from the Goodbye World widget in the /Developer/Examples/Dashboard/ into your widget. If you chose to copy the files, the file references will be relative to your widget's root: AppleClasses/AppleButton.js, for instance.

The AppleButton.js script creates a Done button based on the parameters that you give it. The AppleInfoButton.js script creates an info button. The AppleAnimator.js script performs the animation of the widget flipping from front to back.

3. Add a JavaScript function to your weathermaps.js file. This runs the scripts whenever the widget loads.

4. You will need to call the JavaScript function from the HTML file. You do this by adding `onload='setup();'` to the BODY tag for the front of the widget. Your weathermaps.html file should look something like the one below.

```
<!DOCTYPE html PUBLIC "-//W3C//DTD XHTML 1.0 Strict//EN"
        "http://www.w3.org/TR/xhtml1/DTD/xhtml1-strict.dtd">
<html xmlns="http://www.w3.org/1999/xhtml">
<head>
  <title>WeatherMaps</title>
<style type="text/css">
  @import "weathermaps.css";
</style>

<script type="text/javascript" src="weathermaps.js" charset='utf-8'/>
<script type="text/javascript"
src="/System/Library/WidgetResources/AppleClasses/AppleButton.js" charset='utf-8'/>
<script type="text/javascript"
src="/System/Library/WidgetResources/AppleClasses/AppleInfoButton.js" charset='utf-8'/>
```

```
<script type="text/javascript" src="/System/Library/WidgetResources/AppleClasses/
AppleAnimator.js" charset='utf-8'/>
</head>

<!-- Front Side of WeatherMaps -->
<body onload='setup();'>
    <div id="front">
  <img span="backgroundImage" src="Default.png">

<div id="radar" onclick='replaceMap("radar")'>Radar</div>
<div id="curTemp" onclick='replaceMap("curTemp")'>Current Temps</div>
<div id="nightTemp" onclick='replaceMap("nightTemp")'>Overnight Temps</div>
<div id="tomorrowHigh" onclick='replaceMap("tomorrowHigh")'>Tomorrow's Highs</div>


<img id="mapImage" src=" " width="432" height="290">
  <div id='flip'></div>
</div>

<!-- Backside of WeatherMaps -->
<div id="back">
<img span="backgroundImage" src="back.png">
<div id="doneButton"></div>
</div>
</body>
</html>
```

How It Works

The HTML file contains the `<div>` markers for the front and back of the widget and contains the IDs within them for the buttons. These IDs tell the JavaScript which side to place the buttons on, for example, but not where to place them. The CSS file has all of the structure and layout information. It specifies exactly where the Done button will be placed on the back side of the widget, for instance. The JavaScript handles drawing the buttons and placing them in the right location based on the rules in the CSS file, and — when you click one of the buttons — the script handles flipping the widget.

The Widget's CSS File

Now that you have made the necessary changes to the HTML file, you can make changes to weathermaps.css for the `<div>` tags you've added. You'll need to add rules for the front and back side IDs of the widget as well as for the IDs of the buttons.

```
/*
pfterry, WeatherMaps, 2005
*/

body {
```

```
    margin: 0;
}

#radar {
    font: 10px "Lucida Grande";
    font-weight: bold;
    color: white;
    position: absolute;
    top: 20px;
    left: 20px;
}

#curTemp {
    font: 10px "Lucida Grande";
    font-weight: bold;
    color: white;
    position: absolute;
    top: 20px;
    left: 75px;
}

#nightTemp {
    font: 10px "Lucida Grande";
    font-weight: bold;
    color: white;
    position: absolute;
    top: 20px;
    left: 170px;
}

#tomorrowHigh {
    font: 10px "Lucida Grande";
    font-weight: bold;
    color: white;
    position: absolute;
    top: 20px;
    left: 280px;
}

#mapImage {
    font: 20px "Lucida Grande";
    font-weight: bold;
    text-align: center;
    color: white;
    position: absolute;
    top: 55px;
    left: 16px;
}

.backgroundImage {
    position: absolute;
    top: 0px;
    left: 0px;
}
```

```
#flip {
  position: absolute;
  top:340px;
  right:25px;
}

#doneButton {
  position:absolute;
  bottom:20px;
  left:400px;
}

#front {
  display: block;
}

#back {
  display: none;
}
```

You should double-check your spelling on each of the selector names that you've added. Verify that they exactly match the `<div id>`s in your weathermaps.html. Some of the most infuriating errors you will encounter while developing widgets will result from simple typos.

The Widget's JavaScript File

In the JavaScript file, you'll need to add the functions to load the scripts and show and hide the preferences. As with the changes to the HTML file, you'll want to group these functions together to make working with them easier.

```
// pfterry, WeatherMaps, 2005
```

```
// Global variables for the info and Done buttons.
var glassDoneButton;
var whiteInfoButton;


// setup() calls the Apple classes in the AppleButton.js and AppleInfoButton.js
// scripts to create controls for the divs in weathermaps.html.
function setup()
{
  glassDoneButton = new AppleGlassButton(document.getElementById("doneButton"),
"Done", hidePrefs);
  whiteInfoButton = new AppleInfoButton(document.getElementById("flip"),
document.getElementById("front"), "white", "white", showPrefs);
}


// showPrefs() is called whenever you click on the info button.
function showPrefs()
{
```

```
    var front = document.getElementById("front");
    var back = document.getElementById("back");

    if (window.widget)
        widget.prepareForTransition("ToBack");
    front.style.display="none";
    back.style.display="block";

    if (window.widget)
        setTimeout ('widget.performTransition();', 0);
}


// hidePrefs() is called whenever you click on the Done button.

function hidePrefs()
{
    var front = document.getElementById("front");
    var back = document.getElementById("back");

    if (window.widget)
        widget.prepareForTransition("ToFront");

    back.style.display="none";
    front.style.display="block";

    if (window.widget)
        setTimeout ('widget.performTransition();', 0);
}
```

```
// simple script to switch between the different maps in the WeatherMaps widget
function replaceMap(mapLink)
{

if (mapLink == "radar") {
var theImage = (src='http://image.weather.com/web/radar/us_mkc_closeradar_large_
usen.jpg');

} else if (mapLink == "curTemp") {

var theImage = (src='http://image.weather.com/images/maps/current/cen_curtemp_
720x486.jpg');

} else if (mapLink == "nightTemp") {

var theImage = (src='http://image.weather.com/images/maps/forecast/map_lotmpf_
night1_3usc_enus_600x405.jpg');

} else if (mapLink == "tomorrowHigh") {

var theImage = (src='http://image.weather.com/images/maps/forecast/map_hitmpf_day2_
3usc_enus_600x405.jpg');
```

```
    }

    document.getElementById("mapImage").src = theImage;
    }
```

The functions for the info and Done buttons are grouped together at the bottom of the JavaScript. These functions use the three JavaScripts from the WidgetResources folder. The setup function creates the buttons whenever the widget loads and stores them in the global variables `glassDoneButton` and `whiteInfoButton`. The `showPrefs` function flips the widget, hides the front, and displays the back side whenever you click the info button. The `hidePrefs` function reverses the previous function; it flips the widget, hides the back, and displays the front side whenever you click the Done button.

Testing Your Changes

As mentioned earlier, you will need to install the widget to test your changes. When you install the widget in Dashboard and move the arrow over it, the info button appears in the lower-right corner. As you pass the arrow over the *i*, the circle appears around it (Figure 6-8).

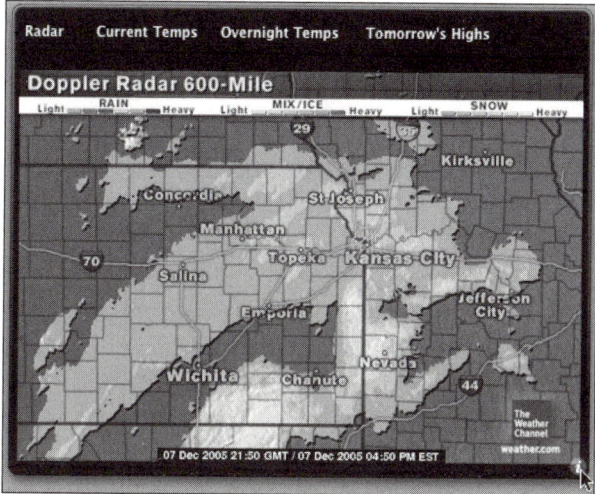

Figure 6-8

Clicking the info button flips the widget over and you can see the back of the widget with the Done button (Figure 6-9). Clicking the Done button flips the widget back to the front.

If the maps or the links for the temperature maps bleed through to the back side of the widget, you need to make certain that they are not included in the back `<div>`.

Figure 6-9

Adding Preferences

Once you have created the back panel, added the JavaScript for flipping the widget, and tested your new features, you are ready to add the preferences user interface. You want to make it as easy as possible for the user to select the maps she is interested in. You may want to use the maps on the weather.com website, but you won't be able to build a query interface to allow the user to look up these maps. However, because you can get the URLs of the different maps, you can build a list of maps for the user.

Perhaps the most concise way of presenting the maps to the user is through pop-up menus. You can collect all the map URLs at weather.com and create a set of menus based on these URLs. Such a menu allows the user to pick a map by its regional name.

Adding Preference Selection

A separate listing of maps is available in the weather map urls.txt file available with the WeatherMaps widget source files for this chapter. The close radar maps are listed by city and follow the 300 and 100-mile radius radar maps for the major cities around the United States. The overnight lows, tomorrow's highs, current temperatures, and severe weather alerts are maps grouped by nine regions around the country: Central, East Central, North Central, South Central, West Central, Northeast, Northwest, Southeast, and Southwest.

The URLs for these maps may have changed. While this widget was being developed, URLs for these maps at weather.com changed three times.

You can add the maps into the back side <div> in the weathermaps.html file as in the following listing, which shows the Current Temperatures maps only. The highlighted section of the code is the listing for the map pop-ups. Full source code including additional regional locations is available at www.wrox.com/dynamic/books/download.aspx.

```
<!-- Back side of WeatherMaps -->
<div id="back">
<img span="backgroundImage" src="back.png" />
```

```
    <div id='popupMenu2'>Current Temperatures</div>
    <select id='cTempMenu' onChange='cTempMap(this.value);'>
      <option value="">Select a regional temperature map...</option>
      <option value="http://image.weather.com/images/maps/current/cen_curtemp_720x486
.jpg">Central</option>
      <option value="http://image.weather.com/images/maps/current/ec_curtemp_720x486
.jpg">East Central</option>
      <option value="http://image.weather.com/images/maps/current/nc_curtemp_720x486
.jpg">North Central</option>
      <option value="http://image.weather.com/images/maps/current/ne_curtemp_720x486
.jpg">Northeast</option>
      <option value="http://image.weather.com/images/maps/current/nw_curtemp_720x486
.jpg">Northwest</option>
      <option value="http://image.weather.com/images/maps/current/sc_curtemp_720x486
.jpg">South Central</option>
      <option value="http://image.weather.com/images/maps/current/se_curtemp_720x486
.jpg">Southeast</option>
      <option value="http://image.weather.com/images/maps/current/sc_curtemp_720x486
.jpg">Southwest</option>
      <option value="http://image.weather.com/images/maps/current/wc_curtemp_720x486
.jpg">West Central</option>
    </select>
```

```
<div id='doneButton'></div>
</div>

</body>
</html>
```

You can see that each pop-up menu is based on a set of menu items contained within a <select> tag. The URLs of the maps are the values in the pop-up menu with the region names providing the item for the user to select. These additions add the names of the five kinds of maps to the back of the widget (Figure 6-10).

With the exception of the Severe Weather Alerts maps, the names of the map groupings correspond to the names on the front of the widget. The pop-up menus appear just below the name of the kind of map (Figure 6-11).

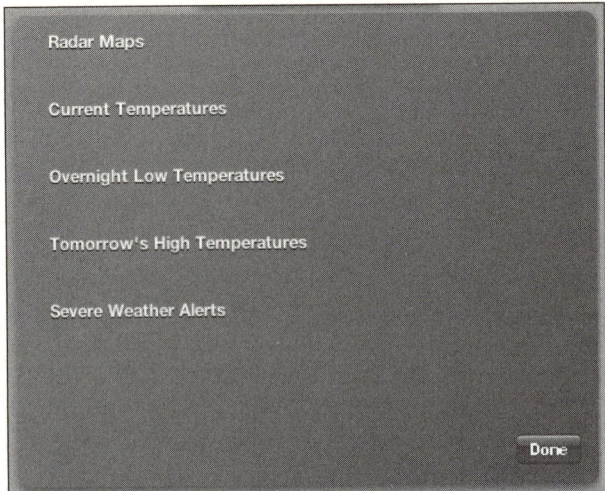

Figure 6-10

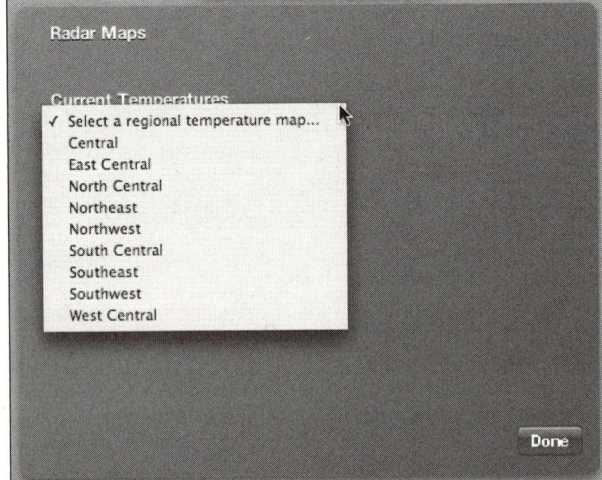

Figure 6-11

The location of the pop-up menus and their connection to the map groups are controlled through rules in the weathermaps.css file. The rules for the pop-up menu placement are grouped at the top of the Cascading Style Sheet. You can see that the names of the map groups are evenly spaced from the top edge of your widget and the top of each map is 9 points beneath the name. The rules also specify the font face, weight, color, and drop shadow. The display names for pop-up menus, like popupMenu1, match the `<div>`s in the HTML file, and the names for the menus match the names in the `<select id>` tags.

```
#popupMenu1 {
    font: 13px "Helvetica Neue";
    font-weight: Bold;
    color: white;
    text-shadow: black 0px 1px 0px;
    position: absolute;
    top: 25px;
    left: 44px;
    z-index: 19;
}

#radarMenu {
    position:absolute;
    top: 34px;
    left: 50px;
    width: 163px;
    height: 30px;
    opacity: 0.0;
    z-index: 20;
}


#popupMenu2 {
    font: 13px "Helvetica Neue";
    font-weight: Bold;
    color: white;
    text-shadow: black 0px 1px 0px;
    position: absolute;
    top: 75px;
    left: 44px;
    z-index: 19;
}

#cTempMenu {
    position:absolute;
    top: 84px;
    left: 50px;
    width: 163px;
    height: 30px;
    opacity: 0.0;
    z-index: 20;
}

#popupMenu3 {
    font: 13px "Helvetica Neue";
    font-weight: Bold;
    color: white;
    text-shadow: black 0px 1px 0px;
    position: absolute;
    top: 125px;
    left: 44px;
```

```
        z-index: 19;
}

#oTempMenu {
        position:absolute;
        top: 134px;
        left: 50px;
        width: 163px;
        height: 30px;
        opacity: 0.0;
        z-index: 20;
}

#popupMenu4 {
        font: 13px "Helvetica Neue";
        font-weight: Bold;
        color: white;
        text-shadow: black 0px 1px 0px;
        position: absolute;
        top: 175px;
        left: 44px;
        z-index: 19;
}

#hTempMenu {
        position:absolute;
        top: 184px;
        left: 50px;
        width: 163px;
        height: 30px;
        opacity: 0.0;
        z-index: 20;
}

#popupMenu5 {
        font: 13px "Helvetica Neue";
        font-weight: Bold;
        color: white;
        text-shadow: black 0px 1px 0px;
        position: absolute;
        top: 225px;
        left: 44px;
        z-index: 19;
}

#sWeatherMenu {
        position:absolute;
        top: 234px;
        left: 50px;
        width: 163px;
        height: 30px;
        opacity: 0.0;
        z-index: 20;
}
```

When the user selects one of the regional names from the pop-up menu, the onChange script passes the value — the URL of the map — to the appropriate function in the weathermaps.js file.

```
<div id='popupMenu2'>Current Temperatures</div>
<select id='cTempMenu' onChange='cTempMap(this.value);'>
  <option value="">Select a regional temperature map...</option>
```

Each pop-up menu has a corresponding JavaScript function. When an item is selected from one of the menus, the selection is returned to the function through the `this.value` variable.

```
// Functions for selecting menu items and setting the preferences
// radarMenu function
function radMap() {
  var rMap = document.getElementById('radarMenu').value;

  if (rMap == '') {
    return;
  }

widget.setPreferenceForKey(rMap,"radarMenu");

}


// cTempMenu function
function cTempMap() {
  var cTMap = document.getElementById('cTempMenu').value;

  if (cTMap == '') {
    return;
  }

widget.setPreferenceForKey(cTMap,"cTempMenu");

}


// oTempMenu function
function oTempMap() {
  var oTMap = document.getElementById('oTempMenu').value;

  if (oTMap == '') {
    return;
  }

widget.setPreferenceForKey(oTMap,"oTempMenu");

}

// hTempMenu function
function hTempMap() {
  var hTMap = document.getElementById('hTempMenu').value;

  if (hTMap == '') {
```

```
            return;
        }

    widget.setPreferenceForKey(hTMap,"hTempMenu");

    }

    // sWeatherMenu function
    function sWeatherMap() {
        var sWMap = document.getElementById('sWeatherMenu').value;

        if (sWMap == '') {
            return;
        }

    widget.setPreferenceForKey(sWMap,"sWeatherMenu");

    }
```

You'll notice that the last line in each function sets the preferences for the widget. What you have to do is modify the current `replaceMap()` function to fetch the maps that the user sets in the pop-up menus. Because you want those settings stored for the next time you open the widget, you can save them as preferences and then change the `replaceMap()` function to load the maps from the preferences. The next section shows you how to write and then read the preferences in your widget.

Saving and Reading Preferences

If you're a long-time Mac user you're familiar with preferences, even though OS X changed them from the OS 9 days. In the bad old days of OS 9, the preferences were locked in the application or in unreadable files. Under OS X, you'll still find preferences in the Preferences folder, but they are stored in XML files that you can read with any text editor as well as the Property List Editor.

Your widget's preferences are stored in its own file: ~/Library/Preferences/widget-com.deadtrees. widget.WeatherMaps.plist. The preferences file is referenced from two Dashboard files — com.apple .dashboard.plist and com.apple.dashboard.client.plist — stored in the ~/Library/Preferences/ folder (Figure 6-12). The first file contains a complete listing of all of loaded widgets (widget-list) and all of the installed widgets (layer-gadgets). The file also contains the developer mode setting. The installed widgets are listed in the layer-gadgets.

Among other items, the second file contains the com.apple.WebKit.searchField:searchHistory and com.apple.WebKit.searchField:Google Maps histories (Figure 6-13).

Clicking the Google recent searches drop-down list in Safari shows you these search histories.

Dashboard has methods for writing and reading preferences into a widget's plist file. These methods reduce all of the effort that you might expend looking for a good place to stash the preference information and then writing functions to write the information out and read it back into the widget. The two methods are:

❑   widget.setPreferenceForKey(preference, key)

❑   widget.preferenceForKey(key)

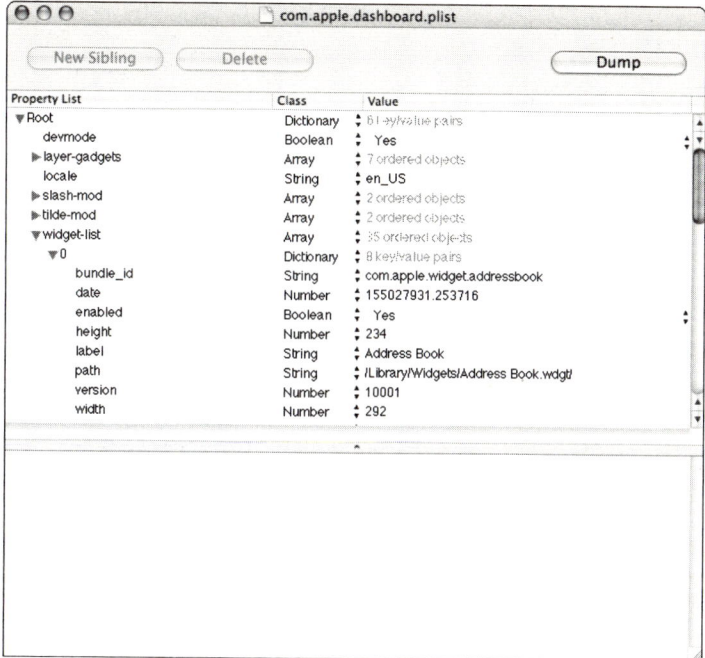

Figure 6-12

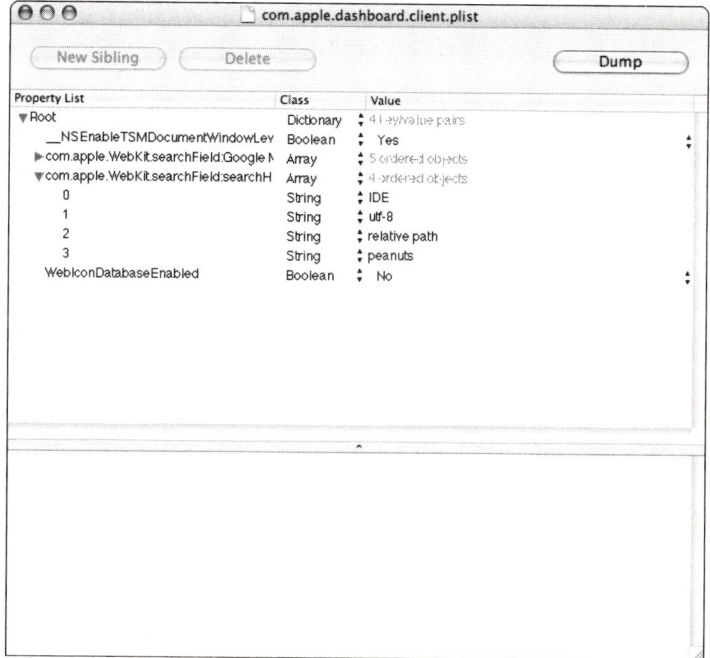

Figure 6-13

When called, the first one writes the preference and a key into the preference file. In the listing of weathermaps.js above, this function

```
// sWeatherMenu function
function sWeatherMap() {
  var sWMap = document.getElementById('sWeatherMenu').value;

  if (sWMap == '') {
    return;
  }

  widget.setPreferenceForKey(sWMap,"sWeatherMenu");

}
```

takes the URL to the map and writes it into the widget-com.deadtrees.widget.WeatherMaps.plist file with the key. The second function reads the preferences back into the widget.

The `widget.setPreferenceForKey` *function has a Cocoa-style parameter ordering: parameters are passed in the order the function names them. When you call this function, you should pass the preference value first and the key second.*

Both the key and the preference must be written as strings. If you try to write the preferences as objects, you will see in the console log an error message stating that the XML data couldn't be generated:

```
DashboardClient[869] CFLog (15): Could not generate XML data for property list
```

In the updated version of the `replaceMap()` function below, your hard-coded URL links to the maps have been replaced with the function to get the stored preferences.

```
// retrieve the map URL from the preferences and display it.
function replaceMap(mapLink) {

  if (mapLink == "radar") {
    if(window.widget) {
      var theImage = widget.preferenceForKey("radarMenu");
    }
  } else if (mapLink == "curTemp") {
    if(window.widget) {
      var theImage = widget.preferenceForKey("cTempMenu");
    }
  } else if (mapLink == "nightTemp") {
    if(window.widget) {
      var theImage = widget.preferenceForKey("oTempMenu");
    }
  } else if (mapLink == "tomorrowHigh") {
    if(window.widget) {
      var theImage = widget.preferenceForKey("hTempMenu");
    }
```

```
  } else if (mapLink == "sWeatherMap") {
    if(window.widget) {
      var theImage = widget.preferenceForKey("sWeatherMenu");
    }
  }

  document.getElementById("mapImage").src = theImage;

}
```

Now whenever a user clicks the map link on the front of the widget, the `theImage` variable is set to the URL, which is read from the preferences file. Your friend in San Antonio will be able to select the maps for her region from the pop-up menus rather than having to change the hard coded links.

Summary

As simple as widgets are designed to be, it makes sense to give the user some options for changing some of the widget's settings. Adding preferences to the widget provides the user with a convenient way of making those changes and gives your widget broader appeal. As you saw in this chapter, adding those additional features to cover the preferences required the JavaScript to do more of the work, but the script took advantage of Dashboard events to perform some of the magic.

In this chapter, you learned:

- ❑   How to flip your widget to display the back side
- ❑   How to add preferences to your widget
- ❑   How to save and reload preferences

Before you turn to Chapter 7 to learn about the widget events that allow you to control the widget in Dashboard, you should run through the exercises below to review what you covered in this chapter.

Exercises

1.   What do you do for an info button if your widget's background is white?

2.   If you see your weather maps appear on the back side of the widget, what is the problem?

3.   Without reading them back in, how can you check your widget's preferences to make certain they are being written properly?

Widget Events

In Chapter 6, you learned what the conventions are for adding preferences to widgets, how to add a panel for the back side, and how to split the contents of the front from the contents of the back of the widget using <div> tags. You also learned how to use JavaScript to save user selectable preferences by writing them into the widget's preferences file, and you learned how to read those preferences in from the preferences file. In this chapter, you are going to learn about the activation events that make the widget work. You'll also learn about control regions.

Whenever you activate Dashboard, some or all of the installed widgets perform actions. You may notice this if you have the Weather widget installed. If it has been a number of hours, that first moment after Dashboard opens the temperature changes in the Weather widget, because it is fetching the current temps as a result of the activation event. In this chapter, you'll learn about the different widget events and how you can use them.

By the end of this chapter, you will know:

- ❑   How to update your widget with the activation event
- ❑   How to check system resources
- ❑   How to remove preferences with the remove event
- ❑   How to use control regions

The Dashboard Activation Event

Most of the time when you invoke Dashboard, your installed widgets fly into view as though nothing has changed. If you blink, you might even miss them refresh their information, but — unless you're the kind of person who invokes Dashboard every minute or so — the widgets probably have to catch up with the latest version of the information. The Stocks widget has to go get the latest quotes and the Weather widget has to get the latest temperature and forecast information.

You have a better chance of seeing the widgets refresh the first time you open Dashboard after you have rebooted your Macintosh (Figure 7-1). Widgets initially load blank because, like any Macintosh application, they use system resources, so widget authors write them so they do not constantly use resources when Dashboard isn't loaded.

Whenever you invoke Dashboard, the activation event loads all of the installed widgets. If those widgets have JavaScript functions associated with the activation event, they will be run as Dashboard loads.

Activation Properties

You can let your widget know when Dashboard activates using the `widget.onshow` property, and when Dashboard is inactive using the `widget.onhide` property. If you look at the Weather.js file, you can see the use of these properties. The script sets up the functions for use when Dashboard is activated.

Figure 7-1

```
if (window.widget)
{
  widget.onremove = onremove;
  widget.onhide = onhide;
  widget.onshow = onshow;
  widget.onreceiverequest = receiverequest;
}
```

The `onshow` function checks to see if the widget has been run before, clears the timer, and runs the animation, then calls the `doLoad` function. The `doLoad` function sets the timer to one minute and then calls the `fetchData` function that uses the Apple parser to get the weather data from AccuWeather.

```
function onshow ()
{

  everBeenCalled = true;

  if (timer != null)
    clearInterval(timer);

  if (windAnimation.animating)
  {
    windAnimation.timer = setInterval ('windAnimate();', 30);
  }
  doLoad ();

}


function doLoad ()
{
  // set timeout to 1 minute for testing
  fetchData();
  timer = setInterval ('fetchData();', timerInterval);

}


function fetchData()
{
  apple_parser.fetchAndExecute (fetchDataInternal);
}
```

When Dashboard is hidden, the `onhide` function clears the Weather widget's timer so that it will not pull weather information while hidden.

```
function onhide () {
  if (timer != null) {
    // we were hidden clear the timer
    clearInterval(timer);
    timer = null;
  }
```

Now that you see how the activation notification works in one of Apple's widgets, you should modify the WeatherMaps widget to take advantage of Dashboard activation to get the latest version of the radar map.

Adding Activation to WeatherMaps

You can add the activation properties to the WeatherMaps widget so it retrieves the latest version of the radar map whenever you activate Dashboard.

1. Open the weathermaps.js file in your text editor.

2. Add the activation properties to the JavaScript.

```
if (window.widget)
{
  widget.onhide = onhide;
  widget.onshow = onshow;
}
```

3. Now you can add the onShow function to get the latest version of the radar map.

```
function onshow ()
{

  var theImage = widget.preferenceForKey("radarMenu");
  document.getElementById("mapImage").src = theImage;

}
```

4. Because we haven't added a function to reload the maps regularly while Dashboard is open, the onHide () function isn't necessary at the moment. You can comment out the widget.onhide statement by adding // to the front of the line.

5. Save your changes to the weathermaps.js file. You'll need to reload the widget to see your changes.

How It Works

When the widget receives the activation event from Dashboard, the onshow function is executed. It sets the variable from the stored WeatherMap preferences so the latest version of the radar map will be loaded the next time you activate Dashboard.

System Resources

As you saw earlier, if your computer has been off or asleep, the first time you activate Dashboard, you may see all of your widgets without their preferences while the information is retrieved. This is a technique for conserving system resources while Dashboard isn't activated.

You can see the impact widgets have on your system if you launch Activity Monitor and leave it running while Dashboard activates. CPU, Disk Activity, and Network usage all spike (Figure 7-2). To monitor widgets, you will need to view All Processes in the Activity Monitor and filter for Dashboard because widgets run as children of Dashboard. Doing this allows you to see the widgets that are installed as well as their resource usage. During the initial spike when Dashboard activates, they use the most CPU and bandwidth.

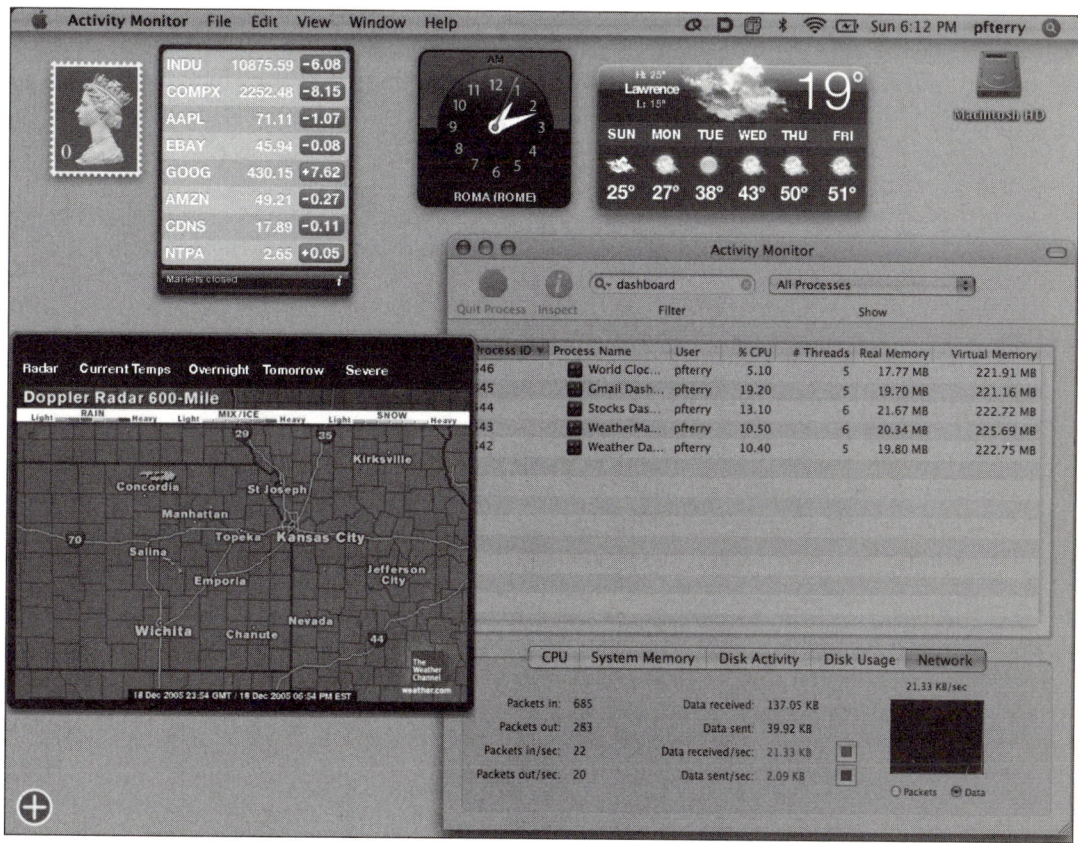

Figure 7-2

Once you close Dashboard, however, the widgets' resource usage falls off, aside from the real and virtual memory that they use (Figure 7-3).

While Dashboard provides an environment for widgets, it does not provide the memory space. Widgets run as child processes of the Dock and are listed individually in the BSD utility top and the Activity Monitor (Figure 7-4). You'll also notice when you look in Activity Monitor that Dashboard doesn't show up as a process.

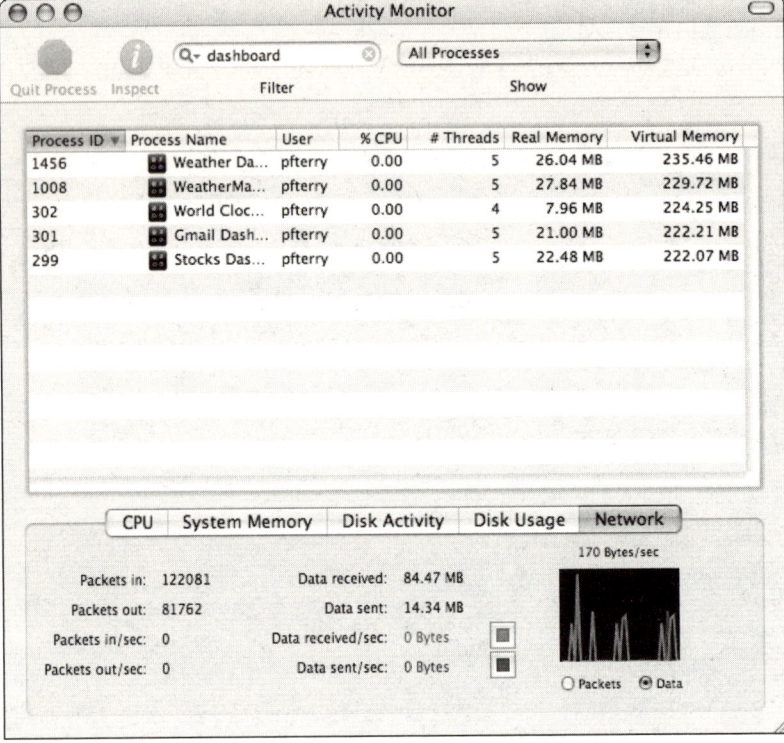

Figure 7-3

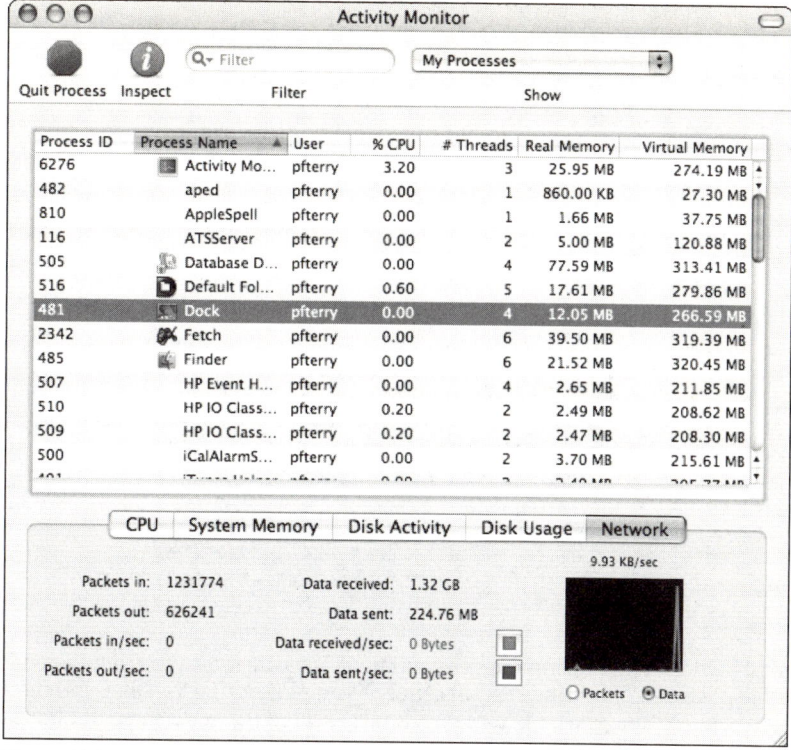

Figure 7-4

Removing Widget Preferences

As you noticed by looking in Activity Monitor at the resources used by widgets, a widget that isn't installed in Dashboard doesn't use any resources. This means that you can lessen system impact by removing unused widgets from Dashboard. You may remember that when you remove a widget from Dashboard by clicking the close box, it is not uninstalled or moved to the trash. It remains in the Widgets folder and visible in the Widgets tray until you need it again.

Widget preferences also hang around unless you explicitly remove them. A removal event handler is available if you want to remove your widget's preferences whenever it is removed from Dashboard. This isn't required, but is just a good housekeeping practice.

If you look at the Weather.js file for the Weather widget, you'll see that I have written it to clear the preferences whenever the widget is removed from Dashboard. The `onremove` statement is set in the same group as the onhide and onshow statements.

```
if (window.widget)
{
  widget.onremove = onremove;
  widget.onhide = onhide;
  widget.onshow = onshow;
  widget.onreceiverequest = receiverequest;
}
```

The `onremove()` function sets the preferences for each one of the options available in the Weather widget to null.

```
function onremove ()
{
  if (window.widget)
  {
    widget.setPreferenceForKey (null, createkey("show-lows"));
    widget.setPreferenceForKey (null, createkey("collapsed"));
    widget.setPreferenceForKey (null, createkey("celcius"));
    widget.setPreferenceForKey (null, createkey("zip"));
    widget.setPreferenceForKey (null, createkey("postal"));
    widget.setPreferenceForKey (null, createkey("savedcity"));
  }
}
```

The effect of this action is that the preferences and their keys are removed from the widget-com.apple .widget.weather.plist file. You can see this in action if you remove the Weather widget. If you check the preferences file before you remove the widget, you'll see all of the keys (Figure 7-5).

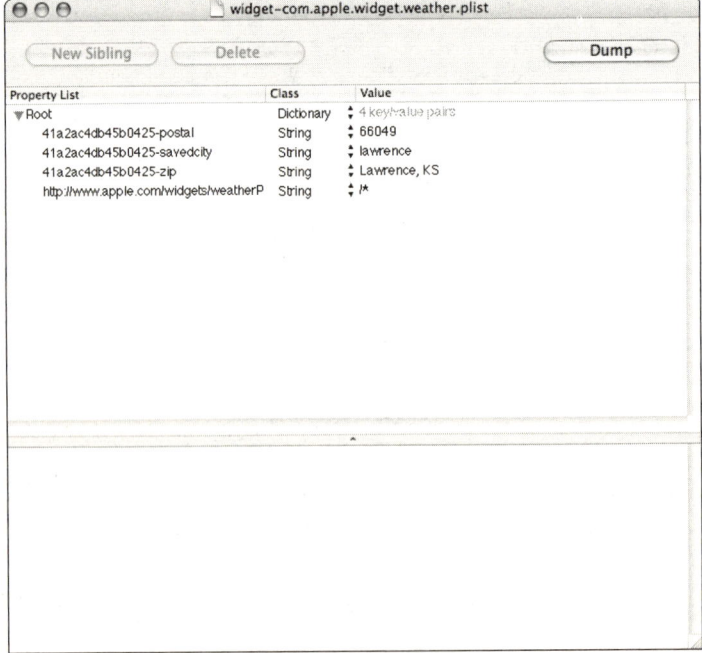

Figure 7-5

When you remove the widget from Dashboard, and open the preferences again, you'll see that they have been removed with the exception of one string (Figure 7-6).

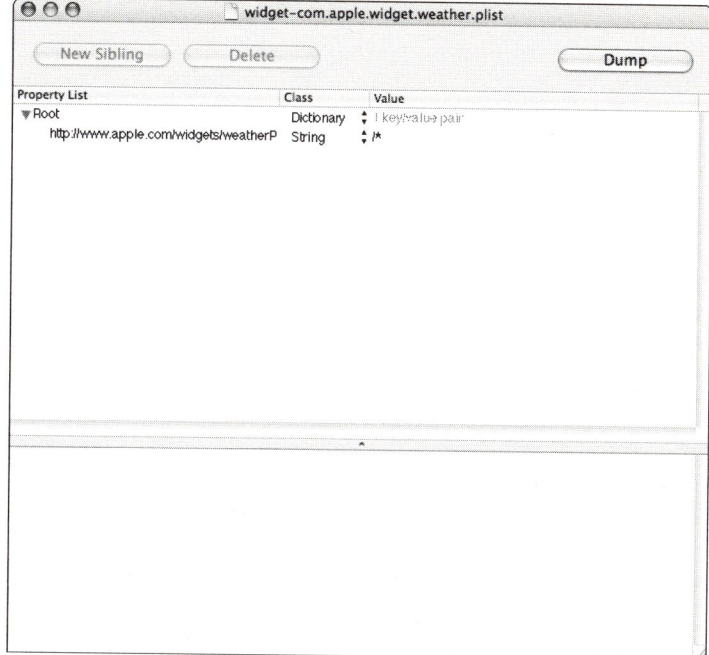

Figure 7-6

If you add the Weather widget back to Dashboard, you'll see that it opens with the default preference settings of Austin.

| Try It Out | Adding onRemove to WeatherMaps |

Add the preferences removal function to the WeatherMaps widget so the preferences are reset whenever the widget is removed from Dashboard.

1. Open the weathermaps.js file in your text editor.

2. Add the remove properties to the JavaScript with the onHide and onShow group.

```
if (window.widget)
{
//   widget.onhide = onHide;
     widget.onshow = onShow;
     widget.onremove = onRemove;
}
```

3. Now you are ready to add the onRemove function to the weathermaps.js file. You'll want to reset each one of the preferences.

```
function onRemove() {
    if (window.widget) {
        widget.setPreferenceForKey(null, "radarMenu");
        widget.setPreferenceForKey(null, "cTempMenu");
        widget.setPreferenceForKey(null, "oTempMenu");
        widget.setPreferenceForKey(null, "hTempMenu");
        widget.setPreferenceForKey(null, "sWeatherMenu");
    }
}
```

4. Save your changes and close the weathermaps.js file. You'll need to reload the widget to make your changes take effect.

5. Hold down the Option key while your arrow is over the WeatherMaps widget and click the close box.

6. Switch to the Finder and open the ~/Library/Preferences/ folder and look for the widget-com.deadtrees.widget.weathermaps.plist. You shouldn't be able to find it. When all of the preferences have been removed, the plist file is removed.

7. Open Dashboard again and you'll see that your WeatherMaps widget is definitely preference-less (Figure 7-7).

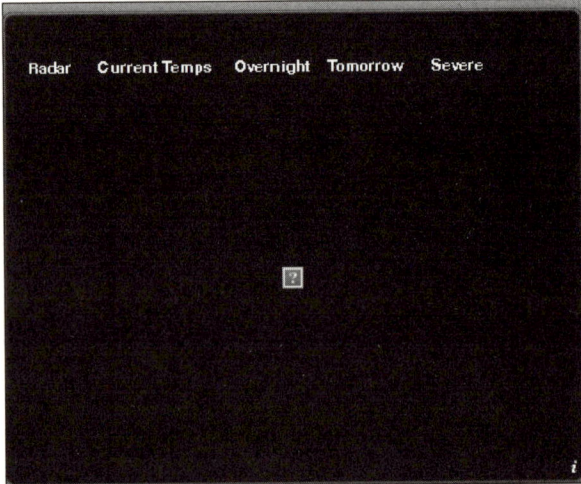

Figure 7-7

The broken link graphic tells you where the radar map should be located if the preference were set.

How It Works

The widget receives the removal event from Dashboard whenever you click in the close box of the widget or use the Widget Manager to remove it. With that, the `onRemove()` function is executed, which removes the preferences. Because you are removing all of the preferences, the WeatherMaps preferences file is removed. (The Weather widget's preferences file isn't removed because it left one key.) When you add WeatherMaps to Dashboard, it opens without any preferences at all; clicking each map link at the top of the widget presents you with the broken link graphic.

You may remember that you are setting the radar map in the HTML file when you establish the `<div>` for the map.

```
<!-- This URL sets the image so the widget comes up with a map the first time it is
launched. -->
<div id="theImages"></div>
   <img id="mapImage"
src="http://image.weather.com/web/radar/us_mkc_closeradar_large_usen.jpg"
width="432" height="290"></img>
   <div id='flip'></div>
</div>
```

This default map is overridden by the execution your new `onShow()` function. Because you haven't set the preference for the Radar map, you see only a broken link. The Weather widget defaulting to Austin makes a little more sense now; better to have the weather conditions of a random U.S. city than an empty widget.

Setting Widget Focus

In addition to activation and remove events, your widgets can also take advantage of events for setting the focus and for tracking drags in Dashboard. For instance, if you want to let the user know when your widget is the front-most widget in Dashboard, you can indicate this through the `widget.focus` and `widget.blur` properties.

You can see this in use in Apple's Calculator widget as well as the PCalc widget. Whenever Calculator has the focus, the screen becomes blue. If another widget is the front-most, the Calculator screen is grey. PCalc does something similar: its screen is a light tan when it has focus and a light grey when it doesn't. If you look at the code in Calculator.js, you'll see two statements that set the properties.

```
window.onfocus = focus;
window.onblur = blur;
```

And here are the two functions that change the screen setting of the Calculator when it has focus.

```
function focus() {
  document.getElementById("lcd-backlight").style.display =  "block";
  document.getElementById("calcDisplay").setAttribute("class", "backlightLCD");
}

function blur() {
  document.getElementById("lcd-backlight").style.display = "";
  document.getElementById("calcDisplay").setAttribute("class", "nobacklightLCD");
}
```

PCalc does this in a slightly different fashion. It also contains functions for setting the widget's focus and blur. However, it uses an image to indicate when the LCD has backlight and when the backlight is off.

In addition to showing when a widget has focus, these handlers can also be used for times when the widget doesn't have focus. The Wimic widget uses the `window.onfocus` handler to minimize the widget when it doesn't have focus (Figure 7-8).

Figure 7-8

Because Wimic retrieves and displays cartoon strips from the Internet, it is rather large when it has focus (Figure 7-9) and minimizing it leaves more space for other widgets you may be running.

Figure 7-9

Dragging a Widget

You can also track your widget's movements through the `ondrag.start` and `ondrag.stop` properties. The `ondrag.start` handler is called as the drag begins and the `ondrag.stop` handler is called when the drag finishes. Besides using these handlers to track the widget's movements, you can also use them for other drag-dependent functions.

The Flight Tracker widget, for instance, uses the `ondrag.start` to close any pop-up menus when the drag starts. The handler calls the `dismissComboBoxes()` function.

```
function ondragstart() {
  dismissComboBoxes();
}
```

The `dismissComboBoxes` function closes any pop-up menus when a drag starts.

```
function dismissComboBoxes()
{
    document.embeds['airlines-input'].dismissPopup();
    document.embeds['departCity-input'].dismissPopup();
    document.embeds['arriveCity-input'].dismissPopup();
}
```

Control Regions

While you're looking at widget events, you should also look at the control regions that Dashboard brings to widgets. You can use the -apple-dashboard-region addition to style sheets to define different parts of your widget for controls. For instance, you can normally click any part of a widget and drag it around the screen. By contrast, application windows have specific regions defined for different functions. Typically, you mouse down on the title bar and drag the window to a new location on screen. Inside the window, however, mousing down and dragging selects the objects or text within the window. If you want to scroll the contents of a document, another region of the window is assigned for that behavior.

You can see an example of the way control regions are used in the Calculator widget. Each of the buttons has a defined region that produces the effect of the buttons of a calculator. Click in one of those regions and you can click the button, but you can't drag the widget. The To Do Tracker widget from Monkey Business Labs also has control regions defined that behave like an application. If you click one of the items in the to-do list, you are able to drag it to a new position in the list (Figure 7-10) rather than dragging the widget. If you want to drag the widget to a new location on screen, you — intuitively — grab the wire ring of the To Do Tracker.

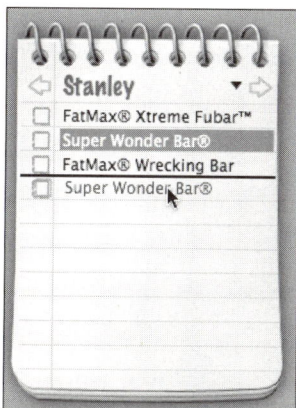

Figure 7-10

When you look in the To Do Tracker.css file, you'll also notice that the previous and next arrows and the resize thumb are defined control regions. The functions for these control regions are apparently in the TDTPlugin and you can't see them, but they could just as easily be created in JavaScript.

The -apple-dashboard-region is a property you add to a CSS selector that specifies the control region for the style. This property takes the parameter dashboard-region(), which requires two parameters: label and geometry. Both of these parameters are required. Label specifies the type of region being defined, and control is the only possible parameter that it can take. As you can easily guess, geometry specifies the shape of the control region. Its parameters are either circle or rectangle. With just this information you can specify a control region. If you look in the To Do Tracker.css file, you see that the wire ring top of the widget is defined with the label control and the geometry rectangle.

The area is specified within the style by the left, bottom, width, and height settings.

In addition to these parameters, you can also specify the boundary offsets in pixels for the control region using four parameters: offset-top, offset-right, offset-bottom, and offset-left. These are the offsets from the edge of the boundary that you have defined in the style. If you do not assign these offsets, Dashboard assumes 0 for all four. Be warned that you cannot specify a negative value for any of these offsets. The wire ring on the To Do Tracker widget is specified as a control region in the TopBar selector in the To Do Tracker.css file. If you added offsets to the TopBar style above, it might look like this.

```
#TopBar {
    position:absolute;
    left:22px;
    bottom:222px;
    width:195px;
    height:25px;
    -apple-dashboard-region: dashboard-region(control rectangle 5px 5px 5px 5px);
}
```

Now that you see how control regions work, let's add one to the WeatherMaps widget.

Try it Out   Adding a Control Region

1. Open the weathermaps.css file.

2. Create a `<div>` for a region on the map widget for the Weather.com logo and define it in the CSS file. It should look something like this:

```
#wLogo {
    position: absolute;
    top:300px;
    right:20px;
    width:50px;
    bottom:30px;
    -apple-dashboard-region: dashboard-region(control rectangle, 0 0 0 0);
}
```

3. Add the `<div>` id to the weathermaps.html file.

```
<div id="wLogo" onclick='weatherLogo();'></div>
```

4. Add the function to the weathermaps.js file.

```
function weatherLogo() {
    if (window.widget) {
        widget.openURL('http://www.weather.com/');
    }
}
```

5. Reload the Weathermaps widget if you have it installed. Now when you click the Weather.com logo on the map, it will open Safari and load the Weather.com website.

How it Works

You define the area in the CSS file. This is similar to defining an area of a graphic on a web page. You attach a function to it using the selector that you created in the CSS file. The function does all of the work. In this case, it closes the Dashboard, launches the browser, and opens the weather.com website in your window. It will be left as an exercise for the programmer, but the function could also load the weather.com page containing the map you just clicked.

Summary

JavaScript may do most of the work in widgets, but it takes the widget events to kick off those scripts. Events allow you to have the latest information without using system resources to continually pull the information in the background. Events also allow you to clean up when the widget is removed.

In this chapter, you learned:

- ❏   How to update your widget with the activation event
- ❏   How to check system resources
- ❏   How to remove preferences with the remove event
- ❏   How to use control regions

In Chapter 8, you'll learn how to resize your widget's window, but you should run through the exercises below before you move on.

Exercises

1.   How do you keep the preferences file if you are removing or resetting the preferences?

2.   Why don't you see Dashboard in the Activity Monitor?

3.   What causes Dashboard to send the removal event?

Adding to the Widget Interface

In Chapter 7, you looked at widget activation events that result from invoking Dashboard. You also looked at the way system resources are affected by widget activation and how the onRemove event could be used to remove widget preferences. In this chapter, you'll learn how to add to the widget interface.

You may have noticed after you installed Tiger and began working with widgets that they usually display a well-defined set of information. Even in cases where the information changes, the widget may not be resizable. In this chapter we'll look at when to make the widget user resizable.

By the end of this chapter, you will know:

❑   When to use absolute or live resizing

❑   How to add resizing to your widget

❑   How to add scrolling to your widget

Resizing

Most widgets display information that can be contained in a small space without the need for any additional space. On the small screens of PowerBooks, iBooks and MacBooks, a widget needs to be a good neighbor and leave enough space for other widgets. The Flight Tracker widget is a good example of this (Figure 8-1).

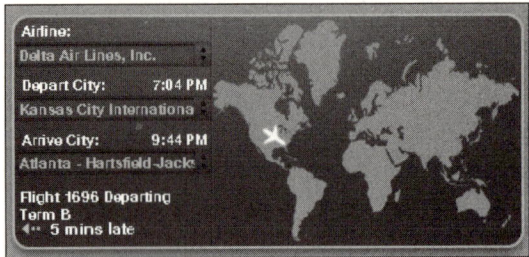

Figure 8-1

In a small space, the Flight Tracker widget allows you to pick the airline, departure and arrival cities, and the flight and then displays the current flight information with a map representing the plane's location. This economy of space is typical of well-designed widgets.

Even when the widget needs to display more information, it can still be done economically. The Stocks widget (Figure 8-2) typically displays the current price and the change.

Figure 8-2

It displays a graph of the historical performance of the stock whenever you click the stock a second time (Figure 8-3). This method of resizing the widget provides the additional space needed for displaying the graph while still maintaining a small screen footprint for most uses.

Sometimes, however, the information may be dynamic and dictate that the widget provides the user with a way to resize it and display additional information. The Widget widget (Figure 8-4), for instance, provides the user with two ways to display more of the widgets installed on his Macintosh. It can be resized to show more widgets in the window and the user can scroll through the list of widgets.

The Stocks widget and the Widgets widget are examples of the two kinds of resizing available for widgets: absolute and relative — or live — resizing, respectively. Each has its own purpose.

Figure 8-3

Figure 8-4

When to Resize the Widget

The information should dictate the kind of resizing that you need to provide. Before you begin by creating a widget for live resizing, you should look at the data to see if you can provide the additional information using absolute resizing. If the additional information is dynamic but consistent like the Stocks widget, you can use absolute resizing. Besides displaying additional information, absolute resizing can also be used for minimizing your widget to preserve screen space. When you examine all of the instances of resizing in your installed widgets, you may find that most of them are absolute resizing, which points out how infrequently you really need to use relative resizing.

However, if your widget needs to display dynamic information that could expand or if your widget displays information that has lots of detail in it, you may want to provide the user with a way of resizing the widget relatively. If your widget displays RSS feeds, for instance, you may want to give the user the option of resizing the widget to get more feeds onscreen. If you are displaying pictures, you may want to give the user the option of resizing the widget to display a larger version of a picture after he has found a picture he wants to view.

How to Resize a Widget

Making your widget resizable requires additions to the HTML, CSS, and JavaScript files. You have to give the user a control for resizing the widget. Typically this is a thumb control that you add to the lower-right corner of the widget, though you may want to provide a different control if you are resizing your widget only vertically. To make the thumb control work, you must provide a control region for it in the widget's CSS file in addition to controlling the placement of the thumb control. Finally, you must include an event handler in the widget's JavaScript that resizes the widget in response to the user's drag.

As you examine how widgets are constructed, you'll see that you have several ways to provide relative resizing. The way you resize your widget depends on the kind of control that you need and the kind of background you are using.

You can make your widget background one whole piece; this is the way most widgets are constructed. Or you can create your widget as a set of tiles that together make up the whole widget, as you can see in this Images folder (Figure 8-5), which contains the separate images for the widget. While this is mainly a matter of personal preference, you should be aware of the differences. If you decide to create your widget in sections, you will have to keep track of the individual pieces in your HTML and CSS file. The individual pieces may give you finer control of the widget interface, but it won't be as straightforward as adding resizing to a widget that is a single panel.

If you are using a picture or a graphic as your background image, you may want to control how the user can resize the widget. If you allow the user to resize the image horizontally as well as vertically, the graphic may become distorted. You can control this by creating the widget with a single background image and then control the way it is resized. For instance, you could allow the user to resize the widget vertically only, like the Apple Events widget shown in Figure 8-6.

If you look in the bottom middle of the widget, you'll see three white lines together on the foreground row of the chairs. This is the resize thumb control. When you resize the Apple Events widget, you'll see that the author controls the way you can resize the widget; you can resize the widget only by making it taller. If you show the contents of the widget and look at the background image, you'll see that it is tuned for resizing vertically (Figure 8-7). Resizing the widget to display more content makes use of the tall background without affecting the foreground seats at the bottom of the image.

Let's look at how a tiled widget would be set up for resizing.

Figure 8-5

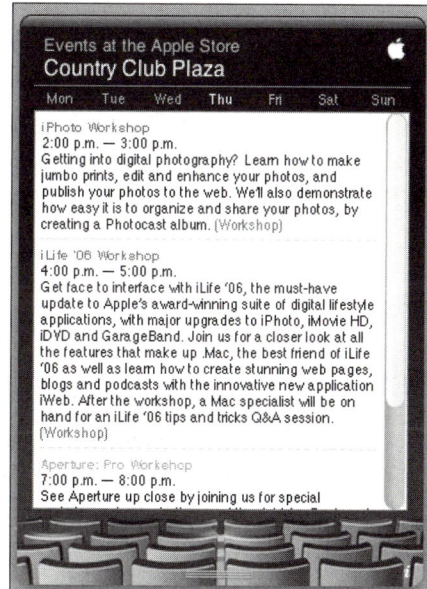

Figure 8-6

Figure 8-7

The HTML File

This rather spare HTML file for our Resize widget shows you how to go about adding the graphics for resizing. If you look under the widget parts comment, you'll see how individual <div>s have been created for each one of the widget tiles. Below the <div>s you'll see that the file URI has been added to link in the resize.png image for the thumb control from Apple's WidgetResources directory.

```
<html>
    <head>
        <style type="text/css">
            @import "resize.css";
        </style>
        <script type='text/javascript' src='AppleClasses/AppleInfoButton.js'
charset='utf-8' />
        <script type='text/javascript' src='AppleClasses/AppleAnimator.js'
charset='utf-8' />
        <script type='text/javascript' src='AppleClasses/AppleButton.js'
charset='utf-8' />
    </head>
    <body onload="init();">
        <div id="front">
            <!-- widget parts -->
            <div id="top">
                <div id="top_left"></div>
                <div id="top_center">
                    <div id="title">tiled resize</div>
                </div>
                <div id="top_right">
                </div>
            </div>

            <div id="middle">
                <div id="middle_left"></div>
                <div id="middle_center"></div>
                <div id="middle_right"></div>
            </div>

            <div id="bottom_left"></div>
            <div id="bottom_center"></div>
            <div id="bottom_right"></div>

            <img id='resize' src='/System/Library/WidgetResources/resize.png'
onmousedown='mouseDown(event);'/>

        <div id="back">
            <div id="prefs">
            </div>
            <div id='doneButton'></div>
        </div>
    </body>
</html>
```

The CSS File

Once you have included the tiled pieces of the widget in the HTML file, you'll need to create selectors for them in the CSS file. This is your way of organizing and joining those tiled images. As with most widget CSS files, the resize.css file contains selectors for the front and back panels of the widget. Between those two selectors and beneath the widget pieces comment, you'll see the selectors for the individual pieces of the widget. Notice that in the selectors the margin settings for all of the tiles are relative to their location and the width of the tile is the important setting being based on the width of the tile (Figure 8-8).

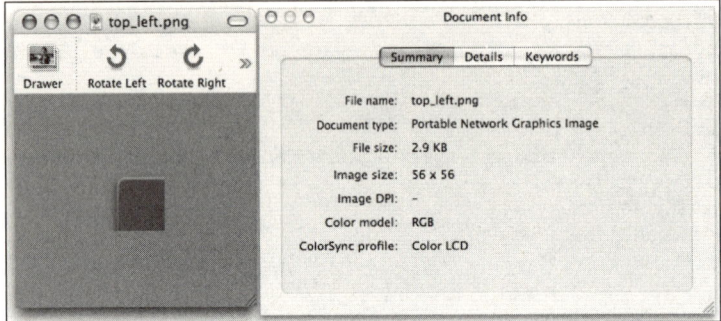

Figure 8-8

For instance, the left margin for the top_left.png is 0 pixels and the right margin for the top_right.png is 0 pixels. The location of the top_middle.png is determined by the width of the left and right tiles and the left and right margins are the width of top_middle.png.

Also notice that the URIs to the tiles is included in the selector rather than in the HTML file. The `background repeat: no-repeat;` setting prevents the image from being tiled across the space. Notice also that each tile that makes up the background is positioned relative to its row and its position in the background. The top_left tile has a top position of 0 and a left position of 0 whereas the top_center tile has a top position of 0 and a left position of 56. This places the left edge of the top_center tile against the right edge of the top_left tile.

```
/*

*/

body {
   margin:0;
}

#front {
   position: absolute;
   top: 0px;
   left: 0px;
   width: 170px;
```

```
  height: 170px;
  display: block;
  text-align: center;
}

#title {
  font: 12px "Helvetica Neue";
  font-weight: bold;
  color: white;
  position: absolute;
  top: 10px;
  width: 100%;
  z-index: 1;
  text-align: center;
}

/*  widget pieces  */

#top {
  position: absolute;
  top: 0px;
  left: 0px;
  right: 0px;
  bottom: 56px;
}

#top_left {
  position: absolute;
  top: 0px;
  left: 0px;
  bottom: 0px;
  width: 56px;
  background-image: url("Images/top_left.png");
  background-repeat: no-repeat;
}

#top_center {
  position: absolute;
  top: 0px;
  left: 56px;
  right: 56px;
  bottom: 0px;
  background-image: url("Images/top_center.png");
  background-repeat: repeat-x;
}

#top_right {
  position: absolute;
  top: 0px;
  right: 0px;
  bottom: 0px;
```

```
    width: 56px;
    background-image: url("Images/top_right.png");
    background-repeat: no-repeat;
}

#middle {
    position: absolute;
    top: 56px;
    left: 0px;
    right: 0px;
    bottom: 56px;
    text-align: center;
}

#middle_left {
    position: absolute;
    top: 0px;
    bottom: 0px;
    left: 0px;
    width: 56px;
    background-image: url("Images/middle_left.png");
    background-repeat: repeat-y;
}

#middle_center {
    position: absolute;
    top: 0px;
    bottom: 0px;
    left: 56px;
    right: 56px;
    background-image: url("Images/middle_center.png");
    background-repeat: repeat;
    }

#middle_right {
    position: absolute;
    top: 0px;
    bottom: 0px;
    right: 0px;
    width: 56px;
    background-image: url("Images/middle_right.png");
    background-repeat: repeat-y;
}

#bottom_left {
    position: absolute;
    left: 0px;
    bottom: 0px;
    width: 56px;
    height: 56px;
    background-image: url("Images/bottom_left.png");
```

```
      background-repeat: no-repeat;
}

#bottom_center {
  position: absolute;
  left: 56px;
  right: 56px;
  bottom: 0px;
  height: 56px;
  background-image: url("Images/bottom_center.png");
  background-repeat: repeat-x;
}

#bottom_right {
  position: absolute;
  right: 0px;
  bottom: 0px;
  width: 56px;
  height: 56px;
  background-image: url("Images/bottom_right.png");
  background-repeat: no-repeat;
}

#resize {
    position: absolute;
    bottom: 18px;
    right: 14px;

    -apple-dashboard-region: dashboard-region(control rectangle, 0 0 0 0);
}


/* widget back */

#back {
  display: none;
  position: absolute;
  top: 0px;
  left: 0px;
  width: 170px;
  height: 170px;
  background-image: url("Backside.png");
}
```

At this point, you have the framework in place for adding resize functionality to your widget. As with any widget, the widget events and the JavaScript perform the resizing animation. The last selector for the front of the widget is the resize selector. It determines where the resize thumb appears on the front of the widget and is measured from the bottom and right side of the widget. The last line of the selector sets the control rectangle. This control region ties all of the resize functionality together through the JavaScript file.

The JavaScript File

Whenever you mouse down on the resize thumb in the control rectangle, the mouse events trigger the appropriate functions in the JavaScript. The control region is linked to the resize thumb in the CSS file and the HTML file links the resize thumb to the mousedown function in the JavaScript file.

```
// tracks where the last mouse position was throughout the drag
var resizeInset;
// the right offset of the grow thumb vs. the edge of widget window
var rightEdgeOffset;
// the bottom offset of the grow thumb vs. the edge of widget window
var bottomEdgeOffset;

// called when the mouse first clicks upon the resize
function mouseDown(event) {
    // begin tracking the move
    document.addEventListener("mousemove", mouseMove, true);
    // and notify when the drag ends
    document.addEventListener("mouseup", mouseUp, true);

    // resizeInset tracks where the actual mouse click happened vs. the right and
    // bottom edges of the widget
    resizeInset = {x:(window.innerWidth - event.x), y:(window.innerHeight - event.y)};

    event.stopPropagation();
    event.preventDefault();
}

// called as the mouse button is down and the mouse moves
function mouseMove(event) {

    // x and y track where bottom-right corner of the widget should be, with relation
    // to the event.
    var x = event.x + resizeInset.x;
    var y = event.y + resizeInset.y;
    // an arbitrary minimum width
    if(x < 105)
      x = 105;
    // an arbitrary minimum height
    if(y < 37)
      y = 37;
    // an arbitrary maximum width
    if(x > 210)
      x = 210;
    // an arbitrary maximum height
    if(y > 210)
      y = 210;

    // resize background
    document.getElementById("front").style.width = x;
    document.getElementById("front").style.height = y;
```

```
document.getElementById("backgroundImage").width = x;
document.getElementById("backgroundImage").height = y;

  // resize the widget
window.resizeTo(x,y);

event.stopPropagation();
event.preventDefault();
}

// called after the mouse button is released
function mouseUp(event) {
  // stop tracking the move
  document.removeEventListener("mousemove", mouseMove, true);
  // and notify if the mouse goes down again
  document.removeEventListener("mouseup", mouseUp, true);

  event.stopPropagation();
  event.preventDefault();
}

// called when the widget loads
function setup() {
}
```

Try It Out   **Relative Resizing with a Single Panel**

In addition to creating a tiled version of your widget background for resizing, you can also use a single background panel and resize it. The additions to your files are basically the same, but you have fewer pieces to keep track of and less code to accomplish the same effect.

1.   Create a single panel background for your widget (Figure 8-9). You can also create a backside.png for the reverse side of your widget.

Figure 8-9

2.   Create a resize.html file similar to the tiled version above. Include the links for the resize.png thumb image and the mouseDown(event).

141

```html
<html>
  <head>
    <style type="text/css">
      @import "resize.css";
    </style>
    <script type='text/javascript' src='AppleClasses/AppleInfoButton.js'
charset='utf-8' />
    <script type='text/javascript' src='AppleClasses/AppleAnimator.js'
charset='utf-8' />
    <script type='text/javascript' src='AppleClasses/AppleButton.js' charset='utf-
8' />
    <script type="text/javascript" src="resize.js" charset="utf-8"></script>
  </head>
  <body onload="setup();">
    <div id="front">
      <img id="backgroundImage" src="Default.png">
      <div id="title">
      resize
      </div>
      <div id="resize" onMouseDown="mouseDown(event);">
        <img id="resizeThumb"
src="/System/Library/WidgetResources/resize.png"></img>
      </div>
    </div>
    <div id="back">
    </div>
  </body>
</html>
```

3. Create a resize.css file with the selector for the resize control and the control rectangle.

```css
body {
    margin:0;
}

/* widget front */

#front {
    position: absolute;
    top: 0px;
    left: 0px;
    width: 170px;
    height: 170px;
    display: block;
    text-align: center;
}

#title {
    font: 12px "Helvetica Neue";
    color: white;
    position: absolute;
```

```
      top: 10px;
      left: 65px;
  }

  #resize {
    position: absolute;
    /*bottom: 22px;
    right: 18px;*/
    bottom: 24px;
    right: 24px;
    width: 12px;
    height: 12px;
    z-index: 2;
    -apple-dashboard-region: dashboard-region(control rectangle 0px 0px 0px 0px);
  }

  /* widget back */

  #back {
  display: none;
  }
```

4. Add the handlers to the JavaScript file for dealing with the user's dragging of the resize box.

```
// tracks where the last mouse position was throughout the drag
var resizeInset;
// the right offset of the grow thumb vs. the edge of widget window
var rightEdgeOffset;
// the bottom offset of the grow thumb vs. the edge of widget window
var bottomEdgeOffset;

// called when the mouse first clicks upon the resize
function mouseDown(event) {
  // begin tracking the move
  document.addEventListener("mousemove", mouseMove, true);
  // and notify when the drag ends
  document.addEventListener("mouseup", mouseUp, true);

  // resizeInset tracks where the actual mouse click happened vs. the right and
  // bottom edges of the widget
  resizeInset = {x:(window.innerWidth - event.x), y:(window.innerHeight - event.y)};

  event.stopPropagation();
  event.preventDefault();
}

// called as the mouse button is down and the mouse moves
function mouseMove(event) {

  // x and y track where bottom-right corner of the widget should be, with relation
  // to the event.
```

```
      var x = event.x + resizeInset.x;
      var y = event.y + resizeInset.y;

      // an arbitrary minimum width
      if(x < 105)
        x = 105;
      // an arbitrary minimum height
      if(y < 37)
        y = 37;
      // an arbitrary maximum width
      if(x > 210)
        x = 210;
      // an arbitrary maximum height
      if(y > 210)
        y = 210;

      // resize background
      document.getElementById("front").style.width = x;
      document.getElementById("front").style.height = y;
      document.getElementById("backgroundImage").width = x;
      document.getElementById("backgroundImage").height = y;

     // resize the widget
     window.resizeTo(x,y);

      event.stopPropagation();
      event.preventDefault();
    }

// called after the mouse button is released
function mouseUp(event) {
    // stop tracking the move
    document.removeEventListener("mousemove", mouseMove, true);
    // and notify if the mouse goes down again
    document.removeEventListener("mouseup", mouseUp, true);

      event.stopPropagation();
      event.preventDefault();
    }

// called when the widget loads
function setup() {{
    }
```

5. Create an info.plist file to make the widget work.

```
<plist version="1.0">
<dict>
  <key>BackwardsCompatibleClassLookup</key>
  <true/>
  <key>CFBundleDisplayName</key>
  <string>resize</string>
  <key>CFBundleIdentifier</key>
  <string>com.deadtrees.widget.resize</string>
```

```
        <key>CFBundleName</key>
        <string>resize</string>
        <key>CFBundleShortVersionString</key>
        <string>1.0</string>
        <key>CFBundleVersion</key>
        <string>1.0</string>
        <key>CloseBoxInsetX</key>
        <integer>13</integer>
        <key>CloseBoxInsetY</key>
        <integer>13</integer>
        <key>MainHTML</key>
        <string>resize.html</string>
    </dict>
    </plist>
```

6.   Add the AppleClasses folder for backward compatibility.

7.   Drop the files in a folder, rename it Resize.wdgt, and then install the widget.

What you'll notice immediately from this example is that the amount of code required for resizing is noticeably smaller than that required for the tiled version of the widget. As stated earlier, how you decide to create the widget background for resizing is a matter of personal preference, but you have to track fewer details and pieces when the widget is constructed from a single panel. That also means this version is easier to debug.

Moving the Close Box

The location of the close box is an issue whether widgets are resizable or not. If you have widgets tightly packed on your screen, when you try to click the close box of one, you may be showing the close box on another (Figure 8-10) if the close box hasn't been properly placed.

Figure 8-10

In situations where you have your widgets overlapping (of course that never happens), you'll experience dueling close boxes. As you try to close one, the other one will flash. This may cause you to accidentally close the wrong widget — an annoying event that you want to avoid.

The improper placement of the close box can become even more pronounced when the widget is being resized. As the widget's size changes, the placement of the close box may need to be moved. Dashboard has a setCloseBoxOffset(x,y) method that allows you to adjust dynamically where the close box is situated.

The *x* and *y* in the method are the coordinates that you give Dashboard and place the close box relative to the top-left corner of the widget. If, for example, you give it the values (0,0), Dashboard places the center of the close box over the widget's top-left corner. Here is an example of the `setCloseBoxOffset(x,y)` method used in Apple's Weather widget.

```
if (lastTopOffset != topOffset || lastLeftOffset != leftOffset)
    {
        // 13 and 10 are the hardcoded start offsets
        widget.setCloseBoxOffset (leftOffset + 13, topOffset+10);
        widget.setPositionOffset (leftOffset, topOffset);
    }
```

Now that you see how to add resizing to your widget, let's turn our attention to another way that you can display more information for the user.

Scrolling

Another way that you can provide the user with more information than what fits within your widget is to add scrolling. If you are displaying text or lists, this allows you to maintain a minimum size for your widget while still accommodating dynamic information.

When to Add Scrolling

You add scrolling to your widget for the same reasons that you add resizing: the information that you want to display in the widget is dynamic and larger than the widget.

You may have noticed that widgets for RSS feeds can be resized and also have a scroll bar. This is the maximum flexibility that you can give the user short of closing Dashboard and opening the browser with the link to the RSS feed. If you want to allow the user to get the information without having to load an application, you can provide your widget with the ability to display the content in a growable window with scrolling.

The HTML File

As with resizing, you'll have to make additions to your widget's HTML, CSS, and JavaScript files. In the HTML file, you need to add Apple's classes for the scroll bar and the scroll area. Like the button classes, the AppleScrollbar.js and AppleScrollArea.js files are part of the WidgetResources directory and provide the functionality for working with scroll bars. You could write your own functions, but you should try using Apple's first.

```
<html>
  <head>
    <style type="text/css">
      @import "resize.css";
    </style>
    <script type='text/javascript' src='AppleClasses/AppleInfoButton.js' charset=
'utf-8' />
    <script type='text/javascript' src='AppleClasses/AppleAnimator.js' charset=
'utf-8' />
```

```
        <script type='text/javascript' src='AppleClasses/AppleButton.js' charset='utf-
8' />
    <script type='text/javascript'
src='/System/Library/WidgetResources/AppleClasses/AppleScrollArea.js'></script>
        <script type='text/javascript'
src='/System/Library/WidgetResources/AppleClasses/AppleScrollbar.js'></script>
        <script type='text/javascript' src='resize.js'></script>
    <body onload="setup();">
      <div id="front">
        <img id="backgroundImage" src="Default.png">
  <div id="title">Reslide</div>
        </div>
        <div id="theImage">
          <img id="png" src="Images/intel_mini.png" height="90px"
width="140px"></img>
      </div>
        <div id="scalerSlider"></div>
        <div id="resize" onMouseDown="mouseDown(event);">
          <img id="resizeThumb"
src="/System/Library/WidgetResources/resize.png"></img>
        </div>
      </div>


      <div id="back">
      </div>
    </body>
</html>
```

The CSS File

In the CSS file of your widget, you'll need to add selectors for the content that you are scrolling and the scroll bar or slider that you are using.

```
body {
    margin:0;
}

/* widget front */

#front {
    position: absolute;
    top: 0px;
    left: 0px;
    width: 170px;
    height: 170px;
    display: block;
    text-align: center;
}

#title {
    font: 12px "Helvetica Neue";
    color: white;
```

```
        position: absolute;
        top: 10px;
        left: 65px;
}
#theImage {
        position: absolute;
        top: 30px;
        bottom: 48px;
        left: 15px;
        right: 15px;
        overflow: auto;
}
#scalerSlider {
        position: absolute;
        bottom: 28px;
        left: 15px;
        right: 15px;
}
```

```
#resize {
    position: absolute;
    bottom: 24px;
    right: 24px;
    width: 12px;
    height: 12px;
    z-index: 2;
    -apple-dashboard-region: dashboard-region(control rectangle 0px 0px 0px 0px);
}

/* widget back */

#back {
display: none;
}
```

Notice that the image file content and the `scalarSlider` selectors are grouped together. As your CSS files become longer, grouping all of the related selectors together makes the file easier to maintain.

The JavaScript File

In the JavaScript file, you will need to add functions for the scroll bar and the content area. If you are using Apple's classes, all of the work is done in them, and your JavaScript needs only to pass the correct values. In this example, variables are added for the `scalarSlider` at the beginning of the file. Notice the use of global variables and how the JavaScript references the selectors used in the HTML file.

```
// tracks where the last mouse position was throughout the drag
var resizeInset;
// the right offset of the grow thumb vs. the edge of widget window
var rightEdgeOffset;
// the bottom offset of the grow thumb vs. the edge of widget window
var bottomEdgeOffset;
// slider variables
```

```
var scalerSlider;
var lastScalerSliderValue;

// called when the mouse first clicks upon the resize
function mouseDown(event) {
  // begin tracking the move
  document.addEventListener("mousemove", mouseMove, true);
  // and notify when the drag ends
  document.addEventListener("mouseup", mouseUp, true);

  // resizeInset tracks where the actual mouse click happened vs. the right and
  // bottom edges of the widget
  resizeInset = {x:(window.innerWidth - event.x), y:(window.innerHeight -
event.y)};

  event.stopPropagation();
  event.preventDefault();
}

// called as the mouse button is down and the mouse moves
function mouseMove(event) {

  // x and y track where bottom-right corner of the widget should be, with relation
  // to the event.
  var x = event.x + resizeInset.x;
  var y = event.y + resizeInset.y;

  // an arbitrary minimum width
  if(x < 105)
    x = 105;
  // an arbitrary minimum height
  if(y < 37)
    y = 37;
  // an arbitrary maximum width
  if(x > 210)
    x = 210;
  // an arbitrary maximum height
  if(y > 210)
    y = 210;

  // resize background
  document.getElementById("front").style.width = x;
  document.getElementById("front").style.height = y;
  document.getElementById("backgroundImage").width = x;
  document.getElementById("backgroundImage").height = y;

 // resize the widget
  window.resizeTo(x,y);

  event.stopPropagation();
  event.preventDefault();
}

// called after the mouse button is released
```

```
function mouseUp(event) {
  // stop tracking the move
  document.removeEventListener("mousemove", mouseMove, true);
  // and notify if the mouse goes down again
  document.removeEventListener("mouseup", mouseUp, true);

  event.stopPropagation();
  event.preventDefault();
}

// called when the widget loads
function setup() {
  alert("entered setup");

  scalerSlider = new AppleHorizontalSlider(document.getElementById("scalerSlider"),
sliderChanged);
  alert("setup: scalerSlider.size: " + scalerSlider.size.toString());
  alert("leaving setup");
}
```

```
function sliderChanged(currentValue) {
  if (currentValue <= 0.01) {
    return;
  } else {
    // check the direction of the slider move:
    if (currentValue < lastScalerSliderValue) {
      // shrinking
      var theImage = document.getElementById("png");
      var preHeight = theImage.height;
      var preWidth = theImage.width;
      var postHeight = preHeight / (1+ scalerSlider.value);
      var postWidth = preWidth / (1+ scalerSlider.value);
      // arbitrary minimum size
      if (postHeight > 90) {
        document.getElementById("png").height = postHeight;
        document.getElementById("png").width = postWidth;
      }
      lastScalerSliderValue = currentValue;
    } else {
      // enlarging
      var theImage = document.getElementById("png");
      var preHeight = theImage.height;
      var preWidth = theImage.width;
      var postHeight = preHeight * (1 + scalerSlider.value);
      var postWidth = preWidth * (1 + scalerSlider.value);
      // arbitrary maximum size
      if (postHeight < 616) {
      document.getElementById("png").height = postHeight;
      document.getElementById("png").width = postWidth;
}

      lastScalerSliderValue = currentValue;
    }
  }
}
```

The `sliderChanged(currentValue)` function at the end of the file tracks the position of the slider and adjusts the size of the image based on the changed values (Figure 8-11).

Figure 8-11

Summary

Though most information can be displayed or summarized in a single widget pane, you may need to display more information occasionally. When you are faced with showing more content, you can use resize and scrolling functionality in your widget.

In this chapter, you learned:

❑ The differences between absolute or live resizing and when to use them

❑ How to add resizing to your widget to provide more information to the user

❑ How to add scrolling to your widget to maintain widget size but provide additional information

Below are a few exercises that you can work through before you move on to adding cut, copy, and paste to your widget.

Exercises

1. Live resizing is also called what?

2. What is relative resizing typically used for in widgets?

3. Where are Apple's scroll bar–related classes stored?

Adding Cut, Copy, and Paste to Your Widget

Cut, copy, and paste are key components of any Macintosh application and are quintessentially Mac. Just like the Finder's Clipboard, Dashboard has a pasteboard that can be used to pass data. When you add the cut, copy, and paste functions to your widget, you give the user an easy way to move data between applications and widgets.

By the end of this chapter, you will know:

❑ What the pasteboard operations are in Dashboard

❑ How the cut, copy, and paste functions work

❑ How to add cut, copy, and paste operations to your widget

Pasteboard

JavaScript in Dashboard supports two constants that are pasteboards for the event object. If you are performing cut, copy, and paste operations in JavaScript, you will use the clipboardData constant. If you are performing drag-and-drop operations in Javascript, you will use the dataTranser constant.

Pasteboard Events

Six JavaScript events provide support for pasteboard operations that can be applied to any element in your widget. Three of the events provide the usual cut, copy, and paste functionality: `oncut`, `oncopy`, and `onpaste`. The other three allow you to manipulate the data beforehand: `onbeforecut`, `onbeforecopy`, and `onbeforepaste`.

All six of these events can be attached to any HTML element in your widget that supports them. In the case of these events, you will register them in the <body> tag so they are called when the body of the widget finishes loading. To implement the cut, copy, and paste functions, you must write handlers that work with the data. You will also need to pass the information about the event to the handler using the event variable.

Pasteboard Handlers

While not all widgets support the cut, copy, and paste functions, those that do perform just like their application counterparts. If you perform a calculation on the Calculator widget, for instance, then press Command-C, you can switch to Text Editor and paste in the result of the calculation. Notice in the widget that the number remained in the display area (Figure 9-1).

Figure 9-1

Modify the number in the Text Editor document and cut it. Activate Dashboard, set the focus on the Calculator and press Command-V. You'll see that the number you cut from Text Editor is pasted in. Divide that number by some amount and then press Command-X. Now you'll see that the number in the Calculator display has been replaced by a 0 (Figure 9-2).

Figure 9-2

This lets you know that the contents of the display have been removed.

When you examine the source files for the Calculator widget, you can see how cut, copy, and paste are implemented. The events are registered in the <body> tag of the Calculator.html file.

```
<body oncut='docut(event);' oncopy='docopy(event);' onpaste='dopaste(event);'>
```

The three event handlers are in the Calculator.js file. The `docut` function sets the pasteboard to MIME type plain text and passes the data from the Calculator display, then calls the `clearDisplay` and the `updateDisplay` functions. This has the same effect as using the Cut command in the Calculator application. The `docopy` function also sets the pasteboard to the plain text MIME type, but it does not clear the display. Both of these functions end with the `event.preventDefault()` and `event.stopPropagation()` functions. You use the `event.preventDefault()` function to prevent Dashboard's default behavior and allow your handler to incorporate the data. You use the `event.stopPropagation()` to stop the event from continuing.

```
function docut(event) {
  event.clipboardData.setData('text/plain', display);
  clearDisplay();
  updateDisplay();
  event.preventDefault();
  event.stopPropagation();

}

function docopy (event) {
  event.clipboardData.setData('text/plain', display);
  event.preventDefault();
  event.stopPropagation();
}

function dopaste (event) {
  var clip = event.clipboardData.getData('text/plain');

  // remove any commas
  clip = clip.replace(/,/g, '');

  if (!directInput) {
    display = evaluator(clip);
    updateDisplay();
  } else
    document.getElementById("calcDisplay").innerText = clip;

  event.preventDefault();
  event.stopPropagation();
}
```

The `dopaste` function uses the `getData` method instead of the `setData` method because it is getting the data for the event. The MIME type parameter for `getData` is set to `text/plain`—the type of data that the Calculator is expecting to receive. It puts the data in the `clip` variable.

For security reasons, the `getData` *method can be called from* `ondrop` *and* `onpaste` *event handlers only.*

The function replaces any commas in the `clip` variable using a regular expression and then inserts the number in the display.

Adding Pasteboard Handlers

Now that you see how the pasteboard events and handlers work together in a widget, you are ready to add copy functionality to your widget. You can take the WeatherMaps widget that you have been working on and make a few changes to it and add a copy command so you can copy the current image from the widget. Because the WeatherMaps widget contains images instead of text, you'll have to use a different MIME type.

Try It Out   **Add Copy to Your Widget**

1.   Open the weathermaps.html file in your text editor.

2.   Add `oncopy='docopy(event);'` to the `<body>` tag. The line should look like this:

```
<body onload='setup();' oncopy='docopy(event);'>
```

3.   Save and close the weathermaps.html file.

4.   Open the weathermaps.js file in your text editor.

5.   Add the global variable `radarURL = "";` beneath the two button variables at the top of the file.

6.   In the `setup()` function, add a line to set the `baseURL` variable from the `radarMenu`:

```
var theImage = widget.preferenceForKey("radarMenu");
radarURL = widget.preferenceForKey("radarMenu");
if (theImage == "") {
  radMap();
```

7.   Now add the `oncopy` function to the file.

```
function docopy (event) {
    event.clipboardData.setData('image/pict',
document.getElementById("mapImage").src);
    event.clipboardData.setData('text/plain', radarURL);

    event.preventDefault();
    event.stopPropagation();
}
```

8.   Save and close the weathermaps.js file.

9.   Activate Dashboard and reload the WeatherMaps widget if you have it installed.

10.   Select the radar map, and then press Command-C to copy it.

11.   Close Dashboard, switch to your word processor, open a new document, and paste.

The radar map URL that you selected in the WeatherMaps widget will be pasted into the document.

How It Works

The `oncopy` event is registered in the `<body>` tag so the `docopy` handler in the JavaScript responds to the standard Macintosh copy keystroke: Command-C. When the widget has focus in Dashboard and the keystroke is pressed, the `docopy` handler is called. The `setData` instance, as you might guess, sets the data from the event's `clipboardData` and the MIME type parameter text/plain is set to the MIME type of the data, which is the URL for the radar map from the widget. Notice that you did not use `var` when setting the global variable. The radarURL variable isn't set until it is read from the preferences during the `setup()` function when it is local to that function. To reference the local variable globally, you set it without the `var`.

Summary

Widgets are not supposed to be small applications, but they should have some of the same basic functionality as Macintosh applications to maintain a consistent user interface. A user who selects text in a widget naturally expects to be able to copy or cut the text. If your widgets support selecting text, you should allow the user to work with it the same way she would in an application.

In this chapter, you learned:

❑   What the pasteboard operations are in Dashboard

❑   How the cut, copy, and paste functions work

❑   How to add cut, copy, and paste operations to your widget

Before moving on to Chapter 10, take a moment to run through these exercises.

Exercises

1.   Which events can you use the `getData` method with?

2.   How do you get information about the event into the handler?

3.   What parameters do you pass the `event.stopPropagation()` function in the handlers for the `oncut`, `oncopy`, and `onpaste` events?

Adding Drag and Drop to the Widget

You could say that Apple brought the notion of drag and drop to the personal computer with the Trashcan in the Macintosh OS. Using direct manipulation, the user was able to grab any file, folder, or application and drag it into the Trashcan and then empty the Trash to remove the item. Dragging and dropping a file is more intuitive than typing `rm -r mycherishedfiles/` in a Terminal window. Dragging and dropping text or graphics was ushered into the operating system in 1994 with System 7.5 and has been incorporated into OS X and extended.

In OS X, the drag-and-drop interface has been extended to cover more applications and data types. In addition to dragging graphics and text files — or just graphics and text — onto the application icons in the Dock, you can drag lists. You can drag lists of songs in iTunes — you even get to see the number of songs you are about to drop on a playlist (Figure 10-1).

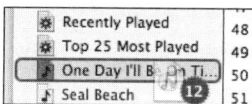

Figure 10-1

In Chapter 9 you saw how to add cut, copy, and paste functionality to your widget. In this chapter, you learn how to add support for drag and drop to your widget using JavaScript. Using WebKit handlers, you can drag text and pictures between widgets as well as drag objects from the Finder to widgets.

By the end of this chapter, you will know:

❑ How to use the drag-and-drop events

❑ How to incorporate drag and drop between the Finder and widgets

❑ How to provide feedback to the user during a drag

Drag-and-Drop Events

So that widgets can perform the some of the same functions as a compiled application, Dashboard provides events that you can use to trigger the drag-and-drop behavior. You can also add handlers to your widget's JavaScript so you can change the image when the object you are dragging reaches its destination.

Dragging and Dropping from the Finder

The Drag-and-Drop Overview section of Apple's OS X Human Interface Guidelines describes the feedback a user should receive. During the drag and drop, the user should receive immediate feedback when the data is selected, during the drag, when the destination is reached, and when the data is dropped.

In the Dashboard Examples from the Developer installation, you'll find a Dropper widget. This widget takes a file dropped on it from the Finder and displays the path to the file, much as you can do in Terminal. The Finder provides most of the feedback for the user when a file is selected and dragged into Dashboard. The JavaScript in the widget provides the feedback when the destination is reached and when the file is dropped.

When you install the widget and activate Dashboard, you'll see that you begin the drag in the Finder before dropping it on the widget (Figure 10-2).

Figure 10-2

Close Dashboard and begin dragging a file and then press F12 to display Dashboard (Figure 10-3).

Figure 10-3

When you get the file over the Dropper widget, you'll see a plus added to the cursor to let you know that you have reached your destination and can drop the file (Figure 10-4).

Figure 10-4

Release the file and the display box in the widget is updated with the path URL to the file (Figure 10-5).

Figure 10-5

This is very straightforward and something you do unconsciously in your daily use of the Macintosh. Let's take a look at the widget's support for drag and drop.

Using Drag and Drop

You may have noticed that whenever you drag a file in the Finder, you see a lighter representation of it. The application icon highlights whenever you drag the file over an application that may be able to work with it in some fashion. Dashboard provides the ability to mimic this same behavior through a set of events. Support for drag and drop in widgets is provided through three events and can be applied to the individual elements of the HTML page in your widget: `ondragstart`, `ondrag`, and `ondragend`.

When you begin dragging an object, the `ondragstart` event is called. As you drag, the `ondrag` event is sent repeatedly to the object you are dragging. Once you reach the destination and drop the object, it is sent the `ondragend` event and it reports the status of the drop — either successful or unsuccessful.

While a drag is in process, any element that has the potential to receive the drop is sent an event whenever the object is dragged is near it. These events allow you to provide feedback to the user about the progress of the drag by changing the cursor during drag or changing the widget to let the user know that the drop can or cannot be accepted. The events are `ondragenter`, `ondragover`, `ondragleave`, and `ondrop`.

The `ondragenter` and `ondragleave` events let the element that might receive the drop know when the object is entering its boundaries or when the object has left the element's boundaries. The `ondragover` event lets the element know that the object could drop on it. The `ondrop` event is sent to the element whenever the object is dropped and allows the widget to respond to the drop.

If you show the contents of the Dropper widget and take a look at the source files, you can see how these events are tied to the elements in the HTML and CSS files through the JavaScript.

HTML

When you examine the HTML file you can see the basic structure with the CSS and JavaScript files incorporated in the Head section. The `ondragenter`, `ondragover`, and `ondragleave` events are included in the `<body>` tag, and each of these events has its own handler assigned to it as well. Whenever a file enters within the body of the widget these handlers are called and any action assigned in them will be executed.

```
<html>
<head>

<!-- The CSS for this widget -->
<style type="text/css">
  @import "Dropper.css";
</style>
<!-- The JavaScript for this widget -->
<script type='text/javascript' src='Dropper.js' charset='utf-8'/>
</head>

<!-- Note the drag and drop handlers set up for body; if any of these events
happen, the relevant handler is called -->
<body ondragenter='dragenter(event);' ondragover='dragover(event);'
ondrop='dragdrop(event)' ondragleave='dragleave(event)'>

  <img id="arrow" src="Default.png" >  <!-- The background image for the widget -->

  <!-- The "info window" that shows the information that this widget outputs -->
  <div class="theInfo">
    <img src="images/top.png">
    <div class="infoWrap">
      <div id="infoLabel">Drag an item from Finder, show Dashboard, and drop it on
this Widget.</div>
      <div id="infoURL"></div>
    </div>
```

```
        <img src="images/bottom.png">
    </div>
  </body>
  </html>
```

Like the Fortune widget, Dropper has a graphic with default text that is replaced by the file URL. The default text is included in the infoLabel `<div>` and the infoURL `<div>` holds the file URL whenever the file is dropped on the widget.

CSS

The CSS file for the Dropper widget contains a header with information about how the styles are used. If the style is going to remain static, you begin it with a period. If the style is going to change programmatically, you begin it with a hash.

```
  */
  /*  Styles
   *  Style sheets allow for precise control of elements within your widget.
   *  All style information is contained within the <style> tags. If you want to
   *  utilize style information, use the class or id attributes on most any tag, and
   *  set them equal to one of your defined styles. Use the class attribute when a
   *  style is to remain static, and id if you change the style in your scripts.
   *  When defining the style, begin the style with a period (.) if it is to remain
   *  static, and a hash (#) if it is going to be altered programatically.
   */


  body {
    margin: 0;
  }

  .theInfo {
    opacity: 1.0;
    position: absolute;
    top: 60px;
    left: 25px;

  }

  .infoWrap {
    background: url("images/middle.png");
    padding-right: 9px;
    padding-left: 9px;
    width: 134px;
  }

  #infoLabel {
    font: 9px "Lucida Grande";
    font-weight: bold;
    color: white;
    padding-top: 4px;
    padding-bottom: 2px;
    text-align: center;
```

```
  }

  #infoURL {
    font: 11px "Courier New";
    font-weight: bold;
    color: white;
    word-wrap: break-word;
    padding-top: 2px;
    padding-bottom: 4px;
  }
```

In the Dropper widget, `theInfo` and `infoWrap` styles are both defined as static. If you refer to the HTML file, `theInfo` begins with the top part of the rectangle graphic (images/top.png) where the file URL will be placed and ends with the bottom portion of the rectangle graphic (images/bottom.png). The `infoWrap` style is also static and contains the middle portion of the graphic.

The `infoLabel` and `infoURL` styles are defined to be modified programmatically. The `infoLabel` contains the default text that is replaced by a new label when a file is dropped, and the `infoURL` holds the file URL.

JavaScript

The JavaScript file contains the event handler to do the work whenever an item or items are dropped on the widget. The `dragdrop` function begins by setting the variable `uri`, which will hold the file URL, to null. This ensures that the variable is cleared each time a new item is dropped on the widget. When the user releases the mouse button over the widget, the variable is set by `event.dataTransfer.getData ("text/uri-list")`, which gets the path to the file in URL format. The function also changes the label text.

The default behavior for WebKit with an `ondrop` event is to receive and incorporate the data. The `event.preventDefault()` in the `dragdrop` function prevents this default behavior and allows your handler to receive the data. You don't have to pass any parameters for this method. The `event.stopPropagation()` is a method that also doesn't require any parameters. Calling it keeps the event from continuing. If you want to cancel a drag, call the `cancelDefault()` method.

```
/******************/
// Drag and drop code
// This code handles the various drag and drop events
/******************/

// The event handler for the image drop.  This handles fetching the image URL and
// trying to place it inside of the widget.

function dragdrop (event)
{
  var uri = null;
  try {
      uri = event.dataTransfer.getData("text/uri-list");
// attempt to load the URL
  } catch (ex)
  {
```

```
   }

   // if the acquisition is successful:
   if (uri)
   {
      document.getElementById("infoLabel").innerText = "That item's URL is:";    //
Add the new label text
      document.getElementById("infoURL").innerText = uri;                  // And display
the file's URL
   }

   event.stopPropagation();
   event.preventDefault();

}


// The dragenter, dragover, and dragleave functions are implemented but not used.
// They can be used if you want to change the image when it enters the widget.

function dragenter (event)
{
   event.stopPropagation();
   event.preventDefault();

}

function dragover (event)
{
   event.stopPropagation();
   event.preventDefault();
}

function dragleave (event)
{
   event.stopPropagation();
   event.preventDefault();
}
```

The remaining three functions that you saw referenced in the <body> tag of the HTML file for indicating when a drag is over or inside of the widget boundaries have been stubbed at the bottom of the script but no actions have been assigned to them.

Try It Out   **Adding the dragover Event**

Now that you see how the drag events work, modify the Dropper.js file to change the image of the Dropper widget as you drag an item over it.

1.   Show the contents of the Dropper widget.

2.   Open the Dropper.js file and scroll to the bottom of the file.

3.   In the dragover function, add JavaScript to change the image of the object you are dragging whenever it is over the body of the widget. Your code might look like this:

```
function dragover (event)
{
document.getElementById("arrow").src = "images/drop.png";
   event.stopPropagation();
   event.preventDefault();
}
```

4. Save your changes to the Dropper.js file and close it.

5. Open the Dropper.html file and scroll to the body tag.

```
<body ondragenter='dragenter(event);' img src='dropit.png'
ondragover='dragover(event);' ondrop='dragdrop(event)'
ondragleave='dragleave(event)'>
```

6. Add the image source information for the `dragover` event. Use the additional image included with the widget if you do not have one of your own.

7. Save and close the file.

8. Activate Dashboard and reload the widget to load your changes.

How It Works

Whenever you perform a drag within Dashboard, WebKit provides feedback by showing you an image of what you are dragging. WebKit does this by using a snapshot of the element you are dragging. Your modifications to the JavaScript and HTML files provide an image that WebKit can substitute for this snapshot.

Dragging Between Widgets

You may have also noticed that you can drag between widgets. Not every widget supports drag and drop, and only dragging of text objects is supported. For example, the To Do Tracker from Monkey Business Labs (Figure 10-6) and the Wikipedia widget both support drag and drop for text. When you begin dragging a text object, Dashboard gives you the standard feedback of showing the text you are dragging.

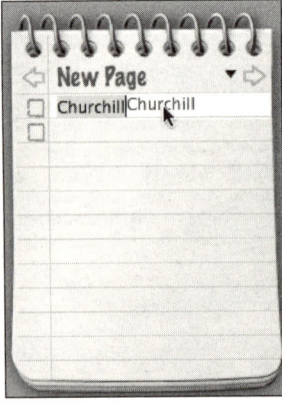

Figure 10-6

When you are over the text entry field in the Wikipedia widget, you get cursor feedback with the plus added to the arrow to let you know that you can drop the object (Figure 10-7).

Figure 10-7

Summary

You probably use drag and drop most days and never think about it. You may unconsciously drag text and graphics from your word processor to the Finder desktop or links from your browser to your word processor or another browser window. Your widget may not need drag-and-drop capabilities, but you should think about how the user will use it. Drag-and-drop functionality is ingrained in the way we use our Macs and would be conspicuous in its absence.

In this chapter, you learned:

- ❑ How to use the drag-and-drop events
- ❑ How to incorporate drag and drop between the Finder and widgets
- ❑ How to provide feedback to the user during a drag

In Chapter 11, you'll look at how access keys enable your widget to work with resources on your Mac and the Internet. First, you should review some of the things you learned in this chapter by running through these exercises.

Exercises

1. What method do you call if you want to cancel a drag?

2. What parameters are passed to the `event.stopPropagation()` method?

3. When was drag-and-drop functionality added to the Macintosh?

Access Keys

In Chapter 10, you learned about the different drag-and-drop events available to widgets as well as how to add drag-and-drop functionality to a widget. In this chapter, you'll look at the access keys that are part of the widget Info.plist file. If your widget needs access to any content outside of its bundle, you will need to allow it to access those resources by specifying the kind of access that it needs.

By the end of this chapter, you will know:

- ❏ What access keys are
- ❏ How to use all of the access keys
- ❏ When access keys are appropriate

Using Access Keys

In Chapter 2, you had a brief look at a widget with a plugin and the widget properties including access keys that are specified in the Info.plist file. You have probably looked at other widget properties as you've worked through the WeatherMaps example. At this point, you are familiar with the idea that if your widget retrieves web pages or maps from the Internet, you have to declare network access or it will not be able to retrieve those web pages. If your widget needs access to any files or applications outside of its bundle, you must declare that access.

Widgets have seven access keys that provide them with varying levels of access to your Macintosh, command-line utilities, your network, and the Internet. Those keys are `AllowFileAccessOutsideOfWidget`, `AllowSystem`, `AllowNetworkAccess`, `AllowInternetPlugins`, `Plugin`, `AllowJava`, and `AllowFullAccess`. The following sections explain each of these and provide examples.

File System Access

The `AllowFileAccessOutsideOfWidget` access key allows your widget to open files and applications outside of the widget bundle. For example, the Tile Game widget that is part of Tiger has the `AllowFileAccessOutsideOfWidget` access key set so that it can use pictures that you drag on it (Figure 11-1).

Figure 11-1

If you remove the `AllowFileAccessOutsideOfWidget` key, you can't drag another image onto the Tile Game. Even though you can grant your widget access outside of its bundle, that access will be limited to your access permissions on the file system. A good rule of thumb is that if you can open the file or application without having to enter the Administration password, your widget should be able to as well.

The `AllowFileAccessOutsideOfWidget` is a Boolean key. If you look in the Tile Game Info.plist file with the Property List Editor, you'll see key and settings (Figure 11-2).

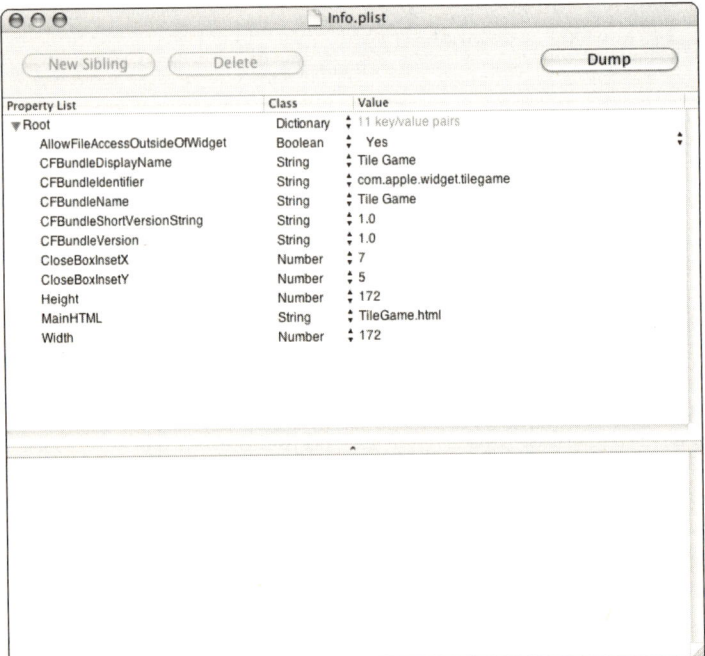

Figure 11-2

If you are editing the Info.plist file with BBEdit or another text editor, the access key is entered between key tags and the Boolean value is set on the line below as in the shaded portion of the Tile Game property list below.

```
<plist version="1.0">
<dict>
  <key>AllowFileAccessOutsideOfWidget</key>
  <true/>
  <key>CFBundleIdentifier</key>
  <string>com.apple.widget.tilegame</string>
  <key>CFBundleName</key>
  <string>Tile Game</string>
  <key>CFBundleDisplayName</key>
  <string>Tile Game</string>
  <key>CFBundleShortVersionString</key>
  <string>1.0</string>
  <key>CFBundleVersion</key>
  <string>1.0</string>
  <key>CloseBoxInsetX</key>
  <integer>7</integer>
  <key>CloseBoxInsetY</key>
  <integer>5</integer>
  <key>Height</key>
  <integer>172</integer>
  <key>MainHTML</key>
  <string>TileGame.html</string>
  <key>Width</key>
  <integer>172</integer>
</dict>
</plist>
```

If your widget has preferences, you don't need to set the AllowFileAccessOutsideOfWidget *in the Info.plist file in order to save the preferences to the filesystem. That functionality is incorporated in the* widget.preferenceForKey() *and* widget.setPreferenceForKey() *methods so that you don't have to add the access key yourself.*

Command-Line Access

If your widget needs access to the command line to run utilities or scripts, you would enter the AllowSystem access key in your Info.plist file. The Uptime widget that is included in the Dashboard examples with the Developer Tools installation calls a command-line utility to get the length of time your Macintosh has been running.

The AllowSystem access key is also binary. Like the AllowFileAccessOutsideOfWidget, your Info.plist file would contain the access key on a single line.

```
<plist version="1.0">
<dict>
  <key>AllowSystem</key>
  <true/>
```

```
    <key>CFBundleDisplayName</key>
    <string>Uptime</string>
    <key>CFBundleIdentifier</key>
    <string>com.apple.widget.uptime</string>
    <key>CFBundleName</key>
    <string>Uptime</string>
    <key>CFBundleShortVersionString</key>
    <string>1.1</string>
    <key>CFBundleVersion</key>
    <string>1.1</string>
    <key>CloseBoxInsetX</key>
    <integer>2</integer>
    <key>CloseBoxInsetY</key>
    <integer>2</integer>
    <key>MainHTML</key>
    <string>Uptime.html</string>
  </dict>
</plist>
```

To take advantage of this access key, your JavaScript file must include the widget.system method with the call to the script or utility in the form `widget.system("command", handler)`. The command is the relative or absolute path to the command-line utility or the script that you want to run. If you need to pass switches to the utility, you would do that as part of the command. For instance, if you wanted to return the current date in Universal Time format you would pass the date with the appropriate switch as part of the command: `/bin/date -u`.

The handler parameter is the function that you want to pass the output from the utility or script to after it executes. If you don't want to call a handler, you enter the value null for the handler parameter.

If you look at the Uptime.js file, you'll see an example of the `widget.system` method.

```
function uptime()
{
  if(window.widget)
  {
    document.getElementById("outputText").innerText =
(widget.system("/usr/bin/uptime", null).outputString);
  }
}
```

The widget.system calls the Uptime utility. Notice that it gives the absolute path to the utility to ensure that the version of Uptime shipped with OS X and not a user-installed version is called.

If you don't know the absolute path to the command that you want to run, you find it using the which *command in the Terminal:* [offhook:~]pfterry%which uptime.

The Uptime widget also doesn't have a handler specified. The `outputString` property allows you to capture the output from the `uptime` command and put it in the widget window using `getElementById("outputText").innerText`. You would normally see this output if you run the utility in Terminal.

```
[offhook:~] pfterry% uptime
1:31  up 8 days,  10:04, 3 users, load averages: 1.79 0.42 0.14
```

The Uptime widget displays this information in the widget window (Figure 11-3).

| Uptime | 1:31 up 8 days, 10:04, 3 users, load averages: 1.79 0.42 0.14 |

Figure 11-3

Synchronous Usage

To explain a bit more about the syntax, you can use the `widget.system()` method either synchronously or asynchronously to accommodate the kind of command-line utility you are working with. In other words, if your widget needs to wait for the result of the command, you would use null for the handler parameter as in the Uptime widget. This works best for command-line utilities that execute and return the results of the execution quickly.

The `outputString` used in the Uptime widget captures what is normally written to `stdout`, or the Terminal window. You can also capture error and status information from the `widget.system()` method.

If you want to capture the command's exit status, you would use the status property instead of outputString.

```
    document.getElementById("outputText").innerText =
(widget.system("/usr/bin/uptime", null).status);
```

Every command has an exit, or return, status. If the command runs successfully, it returns a 0. If a command does not exit successfully, it returns a number greater than 0, which is the error code.

If a command does not run successfully and exits with an error code, the information is written to `stderr`. To capture what would normally be written to `stderr`, use the `errorString` property. For example, if the Uptime utility were to return an error code, that code would be written to `stderr`.

```
    document.getElementById("outputText").innerText =
(widget.system("/usr/bin/uptime", null).errorString);
```

Asynchronous Usage

If the command that you are calling from your widget takes a long time to execute or continues executing until you stop it, you will want to use the widget.system() method asynchronously. This allows your widget to function while the command is executing. To do this, you provide a handler as the second argument to `widget.system()` instead of the null that you provided in synchronous mode. For instance, the command might look like this.

```
widget.system("/usr/bin/tail -f /var/log/system.log, outHandler);
```

The tail command prints any lines as they are added to the system.log file and the `-f` switch instructs tail to follow, or keep printing the lines, until it is told to stop. The `outHandler` should accept a single object as a parameter that will contain the output from the command when it finishes executing. In the same way that you can get what is printed to `stdout`, `stderr`, and the status

173

message when `widget.system()` is run synchronously, you can use the `object.outputString`, `object.errorString`, and `object.status` parameters to retrieve the results of the asynchronous use.

If the command you are calling requires interaction, asynchronous use also supports that. You have three methods for interacting with the command. You can provide input to the command through `write(string)`. For example, you could use the `write(string)` to pass the number of lines that you want the tail command to give from the file that you are tailing.

```
    tailCmd.write(200);
```

with

```
function outHandler(tailCmd) {
    tailCmd.write(200);
}
```

In the tail –f example, the command runs until you cancel it. You use the cancel method to halt the execution of the command.

```
    tailCmd.cancel()
```

You can stop the command from running by sending it an end-of-file (EOF) command. You do this with a close command.

```
    tailCmd.close()
```

When you are using the `widget.system()` method, you should consider how long it will take the command-line utility to finish executing. If the utility runs continuously or may pause for long periods while it is running, you should use the asynchronous mode.

Network Access

If your widget needs access to any resources that it has to get through the network or from the Internet, you must use the `AllowNetworkAccess` key. The WeatherMaps widget, for example, uses the `AllowNetworkAccess` to retrieve maps from a remote website.

```
<dict>
    <key>AllowNetworkAccess</key>
    <true/>
    <key>CFBundleDisplayName</key>
    <string>WeatherMaps</string>
    <key>CFBundleIdentifier</key>
    <string>com.deadtrees.widget.weathermaps</string>
    <key>CFBundleName</key>
    <string>WeatherMaps</string>
    <key>CFBundleShortVersionString</key>
    <string>.8</string>
```

```
   <key>CFBundleVersion</key>
   <string>.8</string>
   <key>CloseBoxInsetX</key>
   <integer>12</integer>
   <key>CloseBoxInsetY</key>
   <integer>12</integer>
   <key>MainHTML</key>
   <string>weathermaps.html</string>
</dict>
</plist>
```

References to remote web pages can be loaded in the WeatherMaps widget because this access key is set. In the WeatherMaps widget, the URLs are included in the menus of the HTML file and are set for the different map links in the setup() function.

```
<div id='popupMenu2'>Current Temperatures</div>
<select id='cTempMenu' onChange='cTempMap(this.value);'>
    <option
value="http://image.weather.com/images/maps/current/acttemp_600x405.jpg">Select a
regional temperature map...</option>
    <option
value="http://image.weather.com/images/maps/current/cen_curtemp_720x486.jpg">
Central</option>
    <option
value="http://image.weather.com/images/maps/current/ec_curtemp_720x486.jpg">East
Central</option>
    <option
value="http://image.weather.com/images/maps/current/nc_curtemp_720x486.jpg">North
Central</option>
    <option
value="http://image.weather.com/images/maps/current/ne_curtemp_720x486.jpg">
Northeast</option>
    <option
value="http://image.weather.com/images/maps/current/nw_curtemp_720x486.jpg">
Northwest</option>
    <option
value="http://image.weather.com/images/maps/current/sc_curtemp_720x486.jpg">South
Central</option>
    <option
value="http://image.weather.com/images/maps/current/se_curtemp_720x486.jpg">
Southeast</option>
    <option
value="http://image.weather.com/images/maps/current/sc_curtemp_720x486.jpg">
Southwest</option>
    <option
value="http://image.weather.com/images/maps/current/wc_curtemp_720x486.jpg">West
Central</option>
</select>
```

If you remove the AllowNetworkAccess key, the maps in the widget are replaced with broken graphic icons.

The `AllowNetworkAccess` key is not required, however, if your widget is going to pass the URL to your browser to open the web page. In this case, you would use the `widget.openURL()` method and pass it the URL, like so.

```
widget.openURL('http://www.peets.com/');
```

If you click a text link or a button that contains this method, your default browser is opened and the URL is loaded.

WebKit and Internet Plugin Access

As you saw in Chapter 2, Dashboard widgets can include plugins in the same way that Safari and other browsers do. The main difference between plugin use in browsers and widgets is that the plugins are part of the widget bundle. As with the original browser plugin architecture; widget, WebKit, and standard browser plugins allow your widget to incorporate content from other sources that it wouldn't be able to access natively. Flash animations and QuickTime movies, for instance, can be displayed in a widget making use of plugins. If your widget needs to access content beyond the widget bundle, file system, or network or needs to interact with applications, you will want to use a plugin.

Because Dashboard is based on the same WebKit technologies as Safari, you are able to incorporate WebKit plugins in your widget. To do this, you provide an access key, and you specify the name of the plugin. The access key for a WebKit plugin is `AllowInternetPlugins` and is a Boolean value. You can see this in the Info.plist for a widget that uses the QuickTime plugin.

```
<plist version="1.0">
<dict>
    <key>AllowInternetPlugins</key>
    <true/>
    <key>BackwardsCompatibleClassLookup</key>
    <true/>
    <key>CFBundleDisplayName</key>
    <string>QT Movie</string>
    <key>CFBundleIdentifier</key>
    <string>com.deadtrees.widget.qtmovie</string>
    <key>CFBundleName</key>
    <string>QT Movie</string>
    <key>CFBundleShortVersionString</key>
    <string>1.0</string>
    <key>CFBundleVersion</key>
    <string>1.0</string>
    <key>CloseBoxInsetX</key>
    <integer>14</integer>
    <key>CloseBoxInsetY</key>
    <integer>16</integer>
    <key>MainHTML</key>
    <string>QTMovie.html</string>
</dict>
</plist>
```

You don't have to enter the plugin name in the Info.plist file, because Internet plugins are automatically picked up by Dashboard.

Widget Plugin Access

The Widget plugin access key allows you to incorporate a plugin specifically written for your widget. Plugins allow your widget access to other files and applications that it does not access natively. As you saw with the Fortune widget earlier in the book, a widget plugin is a Cocoa bundle with its own Info.plist file. It is included in your widget's root directory and your widget is able to communicate with it by using JavaScript to a script object.

The access key syntax specifies a widget plugin. If you look in the Easy Envelope widget's Info.plist file, you'll see the plugin access key. This key uses a string instead of a Boolean value, and the plugin key is followed by the name of the plugin.

```
<dict>
  <key>AllowFullAccess</key>
  <true/>
  <key>CFBundleDisplayName</key>
  <string>EasyEnvelopes</string>
  <key>CFBundleGetInfoString</key>
  <string>1.0.2 Copyright ©2005 by Ambrosia Software, Inc.</string>
  <key>CFBundleIdentifier</key>
  <string>com.ambrosiasw.widget.easyenvelopes</string>
  <key>CFBundleName</key>
  <string>EasyEnvelopes</string>
  <key>CFBundleShortVersionString</key>
  <string>1.0.2</string>
  <key>CFBundleVersion</key>
  <string>1.0.2</string>
  <key>CloseBoxInsetX</key>
  <integer>5</integer>
  <key>CloseBoxInsetY</key>
  <integer>6</integer>
  <key>MainHTML</key>
  <string>EasyEnvelopes.html</string>
  <key>Plugin</key>
  <string>EEWPlugin.widgetplugin</string>
</dict>
</plist>
```

The EEWPlugin is called numerous times in the EasyEnvelopes.js file. As in the example that follows, each time the widget needs information from the plugin, it is called through the JavaScript. In the `grabClipboardAddress()` function, the JavaScript uses the plugin to check the clipboard for an address. If it finds one, the JavaScript places the address in the widget's address field.

```
function grabClipboardAddress() {

  if ( EEWPlugin ) {
    window.setTimeout("EEWPlugin.call('focusOnSearchField')", 0);
    if ( document.getElementById("back").style.display == "block" )
      EEWPlugin.toggleWithBool("frontIsShowing", false);
    else
      EEWPlugin.toggleWithBool("frontIsShowing", true);
  }

  if ( document.getElementById("back").style.display == "block" ) {
    if (returnAddressIndex == kCustomReturnAddress ) {
```

```
        document.getElementById("backReturnAddressCustomText").focus();
        document.getElementById("backReturnAddressCustomText").select();
          }
      }

    if (EEWPlugin) {
      var string = EEWPlugin.analyzePasteboard();
      if (string != "" ) {
        document.getElementById("addressText").innerHTML = string;
        if (EEWPlugin ) {
          var color = EEWPlugin.get("fontColorInfo");
          setAddressColor(color[0], color[1], color[2]);
        }
        setAddressFont(addressFontName, addressFontSize);
      }
    }
  }
```

Java Applet Access

In addition to being able to incorporate plugins into your widget, the `AllowJava` access key gives you access to Java applets. You can include them in your widget in the same way you would include them in a web page that you create.

This is a Boolean access key. You include it in the widget's Info.plist file as follows:

```
<key>AllowJava</key>
<true/>
```

The Distorter widget, which is available from the Dashboard downloads website, includes a Java applet that the widget author found and embedded in the widget. If you show the contents of the widget, you can see the Java classes that the author included (Figure 11-4).

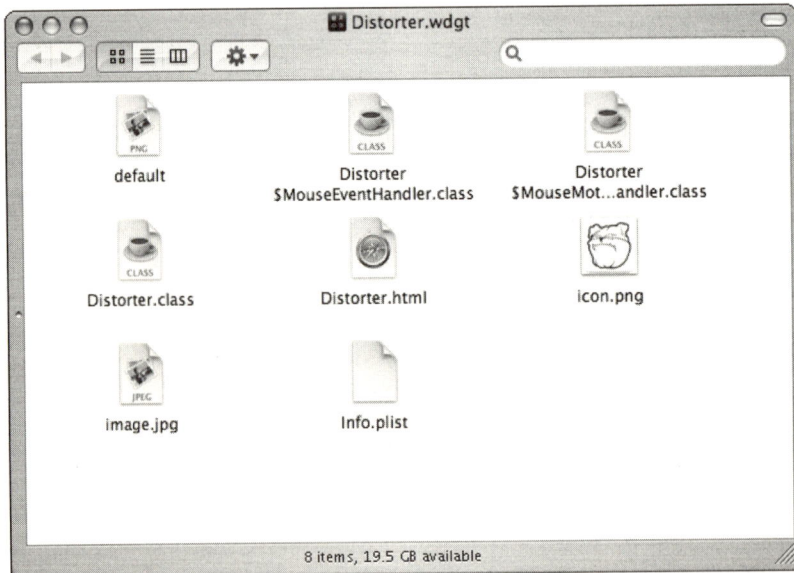

Figure 11-4

When you examine the HTML for the widget, you can see where the applet code is referenced.

```
<applet code="Distorter.class" width="262" height="244">
  <! ATTENTION: Do not forget to enter the width and height of the image you use in
the line above!!! >
  <param name="auto"           value="on" > <! on/off; when on, an automatic motion
will start if mouse is not moved>
  <param name="autoWait"       value="50" > <! How long to wait until the auto-
motion starts when the mouse does not move>
  <param name="autoChange"     value="180"> <! How fast the mode is changed to auto
and back (high values -> soft transition)>
  <param name="autoStrengthX" value="20"> <! in %;   the horizontal strength
(amplitude) of the auto-motion>
  <param name="autoStrengthY" value="30"> <! in %;   same for vertical>
  <param name="autoSpeedX"    value="50"> <! horizontal speed of the auto-motion>
  <param name="autoSpeedY"    value="120"> <! same for vertical>

  <param name="zoom"          value="100"> <! in %;    strength of the zoom>
  <param name="zoomSpeed"     value="20"> <! how fast the zoom works when a mouse-
button is pressed>

  <param name="Imagefile"     value="image.jpg"> <! filename of the image>
</applet>
```

Full Access

While this chapter is primarily about giving widgets access to resources on your Macintosh and the network, you can also think about access from a security point of view of restricting what a widget has access to on your Macintosh. Access keys are widget security. All of the access keys above limit a widget to specific resources. The AllowFullAccess key provides access to everything: file system, command-line utilities, network resources, plugins, and Java applets. If you entered AllowFullAccess for your widget, you won't have to enter the individual access keys for each resource (Figure 11-5).

However, you probably don't want to use AllowFullAccess unless your widget really needs access to multiple access keys. Widgets play in their own sandbox, but you don't need to allow more access than required. You should allow access to only those resources that your widget needs.

AllowFullAccess is useful if your widget needs access to several resources. For instance, if it needs to run a Unix command, access information from an application using a plugin, and access network resources, you may want use AllowFullAccess in the same way Easy Envelopes does.

If you show the contents of the Easy Envelopes widget, you'll see that it contains a plugin, so it would need the Plugin access key.

Including only the AllowFullAccess *key in your widget's Info.plist file doesn't allow the widget plugin to work. You have to explicitly enter the plugin name in your Info.plist file as well.*

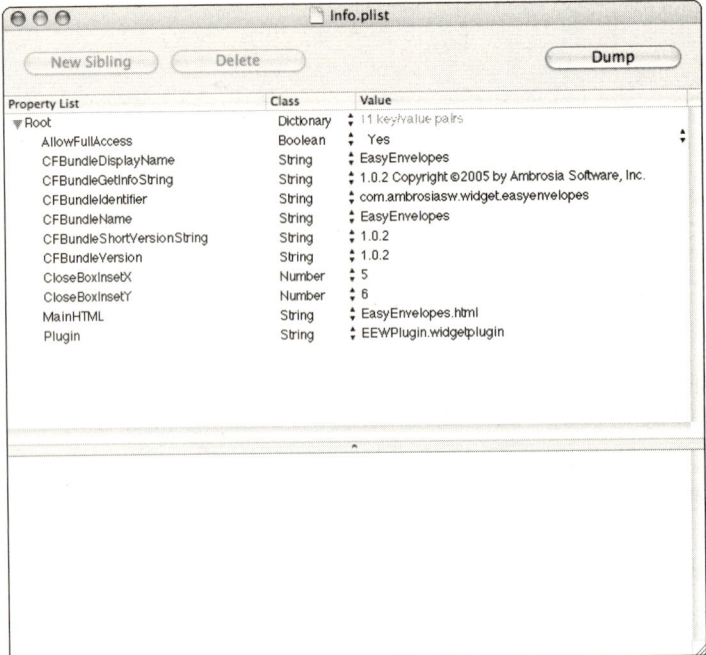

Figure 11-5

You'll find many references to the EEWplugin in the EasyEnvelopes.js file. For example:

```
function toggleBarcodes(showBarcodes) {

  EEWPlugin.toggleWithBool("barcodes", showBarcodes);

  widget.setPreferenceForKey(showBarcodes, "showBarcodes");
}
```

Because it prints the envelope and needs access to the printer, the Easy Envelopes widget needs the `AllowNetworkAccess` key. The `AllowNetworkAccess` key also gives the widget access to the Internet when you click the wax seal and go to the Easy Envelopes section of Ambrosia Software's website.

```
function launchSite() {
  if ( isLinkButtonDown )
      widget.openURL('http://www.AmbrosiaSW.com/utilities/easyenvelopes/');

  isLinkButtonDown = false;
}
```

Summary

In this chapter, you have seen how the level of access that you provide to your widget allows it to access resources on your Macintosh and beyond.

In this chapter, you learned:

❑   What access keys are

❑   How to use all of the access keys

❑   When access keys are appropriate

In Chapter 12, we'll look at incorporating plugins in your widget, but before you move on, you may want to run through these exercises.

Exercises

1.   If your widget calls the traceroute utility, should you use the `widget.system()` method in synchronous or asynchronous mode?

2.   What access key would you use if you wanted to create a widget that displays a QuickTime movie?

3.   Should you use the `AllowFullAccess` key if your widget needs to display the contents of a file in your home directory?

Using Plugins and Applets

In Chapter 11, you learned about the different access keys that allow your widget to gather information from outside of its bundle. In the course of looking at access keys, you even spent some time looking at the different kinds of plugins associated with their access keys: widget, WebKit, and browser plugins. In this chapter, you are going to look at the use of plugins in your widget.

By the end of this chapter, you will know:

- ❑   Why you might want to use a plugin
- ❑   How to incorporate a plugin into your widget
- ❑   How to incorporate a Java applet into your widget

Plugins, Widgets, and Sharing

A discussion of plugins may seem beyond the scope of a book about beginning Dashboard widget development because plugins are compiled executables written in Objective C. Objective C is an object-oriented programming language that can be written and compiled in Apple's IDE Xcode. Even if you don't know Objective C and can't write your own plugin, you can still gain some benefit from plugins if you know how widgets get information from them or send information to them. In some cases, you can take an existing WebKit or browser plugin and incorporate it into your widget. Some widget plugins may also be available for you to use in your widget. As you saw with Java applets in Chapter 11, you may be able to find an applet or plugin that is freely available for your use.

Sharing Etiquette

Because it is so easy to look at the code in a widget, you should remember to credit others when you borrow their code. If they have created a plugin for their widget that is general enough that you could make use of it in yours, you should check with the author to see if it is okay to distribute her code with your widget. For example, the iPhotoLoader.widgetplugin that Jesus de Meyer created for iPhoto Mini was used without his permission. He decided then that subsequent versions of the plugin would be copy-protected so it could not be used outside of the iPhoto Mini widget. Some authors give permission to use their code. Jason Yee says in the HTML header of his iTunes Connection Monitor widget that it is freely distributable under the terms of the GNU GPL. In the readme file included in his Bart widget, Bret Victor says that it is licensed under the MIT license "which basically says that I get the copyright and you get everything else." Even if the author offers a blanket grant of permission, it's always a good practice to ask.

Why Use Plugins?

Because JavaScript, widget events, and the access keys provide most of the capabilities that you need, why would you want to incorporate a plugin into your widget? At least three reasons exist: you may not be able to accomplish what you want to in JavaScript, JavaScript may not be fast enough, and you may not want someone to read your JavaScript code and use it for their own project. You may be able to accomplish most programming tasks in JavaScript, but some things JavaScript cannot do. It can't communicate with other applications without assistance, for example. You can write shell scripts or AppleScripts that provide the information to your widget's JavaScript. If you need to get the information directly from an application or an application's files, plugins are the way to add features to your widget that you can't get through JavaScript, command-line utilities, or scripts.

You may just choose to write a plugin for your widget if speed is an issue. For example, you may be able to read all of the files in from a directory, sort them by name or date, and then display them in a scrolling list using JavaScript. As the number of files in the directory grows, however, you may find that the JavaScript solution slows down. If you create a plugin to handle the same task, it will be able to handle more files and be quicker.

You may also choose to write a plugin if you need to protect your code. If you are trying to make money with your widget, moving your JavaScript functions into compiled code keeps someone else from using them. While most widgets are free and a number are donationware, a few widgets must be paid for. The NotePad widget from Widget Machine (Figure 12-1) is an example of a widget that must be paid for.

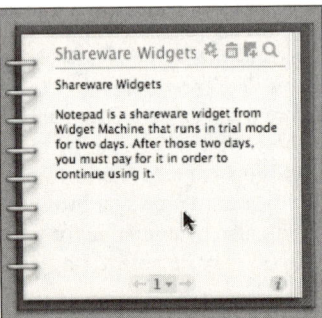

Figure 12-1

When you start it up the first time, it tells you how many days you have left in the trial period (Figure 12-2). Widget Machine controls this behavior through a notepad.widgetplugin that contains a widget registerer application. The price for NotePad is a very reasonable $4.95.

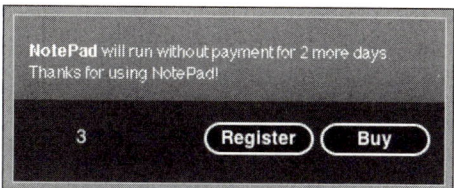

Figure 12-2

Though the overall trend is to give widgets away, Tiger has been out for only a year and we may see more widgets that require payment to unlock full functionality or to continue using them after an initial trial period.

Using Plugins in a Widget

As we saw in Chapter 11, your widget can make use of Internet and WebKit plugins, as well as widget plugins.

Finding Plugins on Your Mac

You'll find Internet plugins inside of the /Library/Internet Plug-ins/ directory. If you look in that directory, you'll see the plugins that your browser uses for websites incorporating QuickTime movies and Flash (Figure 12-3).

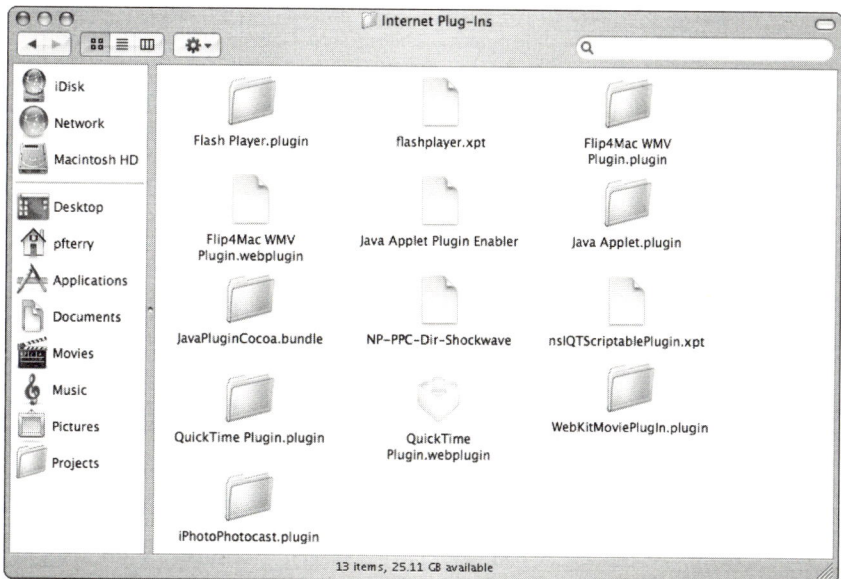

Figure 12-3

You may also see some WebKit plugins installed. In addition to being accessible by your browser, these plugins are available to your widget. Because these aren't part of your widget's bundle, you'll have to make certain they are installed on your users' Macintoshes if you want to use them.

QuickTime

When you install QuickTime, its plugins are installed in the /Library/Internet Plug-Ins directory. This is a common location that any browser or other application on your Macintosh can access. Whenever you play a movie trailer in Safari, it calls the plugin and displays the movie embedded in the web page. If you view the source of the web page, you'll see the embed tags.

You can call the QuickTime plugin to play a movie in your widget. To do this, you need to make the necessary access key changes to the Info.plist file. As you can see in the following code, you'll want to include the `AllowInternetPlugins` access key.

```
<plist version="1.0">
<dict>
    <key>AllowInternetPlugins</key>
    <true/>
    <key>BackwardsCompatibleClassLookup</key>
    <true/>
    <key>CFBundleDisplayName</key>
    <string>QT Movie</string>
    <key>CFBundleIdentifier</key>
    <string>com.deadtrees.widget.qtmovie</string>
    <key>CFBundleName</key>
    <string>QT Movie</string>
    <key>CFBundleShortVersionString</key>
    <string>1.0</string>
    <key>CFBundleVersion</key>
    <string>1.0</string>
    <key>CloseBoxInsetX</key>
    <integer>14</integer>
    <key>CloseBoxInsetY</key>
    <integer>16</integer>
    <key>MainHTML</key>
    <string>QTMovie.html</string>
</dict>
</plist>
```

You also have to add the <embed> tag to your widget's HTML page. Notice that you give the source for the movie in the same way that you link in a graphic. You set the width and height of the movie and then include settings for whether you want the movie to autoplay and loop.

All of the settings available for embedding a QuickTime movie in a page are available at www.apple.com/quicktime/tutorials/embed.html.

In this example, the sample.mov is included in the widget bundle, but you could point to a movie outside of the widget bundle if you include the `AllowFileAccessOutsideOfWidget` access key.

```
<html>
<head>
<style type="text/css">
    @import "QTMovie.css";
</style>
<script type='text/javascript' src='QTMovie.js' charset='utf-8'/>

<!-- The Apple Classes are included at the top level of the widget for pre-10.4.3
compatibility -->
<script type='text/javascript' src='AppleClasses/AppleButton.js' charset='utf-8'/>
<script type='text/javascript' src='AppleClasses/AppleInfoButton.js' charset='utf-
8'/>
<script type='text/javascript' src='AppleClasses/AppleAnimator.js' charset='utf-
8'/>
</head>
<body onload="setup();">
    <div id="front">
        <img span="backgroundImage" src="Default.png">

        <div id="movie">
        <embed src="sample.mov" width="320" height="256" AUTOPLAY=true
LOOP=false></embed>
        </div>

        <div id='infoButton'></div>
    </div>
      <div id="back">
        <img span="backgroundImage" src="Back.png">
        <div id="dtLink">Widget<br><a href="#"
onClick="widget.openURL('http://www.deadtrees.net/');">http://www.deadtrees.net/</a
></div>
        <div id="apLink">Java Applet<br><a href="#"
onClick="widget.openURL('http://www.dataway.ch/~bennet/');">http://www.dataway.ch/~
bennet/</a></div>
        <div id="doneButton"></div>
    </div>
</body>
</html>
```

The embedded movie settings are wrapped in a `<div>` tag that can be referenced by a selector in the CSS file. Using the selector allows you to control the placement of the movie on a background. If you embed the movie in a basic widget, the plugin loads and plays the movie whenever Dashboard loads (Figure 12-4).

If you've used the QuickTime plugin in Safari before, the behavior is the same. Control-clicking the playing movie — or right-clicking, if you have a multibutton mouse — displays the QuickTime plugin pop-up menu.

187

Figure 12-4

Incorporating Widget Plugins

We've already looked at reasons that you would want to use a widget plugin, but probably the best reason is the ability to add features to which you wouldn't otherwise have access. For example, you would not be able to access the keychain to read a password or write a password without a plugin. Some widgets, LiveWidget and GoogleMail to name a couple, have already incorporated keychain access. LiveWidget is for blogging with LiveJournal and it provides a way to log in and post to this site. The GoogleMail widget allows users to log into their GoogleMail and retrieve message summaries.

As with the Java applet, the widget plugin must be installed in the top level of widget. The Info.plist file has to be set for the plugin. The LiveWidget Info.plist file, for instance, shows the PasswordPlugin.

```
<plist version="1.0">
<dict>
    <key>AllowNetworkAccess</key>
    <true/>
    <key>AllowSystem</key>
    <true/>
    <key>CFBundleDisplayName</key>
    <string>LiveWidget</string>
    <key>CFBundleIdentifier</key>
    <string>nz.net.stanton.craig.widget.livewidget</string>
    <key>CFBundleName</key>
    <string>LiveWidget</string>
    <key>CFBundleShortVersionString</key>
    <string>2.1</string>
    <key>CFBundleVersion</key>
    <string>2.1</string>
    <key>CloseBoxInsetX</key>
    <integer>22</integer>
    <key>CloseBoxInsetY</key>
    <integer>15</integer>
    <key>Height</key>
```

```
        <integer>312</integer>
        <key>MainHTML</key>
        <string>LiveWidget.html</string>
        <key>Plugin</key>
        <string>PasswordPlugin.widgetplugin</string>
        <key>Width</key>
        <integer>470</integer>
    </dict>
    </plist>
```

The LiveWidget preferences contain the username and password to gain access to the user's blog (Figure 12-5).

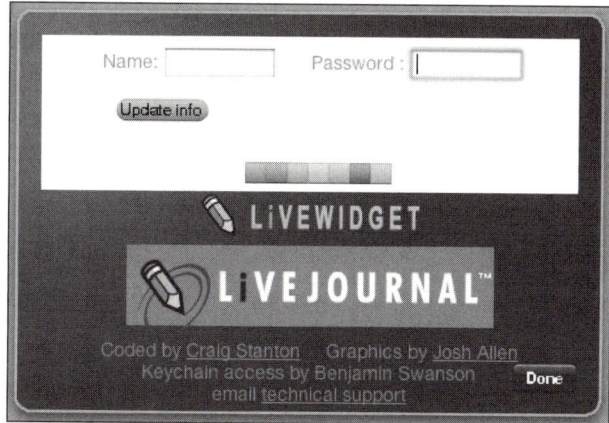

Figure 12-5

The widget takes the username and password and, through the JavaScript, passes it to the PasswordPlugin. The username is passed in the `backForm.username.value` and the password is passed in `backForm.password.value`. You'll also notice that the username is set as a preference so that the next time the user logs in to his blog, he'll have to type only the password.

```
function saveUserLogin(){
    backForm = document.backForm;
    if (window.widget){
        widget.setPreferenceForKey(backForm.username.value, usernameKey);
        //disabled until it is safe
        //widget.setPreferenceForKey(backForm.password.value, passwordKey);

        if (PasswordPlugin){
            PasswordPlugin.makePassword(backForm.username.value,
backForm.password.value, "LiveWidgetPassword");
        }

    }
}
```

The PasswordPlugin also helps restore the user name and password.

```
function restoreUserLogin(){
    backForm = document.backForm;
    theForm = document.mainForm;
    if (window.widget){
        var savedUsername = widget.preferenceForKey(usernameKey);
        if (savedUsername != undefined) {
            backForm.username.value = savedUsername;
            theForm.journals.options.length = 0;
            addOptionToList(theForm.journals, backForm.username.value, '');
            theForm.journals.options.selectedIndex = 0;
            changeList("journals_list", "journals_text");
        }
        if (PasswordPlugin){
            backForm.password.value =
PasswordPlugin.getPassword(backForm.username.value, "LiveWidgetPassword");
        }

        if ((backForm.password.value.length > 0) & (backForm.password.value.length
> 0)){
            startGetInfo();
        }
    }
}
```

As you saw in Chapter 6, JavaScript is the workhorse carrying the information from the form on the back of the widget to the keychain and the preferences.

Using Java Applets

As we saw in Chapter 11, Dashboard includes an access key that allows you to incorporate a Java applet into your widget. Because widgets are basically HTML pages, adding an applet to a widget is just like adding an applet to a web page. As simple as this is, Apple suggests that you not use applets or Flash in your widget because they are so memory heavy.

It is possible to grab a Java applet and incorporate it into a widget. For example, the 3D Clock applet shown in Figure 12-6 is a Java applet available on the Free Java website (www.javafile.com/clocks/coolclock/coolclock.php) or Bennet Uk's website (www.dataway.ch/~bennet/). You can create a simple widget to hold the Java class and display the clock.

Try It Out   **Add a Java Applet to Your Widget**

To see how this would work, let's create a simple widget to hold the Java applet.

1. Create a basic widget background panel (Figure 12-6).

2. Create a folder for the widget and drop all of the widget files in it (Figure 12-7). You can include the AppleClasses directory for backward compatibility and the graphics files for the widget back and icon.

Figure 12-6

3. Drop the Clock3D.class in the root level of the widget.

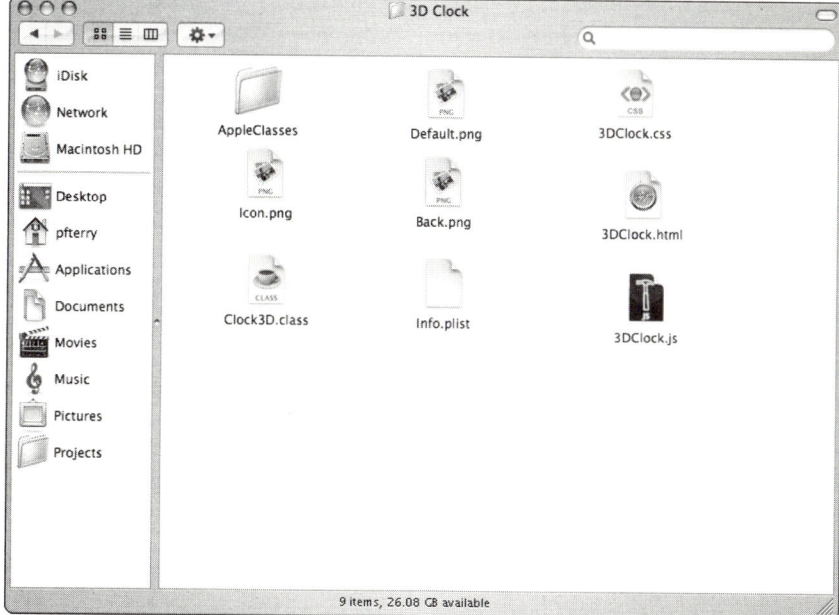

Figure 12-7

4. Create an Info.plist file for the widget like the one that follows. Notice the
BackwardsCompatibleClassLookup key and the AllowJava key will enable
the widget to run the Java applet.

```
<plist version="1.0">
<dict>
    <key>AllowJava</key>
    <true/>
    <key>BackwardsCompatibleClassLookup</key>
    <true/>
    <key>CFBundleDisplayName</key>
    <string>3D Clock</string>
```

```
    <key>CFBundleIdentifier</key>
    <string>com.deadtrees.widget.3dclock</string>
    <key>CFBundleName</key>
    <string>3D Clock</string>
    <key>CFBundleShortVersionString</key>
    <string>1.0</string>
    <key>CFBundleVersion</key>
    <string>1.0</string>
    <key>CloseBoxInsetX</key>
    <integer>14</integer>
    <key>CloseBoxInsetY</key>
    <integer>16</integer>
    <key>MainHTML</key>
    <string>3DClock.html</string>
</dict>
</plist>
```

5. In the HTML file for the widget, you must add the code to call the applet. If the applet has any settings, those must be included. The section containing the applet code needs to be placed inside of a `<div>` tags so you can format it with a selector.

```
<html>
<head>
<style type="text/css">
    @import "3DClock.css";
</style>
<script type='text/javascript' src='3DClock.js' charset='utf-8'/>

<!-- The Apple Classes are included at the top level of the widget for pre-10.4.3
compatibility -->
<script type='text/javascript' src='AppleClasses/AppleButton.js' charset='utf-8'/>
<script type='text/javascript' src='AppleClasses/AppleInfoButton.js' charset='utf-
8'/>
<script type='text/javascript' src='AppleClasses/AppleAnimator.js' charset='utf-
8'/>
</head>
<body onload="setup();">
    <div id="front">
        <img span="backgroundImage" src="Default.png">
        <div id="applet">
        <applet code="Clock3D.class" WIDTH="180" HEIGHT="180">
            <param name="fps" value="18">
            <param name="a1" value="12500">
            <param name="pixd" value="29">
            <param name="pixangle" value="5">
            <param name="radius" value="26">
            <param name="roty" value="-4">
            <param name="rotx" value="0">
            <param name="rotz" value="0.401">
            <param name="irotx" value="0">
            <param name="iroty" value="0">
            <param name="irotz" value="00">
             <param name="style" value="1">
             <param name="color" value="#00FF66">
             <param name="bgcolor" value="#2B2B2B">
             <param name="12hour" value="0">
```

```
            </applet>
          </div>
          <div id='infoButton'></div>
      </div>
        <div id="back">
          <img span="backgroundImage" src="Back.png">
          <div id="dtLink">Widget<br><a href="#"
onclick=widget.openURL("http://www.deadtrees.net/");">http://www.deadtrees.net/</a>
</div>
          <div id="apLink">Java Applet<br><a href="#"
onClick="widget.openURL("http://www.dataway.ch/~bennet/");">http://www.dataway.ch/~
bennet/</a></div>
          <div id="doneButton"></div>
      </div>
  </body>
  </html>
```

6. The CSS file must include a selector to control the placement of the applet on the widget. Without the <div> in the HTML file and its selector in the CSS file, the applet will get loaded, but you will not be able to see it on the widget.

```
body {
    margin: 0;
}

.backgroundImage {
    position: absolute;
    top: 0px;
    left: 0px;
}

#applet {
    position:absolute;
    top:15px;
    left:20px;
}

#infoButton {
    position:absolute;
    bottom: 35px;
    right: 30px;
}

#doneButton {
    position: absolute;
    bottom: 30px;
    left: 90px;
}

#front {
    display: block;
}

#dtLink {
    position:absolute;
    font: 12px "Helvetica Neue";
```

```
        color:white;
        bottom:100;
        left:25;
}

#apLink {
        position:absolute;
        font: 12px "Helvetica Neue";
        color:white;
        bottom:60;
        left:25;
}

#back {
        display: none;
}
```

How It Works

The widget is a container for the Java applet. In the case of the Distorter widget discussed in Chapter 11, the widget contained a bare minimum of the elements that are typically used for a widget. The CSS markup was included in the HTML file and the widget didn't have a JavaScript file because it didn't have a back side. As you can see from the example here, the entry in the Info.plist file, the additions for the applet in the HTML file, and the CSS formatting are all that are needed for the applet. In spite of the simplicity of the 3D Clock widget, it weighs in with 40 megabytes of memory (Figure 12-8).

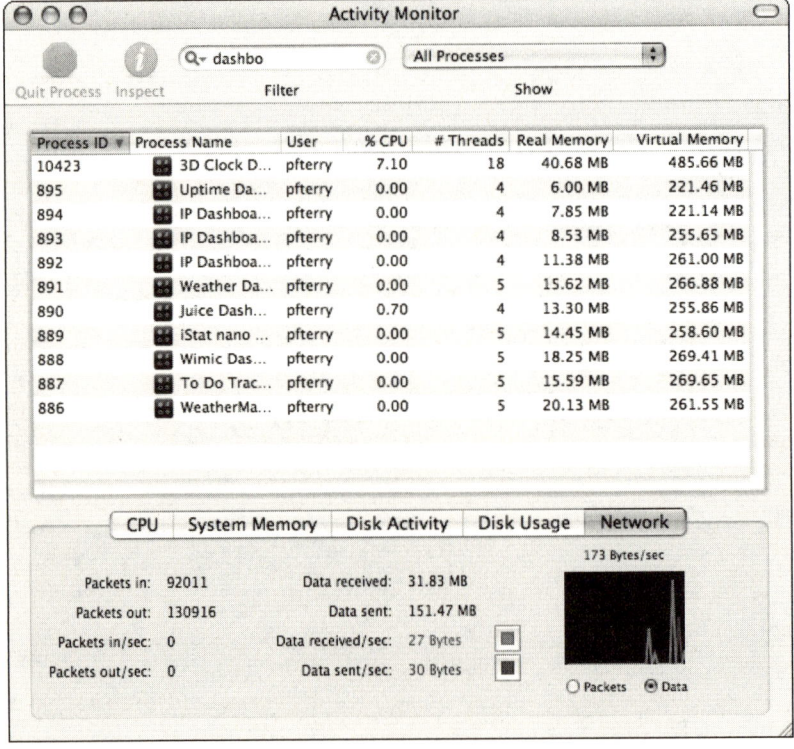

Figure 12-8

Summary

Though you may not be ready to create your own Java applet or custom widget plugin, you can still get the benefits by incorporating them into your widget.

In this chapter, you learned:

❑   Why you might want to use a widget

❑   How to incorporate a plugin into your widget

❑   How to incorporate a Java applet into your widget

Exercises

1.   What differentiates widget plugins from WebKit plugins?

2.   Do you have to add WebKit plugins to your Widget?

3.   Why does Apple suggest that you not include Java applets or Flash in your widget?

Part III
Example Widgets

Easy Envelopes

More than one critic has commented that it would be quicker to open a browser with bookmarks than Dashboard with the different widgets. That may be the case for most web pages, but sometimes you don't want the whole web page and not everything that a widget accesses is a web page. For instance, it is quicker to open a widget to get the particular map you want at weather.com than to load the entire page. You could access system information from the command line with Safari, but a widget is much lighter weight for that task. Sometimes you just can't accomplish in Safari what a widget will do.

Easy Envelopes

Take the Easy Envelopes by Andrew Welch of Ambrosia Software as an example. Several envelope printing applications have been available for the Macintosh during its history and envelope printing templates are available for most of the word processors. Easy Envelopes, however, captures all of the functionality you need in a widget. Perhaps it is because all of the other envelope printing utilities are full-blown applications that Easy Envelopes seems to stretch the idea of a widget a bit.

If a widget is supposed to do one thing well, however, Easy Envelopes is a widget. It may not be a web page for Dashboard the way most widgets are, but it only prints envelopes and it does that extremely well.

The Interface

Easy Envelopes has one of the cleverest interfaces of the 1,700-plus widgets on the Dashboard Downloads site. Not only does it look like an envelope (Figure 13-1), but every graphic on the interface has a use or provides information to the user. The version number of the widget appears above the stamp, the printer name and the envelope size appear in the lower-left corner of the widget.

Figure 13-1

Clicking the printer postage stamp opens the print dialog. Once the widget is configured with the return address, printer, and envelope size, you can print an envelope quickly by entering the address and then clicking the postage stamp (Figure 13-2). The print dialog includes an additional warning to feed the envelope face up.

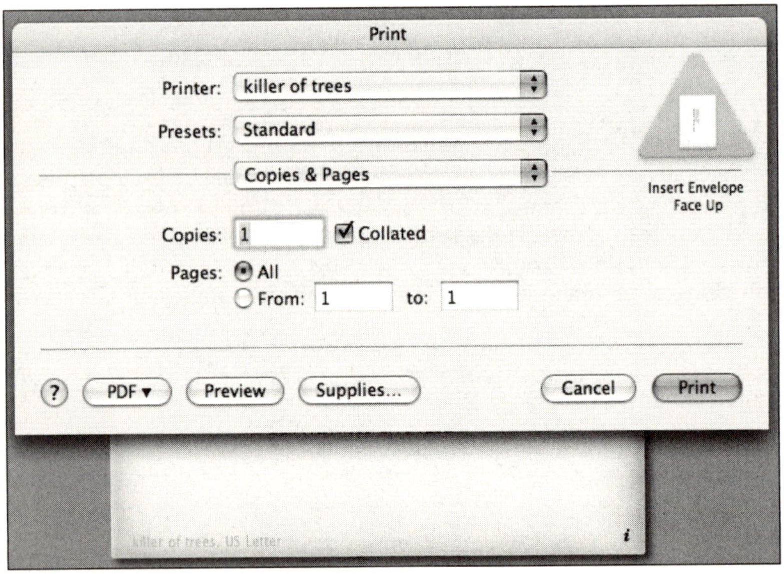

Figure 13-2

In addition to the functionality of the printer postage stamp, clicking the postmark minimizes Easy Envelopes so it takes up less space on your screen (Figure 13-3).

Figure 13-3

The Info button gives you access to the font, envelope size, and other preferences (Figure 13-4). As with the graphics on the front of the widget, each graphic on the back has a function. Clicking the wax seal takes you to the Easy Envelopes page at the Ambrosia Software website. The Done button provides the same function as other widgets with the added benefit that it looks like a post office stamp so it is consistent with the overall interface.

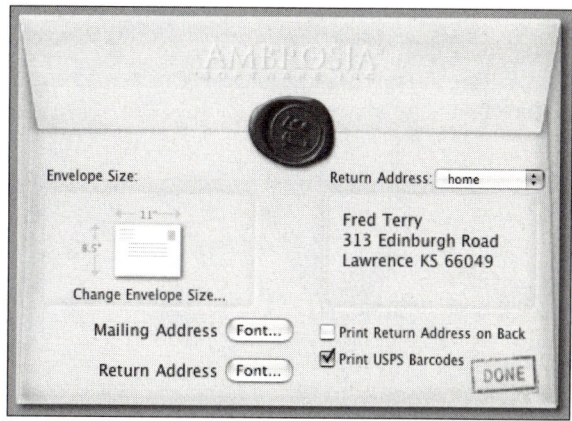

Figure 13-4

Clicking the Change Envelope Size opens the Page Setup dialog box (Figure 13-5) where you can select the size of the envelope that you are printing. The Paper Size pop-up menu includes choices for A4, JB5, #10 Envelope, and Monarch Envelope in addition to US Letter and US Letter Small.

This Page Setup and the Print dialog (Figure 13-2) are indications that the widget is using more than the typical resources available to a widget. In addition to these, the widget uses the Font selection dialog when you click the Font button for the Mailing and Return addresses (Figure 13-6). You'll see how this is accomplished in the following pages.

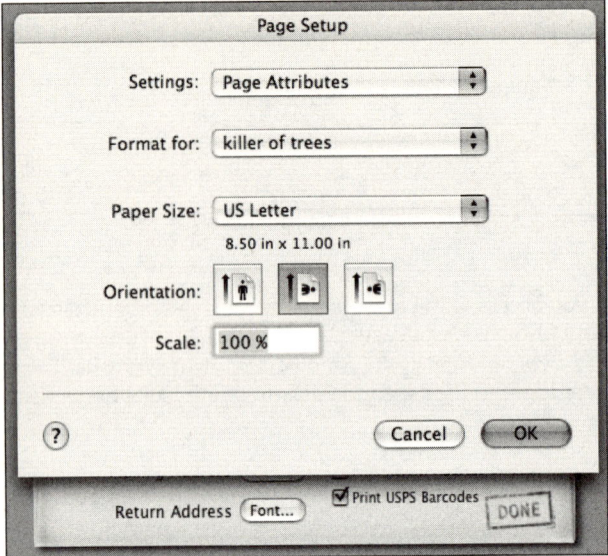

Figure 13-5

Figure 13-6

Besides displaying the Font and Print dialogs, the widget is also able to search the Address Book and insert the found address (Figure 13-7).

Figure 13-7

Easy Envelopes Internals

When you look inside the Easy Envelopes widget, you can see how access to system dialog boxes is accomplished.

Info.plist

When you open the Info.plist file, you can see that the `AllowFullAccess` key at the top of the file is set to true. This gives the widget access to the command line, filesystem, network, and WebKit and standard plugins. Toward the bottom of the file, the plugin EEWPlugin.widgetplugin is included.

```
<?xml version="1.0" encoding="UTF-8"?>
<!DOCTYPE plist PUBLIC "-//Apple Computer//DTD PLIST 1.0//EN"
"http://www.apple.com/DTDs/PropertyList-1.0.dtd">
<plist version="1.0">
<dict>
  <key>AllowFullAccess</key>
  <true/>
  <key>CFBundleDisplayName</key>
  <string>EasyEnvelopes</string>
  <key>CFBundleGetInfoString</key>
  <string>1.0.2 Copyright ©2005 by Ambrosia Software, Inc.</string>
  <key>CFBundleIdentifier</key>
  <string>com.ambrosiasw.widget.easyenvelopes</string>
  <key>CFBundleName</key>
  <string>EasyEnvelopes</string>
  <key>CFBundleShortVersionString</key>
  <string>1.0.2</string>
  <key>CFBundleVersion</key>
  <string>1.0.2</string>
  <key>CloseBoxInsetX</key>
  <integer>5</integer>
```

```
        <key>CloseBoxInsetY</key>
        <integer>6</integer>
        <key>MainHTML</key>
        <string>EasyEnvelopes.html</string>
        <key>Plugin</key>
        <string>EEWPlugin.widgetplugin</string>
    </dict>
</plist>
```

HTML/CSS

When you show the contents of the Easy Envelopes widget and look at the files it is composed of, you see several concepts in use that you learned in the first half of the book. By examining the way these concepts are employed, you may gain a better understanding of them.

In addition to what you would usually see included in the HTML file, that file also contains areas in the front and back `<div>`s that are defined as canvas drawing areas. Two of the areas are where the return addresses can be drawn using JavaScript. The `returnAddressImage` canvas specifies the width and height of the drawing area.

```
<span id="returnAddressText" ></span>
<canvas id="returnAddressImage" width="100" height="70">
```

If you look in the CSS file, you can see the position for the front return address specified as well as the default text specifications for the return address.

```
#returnAddressText {
  font: 12px "LucidaGrande" ;
  font-weight: normal;
  position: absolute;
  top: 20px;
  left: 25px;
}
#returnAddressImage {
  position: absolute;
  top: 20px;
  left: 25px;

  visibility: hidden;

}
#frontReturnAddressImage {
  position: absolute;
  top: 20px;
  left: 25px;

  visibility: hidden;

}
```

The back `<div>` contains the drawing area called the `backReturnAddressImage` along with its height and width.

```
      <span id="backReturnAddressText"></span>
      <canvas id="backReturnAddressImage" width="155" height="80">
      <textarea id="backReturnAddressCustomText"
onblur="changeCustomReturnAddress();"></textarea>
```

And the CSS file contains the canvas and text specifications.

```
#backReturnAddressText {
   font: 12px "LucidaGrande" ;
   font-weight: normal;
   position: absolute;
   top: 145px;
   left: 250px;

   width: 10000px;

   clip: rect(0, 145, 70, 0);
}

#backReturnAddressCustomText {
   position: absolute;
   top: 140px;
   left: 245px;

   width: 145px;
   height: 70px;

   visibility: hidden;
}

#backReturnAddressImage {
   position: absolute;
   top: 135px;
   left: 240px;
   visibility: hidden;
}
```

The other area that has a canvas ID associated with it is in the back div. The three divs envelopeWidth, envelopeHeight, and envelopeLabel open the Page Setup dialog box when the area is clicked in. The following image input is for the wax seal and executes the `canvasDown()` function whenever it is clicked. The canvas ID at the end of the section executes the `showPageSetup()` function, among others, whenever it is clicked.

```
    <div id="envelopeWidth" onMouseDown="canvasDown();" onmouseover="canvasOver();"
onmouseup="showPageSetup();"></div>
    <div id="envelopeHeight" onMouseDown="canvasDown();" onmouseover="canvasOver();"
onmouseup="showPageSetup();"></div>
    <div id="envelopeLabel" style="font: 10px 'Lucida Grande'; position: absolute;
left: 46px; top: 205px;" onMouseDown="canvasDown();" onmouseover="canvasOver();"
onmouseup="showPageSetup();"></div>

       <input type="image" style=" opacity: 0; clip: rect(0, 155, 83,0);
position:absolute; top: 135; left: 25;" onMouseDown="canvasDown();"
src="Images/wax_seal_normal.png">
```

```
    <canvas id="envelopeCanvas" onMouseDown="canvasDown();"
onmouseover="canvasOver();" onmouseout="canvasUpOut();"
onmouseup="showPageSetup();" width="155" height="83"/>
```

The envelopeWidth, envelopeHeight, and envelopeLabel divs along with the canvas ID envelopeCanvas correspond to envelopeCanvas at the top of the CSS file.

```
#envelopeCanvas {
  position: absolute;
  top: 135;
  left: 25;
}
```

The area on the left side of the widget back contains the envelope icon.

```
    <div>
      <input id='recipientText' type=search size="30"/>
    </div>

    <textarea onkeydown="handleManualEdit(event);" onfocus="turnWhite();"
onblur="exitAddressText();" id="addressText" WRAP=OFF></textarea>

    <script  type="text/javascript">
    document.getElementById("addressText").blur();
    </script>

    <form  name="namesForm">
    <select id="listPoint" name="namesList" onChange="keepCursorAtEndOfInput()"
onMouseUp="setAddressFromMenu(event)">
    </select>
    </form>
```

JavaScript Functionality

The Easy Envelope JavaScript file is well organized so you can find the functions associated with the features in the widget. The button functions are grouped together at the top of the file, and the canvas functions are similarly grouped together. Easy Envelopes has a plugin that provides the application-like functionality with the Print, Page Setup, and Font dialog boxes, but JavaScript links the widget to the plugin. In addition to providing a bridge between the widget and the plugin, other functionality in the widget is based on the use of JavaScript. For instance, the minimize feature is completely implemented in JavaScript.

Minimize

The minimize functionality is produced by clicking the postmark. This behavior is established in the HTML file. The img ID contains the reference to the postmark.png file and executes the `minimize(event)` function whenever the area around the postmark is clicked.

```
    <img id="postMark" src="Images/postmark.png" onclick="minimize(event)">
    <input type="image" id="printButtonImage" onmousedown="printButtonDown();"
    onmouseover="printButtonOver();" onmouseout="printButtonUpOut();"
    onmouseup="print();" src="Images/print_btn_normal.png">
```

The `minimize(event)` function that the `onclick` method is calling is in the JavaScript file. You can see that the function contains animation commands and has error checking so the minimized widget window doesn't go off-screen.

```
// Minimize the widget down to a small icon. Invoked by the postmark image's
onclick method.
function minimize(event)
{
  var multiplier = 1;
  if (event && event.shiftKey)
    multiplier *= 10; // shift key down -> "slow-mo"

  // Make sure minimizing doesn't put the widget entirely offscreen
  if (EEWPlugin.isPointOnscreenForXY(window.screenX, window.screenY))
  {
    resizeAnimation.startHeight = fullSize.height;
    resizeAnimation.startWidth = fullSize.width;
    resizeAnimation.endHeight = minSize.height;
    resizeAnimation.endWidth = minSize.width;

    resizeAnimation.startTime = (new Date).getTime() - 13; // set it back one
frame.
    resizeAnimation.duration = 250 * multiplier;

    // Disallow maximize-during-minimize to avoid concurrency bugs
    minimized.onclick = null;
    resizeAnimation.onfinished = finishMinimize;

    EEWPlugin.call("saveWidgetSnapshot");
    front.style.display = "none";
    EEWPlugin.toggleWithBool("searchFieldVisible", false);
    EEWPlugin.call("prepareForMinimize");
    resizeAnimation.timer = setInterval(animateResize, 13);
    animateResize();
  }
}

function finishMinimize()
{
  minimizedIcon.src = EEWPlugin.finishMinimize();
  minimized.style.display = "block";
  minimized.onclick = maximize;
  widget.setPreferenceForKey("minimized", widget.identifier+"-size");
}
```

If you've noticed that the minimized widget window looks like a miniature version of the original—that is, it contains your mailing address—you can see that the plugin takes a snapshot of the widget window with the EEWPlugin.call(`saveWidgetSnapshot`).

Return Address

Several JavaScript functions take the addresses and draw them on the canvas areas that are set up in HTML and CSS files. The `drawFrontStuff()` function, for example, draws the return address on the front of the envelope.

```
        //draws the return address image on the front
        function drawFrontStuff() {

          /***********************/
            /**** DRAW RETURN ADDRESS IMAGE ON FRONT ****/

            if ( returnAddressIndex == kImageReturnAddress ) {

              var image = new Image();
              image.src = imageFilename;

              var canvas = document.getElementById("returnAddressImage");
              var context = canvas.getContext("2d");

              context.clearRect(0, 0, canvas.width, canvas.height);

              if ( image.width > canvas.width || image.height > canvas.height ) {
                var displayRatio = canvas.width / canvas.height;
                var imageRatio = image.width / image.height;

                var scaleWidth, scaleHeight;
                if( imageRatio > displayRatio ) {
                  var scale = canvas.width / image.width;
                  scaleWidth = canvas.width;
                  scaleHeight = image.height * scale;
                  } else if ( imageRatio < displayRatio )  {
                  var scale = canvas.height / image.height;
                  scaleWidth = image.width * scale;
                  scaleHeight = canvas.height;
                  }

                  context.drawImage(image, 0, 0, Math.floor(image.width),
          Math.floor(image.height), 0, 0, Math.floor(scaleWidth), Math.floor(scaleHeight));


              } else
                context.drawImage(image, 0, 0);
            }

            /***********************/

        }
```

Page Setup and Font Panels

The JavaScript calls the plugin to display the Page Setup and Font dialog boxes through the showPageSetup(), showAddressFontPanel(), and showReturnAddressFontPanel() functions whenever you click their buttons in the widget. The Print dialog is displayed through a different call to the plugin.

```
//shows the page setup panel
function showPageSetup() {

  if ( isCanvasButtonPressed ) {

    if ( EEWPlugin && window.widget) {

      EEWPlugin.call("showPageSetup");

      drawBackStuff();
    }
  }

  isCanvasButtonPressed = false;
}

//shows the font panel for the mailing address
function showAddressFontPanel() {

  if ( isAddressFontButtonDown ) {

    if ( EEWPlugin ) {

      EEWPlugin.showFontPanel(1);
    }
  }

  isAddressFontButtonDown = false;
}

//shows the font panel for the return address
function showReturnAddressFontPanel() {

  if ( EEWPlugin ) {

    EEWPlugin.showFontPanel(2);

  }

  isReturnAddressFontButtonDown = false;
}

function checkFonts() {

}
```

Each of these JavaScript functions gets the selections you make in the dialogs, uses them in the widget, and stores them as preferences. This is a good example of how a plugin can be used to access functionality in the Macintosh OS that is not available to JavaScript.

Summary

Email being the primary form of communication for most computer users, you may not scrawl an address on an envelope more than once a month. But if your constant typing has lead to the decline of your penmanship, Easy Envelopes may ensure that your letters, bills, and birthday cards arrive at the correct destination. Because Easy Envelopes can get your parents' snail mail address from your Address Book, you'll never have to worry about forgetting the ZIP code or house address. While paper mail may be falling out of favor, your postal correctness is provided by a widget whose form suggests its function and can easily be minimized to save space.

14

SecureCopy Widget

In addition to providing web content at your fingertips, widgets can serve as an interface to any of the command-line utilities on your Macintosh. If you have trouble remembering the syntax for a command-line utility, you can easily build a widget that calls the utility using the `widget.system` method and you won't have to remember the syntax for those powerful but infrequently used commands. This chapter looks at a widget that demonstrates building an interface for the scp utility in Darwin.

SSH & scp

FTP may be the most familiar means of transferring files between two computers on the Internet, but it is not the most secure. It sends your password and data in clear text that can easily be intercepted and viewed by malicious users. A more secure means of transferring files is available using SSH, or secure shell. SSH is both a set of command-line utilities and a protocol for gaining access to a remote computer, already built in to the Mac OS. The SSH suite includes slogin, ssh, and scp for securely connecting to a remote machine, running a remote shell, and copying files to a remote machine, respectively. With SSH, client and server connections are authenticated using a digital certificate and passwords. The digital certificate and passwords—and in fact the entire session—are all protected by encryption. The security in SSH comes through RSA public key cryptography.

You may think that because you are copying files between machines within your own local network, you probably don't have need for such strong security. You may be right. But you are overlooking a more mundane use of scp. If you want to copy files or directories between two Macs, your options are burning the data to CD, swapping an external drive, personal file sharing, FTP, or scp. scp allows you to copy files between two Macs without mounting filesystems and incurring the overhead of the Finder dealing with another mounted filesystem.

In true Unix fashion, scp is a command-line utility. To copy a file from one Macintosh to the other using scp, you pass the utility the file you want to copy, the Macintosh you want to copy it to, and the file's name on that computer, like so, using the Terminal application.

```
[offhook:~/.ssh] pfterry% scp traffic.tiff pfterry@desklamp:traffic.tiff
```

You will be prompted for your password on the computer to which you are copying. If this is your first connection to the remote computer, you will be asked to accept its SSH key.

```
[offhook:~/.ssh] pfterry@desklamp's password:
```

When you enter your password and press Return, the file is copied from your Macintosh to the other Macintosh. In the terminal, the filename, percentage of the file copied, and the speed of the copy, and time remaining until the copy is complete are displayed as the file is copied.

```
traffic.tiff                3%   30MB   1.7MB/s   07:48 ETA
```

If you substitute the path to a directory for the file and include a –r switch, scp copies the directory and all of the directories or files in it recursively to the other Macintosh.

You can reverse the process if you know the path to a file or directory on a networked Macintosh that you want copied to your Macintosh.

```
[offhook:~/.ssh] pfterry% scp pfterry@countzero:~/Desktop/traffic.tiff .
```

In this case, you are copying the traffic.tiff file from the desktop of your account on the networked Macintosh to the current directory on your local Macintosh. The dot indicates that you are copying the file to the current directory. You will be prompted for your password on the computer that you are copying from.

```
[offhook:~/.ssh] pfterry@countzero's password:
```

As the file is copied from the remote computer to the local computer, you can see the transfer statistics.

The SecureCopy Widget

The SecureCopy widget takes advantage of the `widget.system` method to perform the same function as the scp command-line utility. It takes advantage of Dashboard's drag-and-drop capabilities so you do not have to enter the full path to the file that you want to copy to a networked Macintosh.

The Interface

The SecureCopy widget provides a Dashboard interface to the scp command-line utility. The interface is a set of text boxes where you can enter the information that you would normally type in your terminal (Figure 14-1). The Host field takes the name or IP address of the computer to or from which you are copying the file. The Filename field takes the path to the file you want to copy. If you are copying the file from your local Macintosh, you can drag the file to the Filename field. The Switches field takes the command-line switches that you would enter to copy a directory. You enter your user name on the remote computer in the User Name field.

Once you have entered the information for the copy in the widget, you can click the Copy To button to copy the local file to the remote computer. If you are copying the file from the remote computer to your local computer, you click the Copy From button.

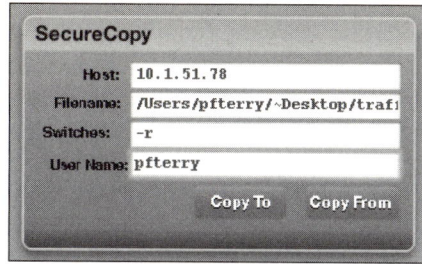

Figure 14-1

The back of the widget contains help information about the switches that are available for scp (Figure 14-2).

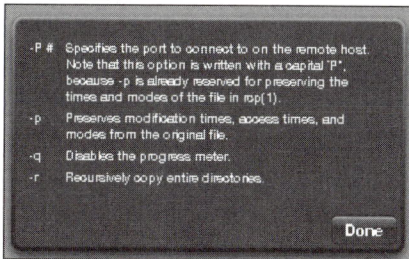

Figure 14-2

SecureCopy Internals

Like most widgets, SecureCopy has the basic set of files required for the widget (Figure 14-3).

Figure 14-3

Info.plist

The widget has the `AllowNetworkAccess`, `AllowSystem`, and `AllowFileAccessOutsideOfWidget` access keys set. It needs these three because it needs access to the network to copy the files and directories, and it needs access to the filesystem to run the scp command-line utility. The widget needs access outside of the widget so you can copy files from anywhere on your hard disk.

```
<plist version="1.0">
<dict>
    <key>AllowFileAccessOutsideOfWidget</key>
    <true/>
    <key>AllowNetworkAccess</key>
    <true/>
    <key>AllowSystem</key>
    <true/>
    <key>CFBundleDisplayName</key>
    <string>SecureCopy</string>
    <key>CFBundleIdentifier</key>
    <string>com.apple.widget.securecopy</string>
    <key>CFBundleName</key>
    <string>SecureCopy</string>
    <key>CFBundleShortVersionString</key>
    <string>.5</string>
    <key>CFBundleVersion</key>
    <string>.5</string>
    <key>CloseBoxInsetX</key>
    <integer>6</integer>
    <key>CloseBoxInsetY</key>
    <integer>6</integer>
    <key>MainHTML</key>
    <string>scp.html</string>
</dict>
</plist>
```

HTML/CSS

The scp.html file isn't very complicated. The text fields for user input are provided through a standard text input form. The Apple Class JavaScripts to animate flipping the widget (for the info button and for the Done button) are imported in addition to the scp.js widget JavaScript. The widget also has front and back `<div>`s, and the form and info button are placed in the front `<div>`.

```
<html>
  <style type="text/css">
    @import "scp.css";
  </style>
    <script type="text/javascript" src="scp.js" />
    <script type="text/javascript" src="AppleClasses/AppleButton.js" charset="utf-
8"/>
    <script type="text/javascript" src="AppleClasses/AppleInfoButton.js"
charset="utf-8"/>
    <script type="text/javascript" src="AppleClasses/AppleAnimator.js"
charset="utf-8"/>
  </head>
```

```
    <body onload="setup()">
    <div id="front">
      <!-- the widget background -->
      <img src="Default.png"></img>

      <!-- the widget title -->
      <span class="windowLabel">SecureCopy</span>

      <!-- the filename label and input -->
      <span class="fileLabel">Local file:</span>
      <input type="text" value="enter unix file path..." id="fileText"
ondragenter="dragenter(event);" ondragover="dragover(event);"
ondrop="dragdrop(event)" ondragleave="dragleave(event)"></input>

      <!-- the host label and input -->
      <span class="hostLabel">Host:</span>
      <input type="text" value="enter name or IP address..." id="hostText"></input>

      <!-- the username label and input -->
      <span class="userLabel">User Name:</span>
      <input type="text" value="enter user name..." id="userText"></input>

      <!-- the switches label and input -->
      <span class="switchesLabel">Switches:</span>
      <input type="text" value="enter switches for the copy..."
id="switchesText"></input>

      <!-- the copy to button -->
      <div id="copyToButton" onmousedown="copyTo();"
onmouseup="buttonUpOut('toButtonImage');"
onmouseout="buttonUpOut('toButtonImage');">
        <img id="toButtonImage" src="Images/Button.png"></img>
        <div id="toButtonText">Copy To</div>
      </div>

      <!-- the copy from button -->
      <div id="copyFromButton" onmousedown="copyFrom();"
onmouseup="buttonUpOut('fromButtonImage');"
onmouseout="buttonUpOut('fromButtonImage');">
        <img id="fromButtonImage" src="Images/Button.png"></img>
        <div id="fromButtonText">Copy From</div>
      </div>
      <div id="flip"></div>
    </div>

  <div id="back">
    <img span=backgroundImage src="Back.png">
    <div id="man">
    <table><tr>
    <td id="r1c1">-P #</td>
    <td>Specifies the port to connect to on the remote host.  Note that
      this option is written with a capital `P', because -p is already
      reserved for preserving the times and modes of the file in
      rcp(1).</td>
    </tr><tr>
```

```
      <td id="r2c1"> -p</td>
      <td>        Preserves modification times, access times, and modes from the
          original file.
      </td></tr><tr>
      <td id="r3c1"> -q</td>
      <td>        Disables the progress meter.
      </td></tr><tr>
      <td id="r4c1"> -r </td>
      <td>        Recursively copy entire directories.
       </td></tr></table>
      </div>
      <div id="doneButton"></div>
    </div>
    </body>
</html>
```

The back `<div>` contains some help information about the switches that the user might want to use with SecureCopy as well as copyright information and the Done button.

The selectors in the scp.css file are grouped according by front and back. All of the buttons are grouped together as well. The table selector at the bottom of the CSS file formats the switch information on the back side of the widget.

```
body {
   margin: 0;
}

#front {
   display: block;
   position: absolute;
   top: 0px;
   left: 0px;
}

.windowLabel {
   font: 15px "Helvetica Neue";
   font-weight: bold;
   color: black;
   position: absolute;
   left: 20px;
   top: 10px;
}

.fileLabel {
   font: 11px "Helvetica Neue";
   font-weight: bold;
   color: black;
   position: absolute;
   left: 34px;
   top: 64px;
}

#fileText {
   font: 12px "Courier New";
```

```
    font-weight: bold;
    color: green;
    position: absolute;
    left: 93px;
    top: 60px;
    width: 205px;
    border-width: 0px;
    border-color: transparent;
    background-color: transparent;
    -apple-dashboard-region: dashboard-region(control rectangle);
}

.hostLabel {
    font: 11px "Helvetica Neue";
    font-weight: bold;
    color: black;
    position: absolute;
    left: 56px;
    top: 43px;
}

#hostText {
    font: 12px "Courier New";
    font-weight: bold;
    color: green;
    position: absolute;
    left: 93px;
    top: 38px;
    width: 205px;
    border-width: 0px;
    border-color: transparent;
    background-color: transparent;
    -apple-dashboard-region: dashboard-region(control rectangle);
}

.userLabel {
    font: 11px "Helvetica Neue";
    font-weight: bold;
    color: black;
    position: absolute;
    left: 31px;
    top: 110px;
}

#userText {
    font: 12px "Courier New";
    font-weight: bold;
    color: green;
    position: absolute;
    left: 93px;
    top: 104px;
    width: 205px;
    border-width: 0px;
    border-color: transparent;
```

```
    background-color: transparent;
    -apple-dashboard-region: dashboard-region(control rectangle);
}

.switchesLabel {
  font: 11px "Helvetica Neue";
  font-weight: bold;
  color: black;
  position: absolute;
  left: 26px;
  top: 86px;
}

#switchesText {
  font: 12px "Courier New";
  font-weight: bold;
  color: green;
  position: absolute;
  left: 93px;
  top: 82px;
  width: 205px;
  border-width: 0px;
  border-color: transparent;
  background-color: transparent;
  -apple-dashboard-region: dashboard-region(control rectangle);
}

#toButtonImage {
  position: absolute;
  left: 140px;
  top: 130px;
  -apple-dashboard-region: dashboard-region(control rectangle);
}

#toButtonText {
  font: 12px "Helvetica Neue";
  font-weight: Bold;
  color: white;
  text-shadow: black 0px 1px 0px;
  position: absolute;
  left: 155px;
  top: 136px;
}

#fromButtonImage {
  position: absolute;
  left: 225px;
  top: 130px;
  -apple-dashboard-region: dashboard-region(control rectangle);
}

#fromButtonText {
  font: 12px "Helvetica Neue";
  font-weight: Bold;
```

```
    color: white;
    text-shadow: black 0px 1px 0px;
    position: absolute;
    left: 230px;
    top: 136px;
}

#flip {
    position: fixed;
    bottom: 32px;
    left: 14px;
}

.backgroundImage {
    position: absolute;
    top: 0px;
    left: 0px;
}

#back {
    display: none;
    position: absolute;
    top: 0px;
    left: 0px;
}

#doneButton {
    position:absolute;
    bottom:20px;
    left:254px;
}

#man {
    font: 10px "Helvetica Neue";
    color: white;
    position: absolute;
    left: 20px;
    top: 20px;
    width: 85%;
}

table {table-layout: auto; width: auto;
font: 10px "Helvetica Neue"; color: white;}
#r1c1 {width:10%; vertical-align: top;}
#r2c1 {width:10%; vertical-align: top;}
#r3c1 {width:10%;}
#r4c1 {width:10%;}

#copyright {
    font: 10px "Helvetica Neue";
    color: white;
    position: absolute;
    left: 75px;
    bottom:20px;
```

JavaScript Functionality

Though the JavaScript is based on the command and switches typed on the command line, it contains other functions to provide standard features. For example, the variables at the top of the JavaScript and the use of the Apple Classes provide the info and Done buttons and the Apple Classes are called in the `setup()` function.

```
// Global variables for the info and done buttonsvar glassDoneButton;
var whiteInfoButton;

function setup()
{
// Setup Apple Classes
    glassDoneButton = new AppleGlassButton(document.getElementById("doneButton"),
"Done", hidePrefs);
    whiteInfoButton = new AppleInfoButton(document.getElementById("flip"),
document.getElementById("front"), "white", "white", showPrefs);
```

The `dragdrop(event)` function takes care of getting the path to the file or directory that you drop on the widget, removing the prefix, and removing the spaces from the path. This converts the path into something the scp utility can use. This method allows you to drop the file or directory over the filename and saves you the trouble of typing the exact path to the file or directory.

```
function dragdrop(event) {
  var uri = null;
  try {
      uri = event.dataTransfer.getData("text/uri-list");
  } catch (ex) {
  }

  alert(uri);

  if (uri) {
    // remove the "file://localhost" uri prefix:
     var theFile = uri.split("file://localhost");
    document.getElementById("fileText").value = theFile[1];
    // remove any spaces "%20". WARNING: NOT ACCOUNTING FOR ALL SPECIAL
CHARACTERS!!!
      theFile = theFile.replace(/%20/, " ")
    document.getElementById("fileText").value = theFile;
  }

  event.stopPropagation();
  event.preventDefault();
}
```

The `copyFrom()` function is the portion of the JavaScript that is based on the command typed in Terminal. The function is executed when the Copy From button is clicked. The command is built from the host, filename, switches, and user fields and sent to the command line through the `widget.system` method.

```
// The copyFrom() function is called when the Copy button is pressed.
// It uses the widget.system call synchronously to execute scp with the command
built from the information in the widget fields.
```

```
function copyFrom() {
  document.getElementById("fromButtonImage").src = "Images/Button_down.png";

  var pathOfFileToCopy = document.getElementById("fileText").value;
  var userName = document.getElementById("userText").value;
  var hostAddress = document.getElementById("hostText").value;
  var destinationFilePath = document.getElementById("fileText").value;

  var scpCommand = "/usr/bin/scp "+ userName + "@" + hostAddress + ":\"" +
pathOfFileToCopy + "\" \"" + destinationFilePath + "\"";


  var sysCommand = widget.system(scpCommand, null);

}
```

The reverse of the `copyFrom()` function is the `copyTo()` function. The `copyTo()` function builds the command from the fields in the widget and copies the file to the remote machine.

```
// The copyTo() function is called when the Copy button is pressed.
// It uses the widget.system call synchronously to execute scp with the command
built from the information in the widget fields.

function copyTo() {
  document.getElementById("toButtonImage").src = "Images/Button_down.png";

  var pathOfFileToCopy = document.getElementById("fileText").value;
  var userName = document.getElementById("userText").value;
  var hostAddress = document.getElementById("hostText").value;
  var destinationFilePath = document.getElementById("fileText").value;

  var scpCommand = "/usr/bin/scp \""+ pathOfFileToCopy + "\" " + userName + "@" +
hostAddress + ":\"" + destinationFilePath + "\"";


  var sysCommand = widget.system(scpCommand, null);
```

Using SecureCopy

Whenever you are connecting to another computer using ssh, you are challenged for a password when you connect. The scp utility functions the same way. If you want to copy a file, you'll have to enter your password to do so. This becomes an immediate problem with the `widget.system` because it cannot respond to a password challenge. Shell scripting doesn't allow for many solutions to respond to a password request and they can break easily.

You can create public and private keys for the Macintoshes that you copy files between and your secure copy can run without the need to respond to a password request. To do this, you create the keys using the sys-keygen command in Terminal (Figure 14-4).

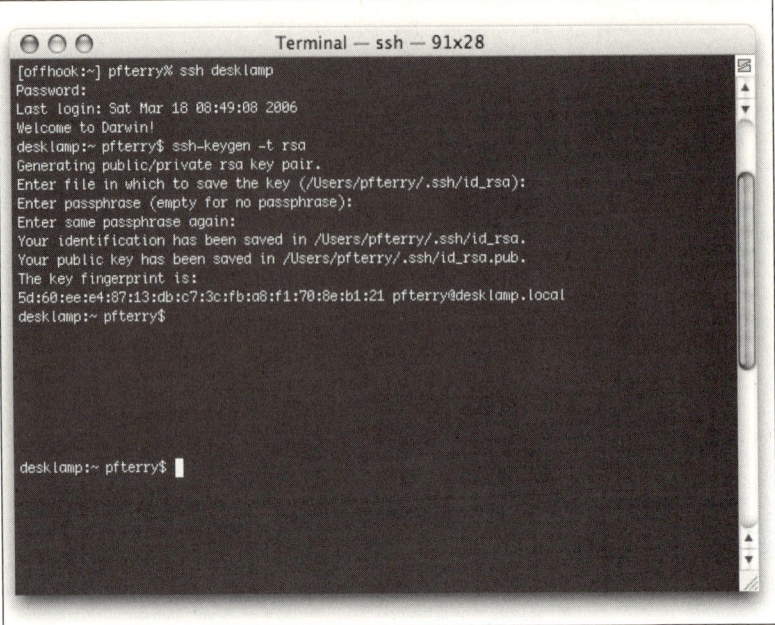

Figure 14-4

Enter **ssh-keygen –t rsa** on the command line in terminal. The –t rsa switch tells the sys-keygen key generator what type of keys to create, in this case, RSA keys. When you are prompted to enter a passphrase, press the Return key. The keys are created in the SSH subdirectory (with .ssh extension) of your home directory. If you don't have an SSH directory, ssh-keygen creates one. When you change to the SSH directory and view the contents, you'll see the keys that you've created.

```
[desklamp:~/.ssh] pfterry% ls
authorized_keys id_rsa        id_rsa.pub      known_hosts
[desklamp:~/.ssh] pfterry%
```

The id.rsa file contains the private key, and the id.rsa.pub file contains the public key. You will need to copy the public key to the Macintosh to which you copy files and add it to the authorized_keys file. Copy the public key file only to the Macintosh; the private key stays on your local Macintosh.

If the authorized_keys file doesn't exist, you can create the file with the copy command.

```
cp  id_rsa.pub authorized_keys
```

If the authorized_keys file already exists, you'll need to append this key to the end of it with the unix cat and redirect commands.

```
[offhook:~/.ssh] pfterry% cat ~/id_rsa.pub >>
authorized_keys
[offhook:~/.ssh] pfterry% rm ~/id_rsa.pub
```

Now when you perform a secure copy, you are not prompted for a password.

Summary

While most widgets may provide help about a particular scripting language or collect the latest RSS feeds from a popular website, widgets can also provide a user friendly interface to command-line utilities through the `widget.system` method. The SecureCopy widget is an example.

Amazon Album Art

iTunes, the music player that ships with OS X, is almost overshadowed by the popularity of the iPod and all of the marketing fuss it has generated. iTunes, however, is the only bridge between Apple's iTunes Music Store; it is a requirement to load music on the iPod. iTunes is probably a stealth sales tool for the iPod.

One of the cool features in iTunes is that it displays the cover art from your iTunes Music Store purchases in the lower-left corner of the iTunes window (Figure 15-1). However, if you have ripped your CD collection into iTunes (or you only purchase music in shrink-wrapped jewel cases), those albums will not include the cover art.

You can fix this manually by searching for your album on Amazon or another website and downloading the cover art. You can then drag the cover art into the album art window inside iTunes. This is a reasonable — if clunky — workaround, but it is time-consuming and too manual. After all, we are working with a Macintosh and it is the most scriptable computing platform available if you count all of the Unix scripting tools and AppleScript. Fortunately, someone realized this and created a widget to automate the process of adding the cover art to all of your ripped albums in iTunes.

Figure 15-1

Amazon Album Art

As the name indicates, Simon Whitaker's Amazon Album Art widget is able to retrieve album artwork from Amazon for you. Moreover, it simplifies the manual process from the beginning by getting the track listing from iTunes and searching Amazon for the album with just a button click. In practice, you can display Dashboard when a track is playing that you know you don't have the artwork for, click the iTunes button, add the album art to the track, and close Dashboard.

The Interface

Like a couple of the other widgets that we've looked at, the Amazon Album Art widget has a minimized interface (Figure 15-2) in addition to a full-sized view displaying the artwork that you are searching for and a back side panel. The real advantage for small screens and laptop users is that you can leave the widget open all of the time without it taking up too much screen real estate.

Figure 15-2

Clicking the info button displays the preferences on the back side of the widget (Figure 15-3). The options let you select from a Preferred Amazon store, that is, a store related to the country in which you live. The Search for menu lets you select between popular and classical music. The Operate on menu allows you to apply the "set as album art action" to the currently playing track, the whole album, or the current selection. You can also choose to save small images (240 × 240) to iTunes and use a local proxy server to connect to the iTunes Music Store.

Figure 15-3

You can query iTunes for the currently playing track by clicking the small iTunes icon (Figure 15-4). Amazon Album Art gets the track information from iTunes and then searches Amazon to get the cover art for the album.

Figure 15-4

When the widget finds the cover art, it expands to display the art in the lower portion of the widget (Figure 15-5).

Figure 15-5

If you want to set the cover art for the track that is currently playing or for the whole album, you can click the "Set as album art in iTunes" banner at the bottom of the screen (Figure 15-6).

Figure 15-6

The widget also allows you to search Amazon for albums by an artist. You can enter the name of the artist in the search field and press the Return key. When an album cover appears in the widget, clicking the thumbnails icon in the upper-right corner of the album cover displays the covers of all of the artist's albums (Figure 15-7). Clicking one of the covers displays a large image of the cover, and then clicking the cover takes you to the album's page on Amazon.

Figure 15-7

If the Amazon Album Art widget can't find the album on Amazon, it gives you the option of searching Google for the cover art (Figure 15-8).

This option doesn't automate inserting the cover art in iTunes, but it does provide the artwork if it can be found.

Figure 15-8

Amazon Album Art Internals

When you look inside the Amazon Album Art widget (Figure 15-9), you see that it looks like any of the widgets that you've worked with. The main default images are at the root level of the widget with the graphics for the logo, search box, back side, and the pieces that are used for the expanded window all placed in an Images folder. Because the widget can search on any of the country-specific Amazon stores, the localization strings are in separate folders for each language (German, French, Netherlands, and Russian, in addition to English).

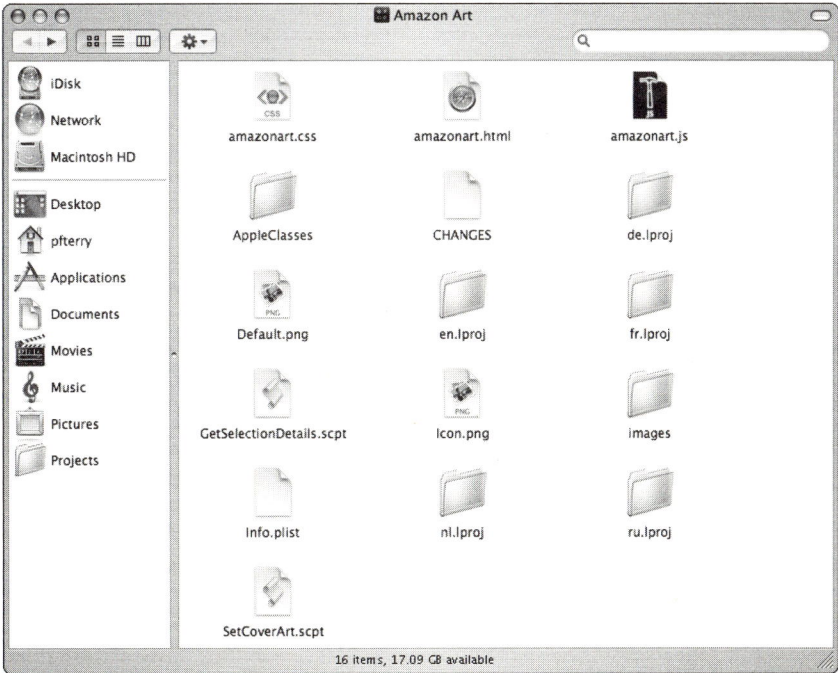

Figure 15-9

You'll notice a couple of different things about the Album Art widget. The Apple Classes contains the AppleAnimator.js, AppleButton.js, and AppleInfoButton.js JavaScript files. You can also see two AppleScript files at the root level of the widget.

Info.plist

In the properties list for the widget, you see that three access keys are set. `AllowFileAccessOutsideOfWidget` is set because the widget needs to interact with iTunes. The `AllowNetworkAccess` key is set because the widget needs to fetch the cover art from Amazon.

```
<?xml version="1.0" encoding="UTF-8"?>
<!DOCTYPE plist PUBLIC "-//Apple Computer//DTD PLIST 1.0//EN"
"http://www.apple.com/DTDs/PropertyList-1.0.dtd">
<plist version="1.0">
<dict>
    <key>AllowFileAcessOutsideOfWidget</key>
    <true/>
    <key>AllowNetworkAccess</key>
    <true/>
    <key>AllowSystem</key>
    <true/>
    <key>CFBundleDisplayName</key>
    <string>Amazon Album Art</string>
    <key>CFBundleIdentifier</key>
    <string>com.widget-foundry.widget.albumart</string>
    <key>CFBundleName</key>
    <string>Amazon Album Art</string>
    <key>CFBundleShortVersionString</key>
    <string>2.0</string>
    <key>CFBundleVersion</key>
    <string>2.0</string>
    <key>CloseBoxInsetX</key>
    <integer>8</integer>
    <key>CloseBoxInsetY</key>
    <integer>4</integer>
    <key>Height</key>
    <integer>56</integer>
    <key>MainHTML</key>
    <string>amazonart.html</string>
    <key>Width</key>
    <integer>216</integer>
</dict>
</plist>
```

Finally, the `AllowSystem` key is included because the widget needs to run the GetSelectionDetails and SetCoverArt AppleScripts in its bundle.

HTML/CSS

The HTML and CSS files for the Amazon Album Art widget are fairly standard. The HTML file imports the CSS file and the JavaScripts for the buttons, localization strings, and the main JavaScript for the widget. The portion of the script that controls the artwork display on the widget's front is the `slidearea`, `fbottom`, and `ftop` `<div>`s.

```
<html>
<head>
<title>Amazon Album Search</title>

<style type="text/css">
  @import "amazonart.css";
</style>

<script type='text/javascript' src='AppleClasses/AppleInfoButton.js' charset='utf-
8' />
<script type='text/javascript' src='AppleClasses/AppleAnimator.js' charset='utf-8'
/>
<script type='text/javascript' src='AppleClasses/AppleButton.js' charset='utf-8' />
<script type="text/javascript" src="localisedStrings.js" charset='utf-8' />
<script type="text/javascript" src="amazonart.js" charset='utf-8' />

</head>
<body onLoad="setup();">
<div id="front">
  <div id="slidearea">
    <div id="slide">
      <div id="art_bg"></div>
      <div id="art"><p>No artwork requested yet</p></div>
      <div id="add_to_itunes_container">
      <div id="add_to_itunes" onClick="setAlbumArt()"><a href="#"
id="add_to_itunes_a">Set as album art in iTunes</a></div>
      </div>
      <div id="show_thumbnails"><a href="#" id="show_thumbnails_a"><img
src="images/show_thumbnails.png" id="show_thumbnails_img"/></a></div>
      <div id="thumbnails"></div>
    </div>

    <div id="fbottom" onClick="toggleSlide();"><img
src="images/front_r3_c1.png"></div>
  </div>

  <div id="ftop" onClick="toggleSlide();">
    <img src="images/front_r1_c1.png" />
    <!-- <img src="images/searchbox_bg.png" id="searchbox_bg" /> -->
  </div>
  <input id="s" type="search" name="s" placeholder="Album details" results="5"
autosave="amazonartwidgetsearch" onsearch="doSearch();">
  <div id="get_from_itunes" onClick="getDetailsFromiTunes();"><a href="#"
id="get_from_itunes_a"><img id="itunes_icon" src="images/itunes_icon.png"
/></a></div>
  <div id='infoButton'></div>
</div>
```

The add_to_itunes div calls the setAlbumArt() function whenever you click the banner at the bottom of the widget after it has found the album art. The show_thumbnails div displays the small thumbnails icon in the upper-right corner of the artwork display. The fbottom and ftop divs contain the toggleSlide() function.

The CSS file contains the rules for the area that slides on the front of the widget. The slidearea at the top of the section shows the size of the widget with the slide extended and album art displayed.

```
/* ----- SLIDING STUFF ----- */

#slidearea /* defines area where slide is visible */
{
  padding: 0px;
  position: absolute;
  height: 218px;
  width: 216px;
  overflow: hidden;
  top: 38px;
  left: 0px;
}

#slide /* The bit that slides up and down */
{
  position: absolute;
  top: 0px;
  left: 0px;
  width: 216px;
  height: 0px;
  overflow: hidden;
}

#art_bg /* The background image - to add drop shadow to album art */
{
  background-image:url(images/front_r2_c1.png);
  position: absolute;
  top: 0px;
  left: 0px;
  width: 216px;
  height: 200px;
}

#thumbnails
{
  position: absolute;
  top: 0px;
  left: 8px;
  width: 180px;
  height: 180px;
  background-color: #000000;
  padding: 10px;
  overflow: hidden;
  visibility: hidden;
}

#thumbnails .thumbnail
{
  float: left;
  margin: 5px;
}

#thumbnails .selected
{
  padding: 2px;
  margin: 2px;
```

```
    border: 1px dashed #999999;
}

#art /* The bit where the album art goes */
{
    position: absolute;
    top: 0px;
    left: 8px;
    width: 200px;
    height: 200px;
    overflow: hidden;
}

#art p
{
    padding: 5px 5px 10px 5px;
    margin: 0px;
    vertical-align: middle;
    text-align: center;
}

#fbottom
{
    padding: 0px;
    position: absolute;
    top: -1px;
    left: 0px;
}

#add_to_itunes_container
{
    position: absolute;
    bottom: 5px;
    left: 13px;
    width: 190px;
    height: 32px;
}

#add_to_itunes
{
    visibility: hidden;
    padding: 2px 5px 2px 5px;
    width: 190px;
    height: 32px;

    background-image:url(images/add_to_itunes_bg.png);

    text-align: center;
    font-family: "Gill Sans", "Helvetica Neue", sans-serif;
    text-shadow: 0px 1px 0px #000000;
    color: #ffffff;
    font-size: 11px;
    font-weight: bold;

    display: table-cell;
      vertical-align: middle;
```

```
}

#add_to_itunes a
{
  color: #ffffff;
  text-decoration: none;
}

#show_thumbnails
{
  position: absolute;
  top: 5px;
  right: 13px;
  visibility: hidden;
}

div
{
  font-family: "Helvetica Neue", sans-serif;
  font-size: 11px;
}
```

The HTML and CSS files set up the slide area and provide the layout, but the amazonart.js script has a section that controls when the widget slides to display the album artwork.

JavaScript Functionality

The portion of the amazonart.js script that controls sliding the widget to display the artwork is marked in the code with a "slide stuff" comment.

```
// ----- SLIDE STUFF -----

function goAmazon(ASIN)
{
  if (window.widget)
  {
    var aa_url;
    switch (gCountry)
    {
      case 'uk':
        aa_url =
"http://www.amazon.co.uk/exec/obidos/redirect?link_code=ur2&tag=netcetera06-21&camp
=1634&creative=6738&path=ASIN%2F" + ASIN + "%2F";
        break;
      case 'ca':
        aa_url =
"http://www.amazon.ca/exec/obidos/redirect?link_code=as2&path=ASIN/" + ASIN +
"&tag=thewidgetfoun-20&camp=15121&creative=330641";
        break;
      case 'fr':
        aa_url =
"http://www.amazon.fr/exec/obidos/redirect?link_code=as2&path=ASIN/" + ASIN +
"&tag=thewidgetfoun-21&camp=1642&creative=6746";
        break;
```

```
        case 'de':
            aa_url =
"http://www.amazon.de/exec/obidos/redirect?link_code=as2&path=ASIN/" + ASIN +
"&tag=thewidgetfo05-21&camp=1638&creative=6742";
            break;
        case 'at':
            aa_url =
"http://www.amazon.de/exec/obidos/redirect?link_code=as2&path=ASIN/" + ASIN +
"%3Fsite-redirect=at&tag=thewidgetfo05-21&camp=1638&creative=6742";
            break;
        case 'jp':
            aa_url = "http://www.amazon.co.jp/exec/obidos/ASIN/" + ASIN;
            break;
        default: // us
            aa_url =
"http://www.amazon.com/exec/obidos/redirect?link_code=as2&path=ASIN/" + ASIN +
"&tag=chubbybat-20&camp=1789&creative=9325";
    }
    widget.openURL(aa_url);
  }
}


function toggleSlide()
{
  if (gOpen)
  {
    slideClosed();
  }
  else
  {
    slideOpen();
  }
}

function slideOpen()
{
  gSlideOpenAnimator.stop();
  gSlideClosedAnimator.stop();

  gOpen = true;
  if (window.widget)
    window.resizeTo(216, 257);
  gSlideOpenAnimator.start();
}

function slideClosed()
{
  gSlideOpenAnimator.stop();
  gSlideClosedAnimator.stop();

  gSlideClosedAnimator.start();
}

function slideIt(animation, current, start, finish)
{
```

```
        gSlide.style.height = current + "px";
        o("fbottom").style.top = current + "px";
    }

    function slideClosedCompleted()
    {
        if (window.widget)
            window.resizeTo(216, 56);
        o("fbottom").style.top = "-1px";
        gOpen = false;
    }
```

In addition to the JavaScript functionality that controls the display of artwork, Amazon Album Art takes advantage of the command line to run AppleScripts and control iTunes to add the cover art to the track and get information about the current selection.

Get Details from iTunes

To get the details of the track that is currently playing or the track that is selected whenever you click the iTunes button in the widget, the widget's JavaScript calls the GetSelectionDetails script. When you look in the JavaScript, you can see the AppleScript called using the osascript utility. The result is passed back to the JavaScript using the outputString.

```
    // ----- GET DETAILS OF CURRENT SELECTION FROM ITUNES STUFF -----

    function getDetailsFromiTunes()
    {
        if (window.widget)
        {
        o("s").value = getLocalisedString("Fetching...");
            var output = widget.system("/usr/bin/osascript GetSelectionDetails.scpt " +
    gMode, null).outputString;
            if (output && output.length > 0)
            {
                output = output.replace(/\s+$/, ""); // remove white space from end of string
    - removes LF that Applescript writes
                o("s").value = output;
                doSearch();
            }
            else
            {
                o("s").value = "";
            }
        }
    }
```

The GetSelectionDetails script checks to see if iTunes is running. If it is, the script checks to see if the mode is set for selection and if it is, to get the artist and album. If iTunes is playing music, the script gets the artist and album of the currently playing track. When it has the information, it copies it to stdout where the JavaScript picks it up in the outputString.

```
    on run argv
        set mode to item 1 of argv
        tell application "Finder"
```

```
      set iTunesRunning to process "iTunes" exists
   end tell

   if iTunesRunning then
     tell application "iTunes"
       try
         if mode is "selection" and selection is not {} then
           set theArtist to artist of item 1 of selection
           set theAlbum to album of item 1 of selection
         else if player state is not stopped then
           set theArtist to artist of current track
           set theAlbum to album of current track
         end if
         copy theArtist & " " & theAlbum to stdout
       end try
     end tell

   else
     -- copy "iTunes must be running, with one or more tracks selected" to stderr
   end if
end run
```

With the information from the script, Amazon Album Art is able to find the album information on Amazon and download the artwork.

Processing the Downloaded Image

In the amazonart.js script, the `processDownloadedImage()` function takes the cover art downloaded from Amazon and adds it to the album in iTunes. The first part of the function sets up an error check to make sure you have selected tracks in iTunes before trying to look them up on Amazon. The `widget .system()` method uses the osascript command to run the SetCoverArt AppleScript and pass it the gLocalJpeg, which contains the cover art, and specifies whether to use small images.

```
function processDownloadedImage(currentStringOnStdout)
{
  if (currentStringOnStdout.length > 0)
  {
    // curl only outputs on error - so if there was output, something went wrong
    gItunesLink.innerHTML = getLocalisedString("Select iTunes tracks first");
    setTimeout(resetAddToiTunesImage, 5000);
  }
  else
  {
    if (window.widget)
    {
      var useSmallImages = o("small_images").checked ? "Yes" : "No";
      var output = widget.system("/usr/bin/osascript SetCoverArt.scpt " +
gLocalJpeg + " " + gMode + " " + useSmallImages, null).outputString;
      if (output && output.substr(0,6) == "Error:")
      {
        gItunesLink.innerHTML = getLocalisedString("Select iTunes tracks first");
        setTimeout(resetAddToiTunesImage, 5000);
      }
      else
```

```
      {
         gItunesLink.innerHTML = '<a href="#" id="add_to_itunes_a">' +
getLocalisedString("Set as album art in iTunes") + '</a>';
      }
    }
  }
}
```

The GetSelectionDetails AppleScript has global variables for the filename, mode, and use small images settings. These are passed to the AppleScript from the JavaScript using the osascript utility.

The first part of the AppleScript has sections for locating iTunes and setting up the cache for the album art in the user's Library folder. It checks to see if iTunes is running and alerts the user if it is not. After the setup, the script attempts to get a list of tracks from iTunes to operate on. The script then proceeds to get the artwork from Amazon and set it for the tracks that are playing or for the selection.

```
global jpeg_filename, mode, use_small_images

on run argv
   set jpeg_filename to item 1 of argv
   set mode to item 2 of argv
   set use_small_images to item 3 of argv
   --set jpeg_filename to "amazonart.jpg"
   --set mode to "selection"
   --set use_small_images to "no"

   -- is iTunes running?
   tell application "Finder"
     set itunes_running to process "iTunes" exists
   end tell
   -- get path to image files
   set jpeg_loc to ((path to home folder) as string) & "Library:Caches:com.widget-
foundry.widget.albumart:" & jpeg_filename
   set pict_loc to convert_jpeg_to_pict(jpeg_loc)

   if itunes_running then
     set_artwork(pict_loc)
   else
     copy "Error: iTunes must be running, with one or more tracks selected" to
stdout
   end if
end run

to set_artwork(pict_loc)
   try
     tell application "iTunes"

        -- get list of tracks on which to operate
        set t to {}

        if mode is "selection" and selection is not {} then
          set t to selection
        else if mode is "current_track" and player state is not stopped then
          set t to {current track}
```

```
            else if mode is "current_album" and player state is not stopped then
                set alb to album of current track
                set t to (file tracks of library playlist 1 whose album is alb)
            end if

            if t is not {} then

                -- show warning if more than 30 tracks are to be processed
                set proceed to "Yes"
                if (count of t) is greater than 30 then
                    set r to display dialog "Set art on all " & ((count of t) as string) & "
tracks - are you sure? This may take some time to complete." buttons {"Yes", "No"}
with icon 2
                    set proceed to button returned of r
                end if

                if proceed is "Yes" then

                    -- get contents of JPEG
                    set file_ref to open for access pict_loc
                    set ott to read file_ref from 513 as picture
                    close access file_ref

                    -- set album art image on tracks
                    with timeout of 600 seconds
                      repeat with a_track in t
                        try
                            set data of artwork 1 of (a_track) to ott
                        on error m
                            copy "Error: " & m to stdout
                        end try
                      end repeat
                    end timeout

                end if

            else
                copy "Error: You need to select some tracks in iTunes first!" to stdout
            end if

        end tell
    on error m
        copy m to stdout
        return
    end try
end set_artwork


to convert_jpeg_to_pict(orig_file)
    try
        set ext_index to (length of orig_file) - 3
        set new_file to text from character 1 to character ext_index of orig_file & "
"pict"

        -- convert to PICT
```

```
   tell application "Image Events"
      launch
      -- open the image file
      set this_image to open orig_file

      if use_small_images is "Yes" then
         -- resize if image is > 240 pixels wide - assume pic is more-or-less square
         copy the dimensions of this_image to {xdim, ydim}
         if xdim is greater than 240 then
            scale this_image to size 240
         end if
      end if

      tell application "Finder" to set new_item to new_file
      save this_image in new_item as PICT
      close this_image
   end tell
   return new_file

  on error m number n
    if n is -1728 then
      copy "Error: Error when converting image for iTunes" to stdout
    else
      copy "Error: " & m to stdout
    end if
  end try
end convert_jpeg_to_pict
```

The last handler in the AppleScript converts the JPEG artwork file to a PICT format for iTunes. As you can see, it uses the Image Events utility for the conversion.

Summary

The Show Artwork command in iTunes is great for purchased music, but it doesn't provide the same experience if your music library is built from your audio CDs. The Amazon Album Art widget provides a way to add the album artwork to your ripped CDs by automating an otherwise manual process. To augment iTunes, it takes advantage of two strengths of widgets: the abilities to retrieve information from a website and to interact with applications.

Timbuktu Quick Connect

Timbuktu is a screen-sharing program from Netopia that runs on both Macs and PCs and allows you to control a remote computer from your Macintosh (Figure 16-1). Though Timbuktu is not at feature parity on the two platforms yet, the Mac version includes file exchange, clipboard exchange, and sending files and messages, and is very scriptable. To connect to another computer, you open the New Connection window in Timbuktu, find the computer to which you want to connect, and then log in to it.

Written by Nick Rogers of Netopia, the Timbuktu Quick Connect widget enables you to jump directly to a connection with a remote computer without having to open the New Connection window in Timbuktu and look for the computer you want to connect to. If you have multiple subnets with a number of computers in each, the Timbuktu Quick Connect widget can save you time because you won't have to look through the subnets to find the computer and you don't have to remember the IP to connect to it.

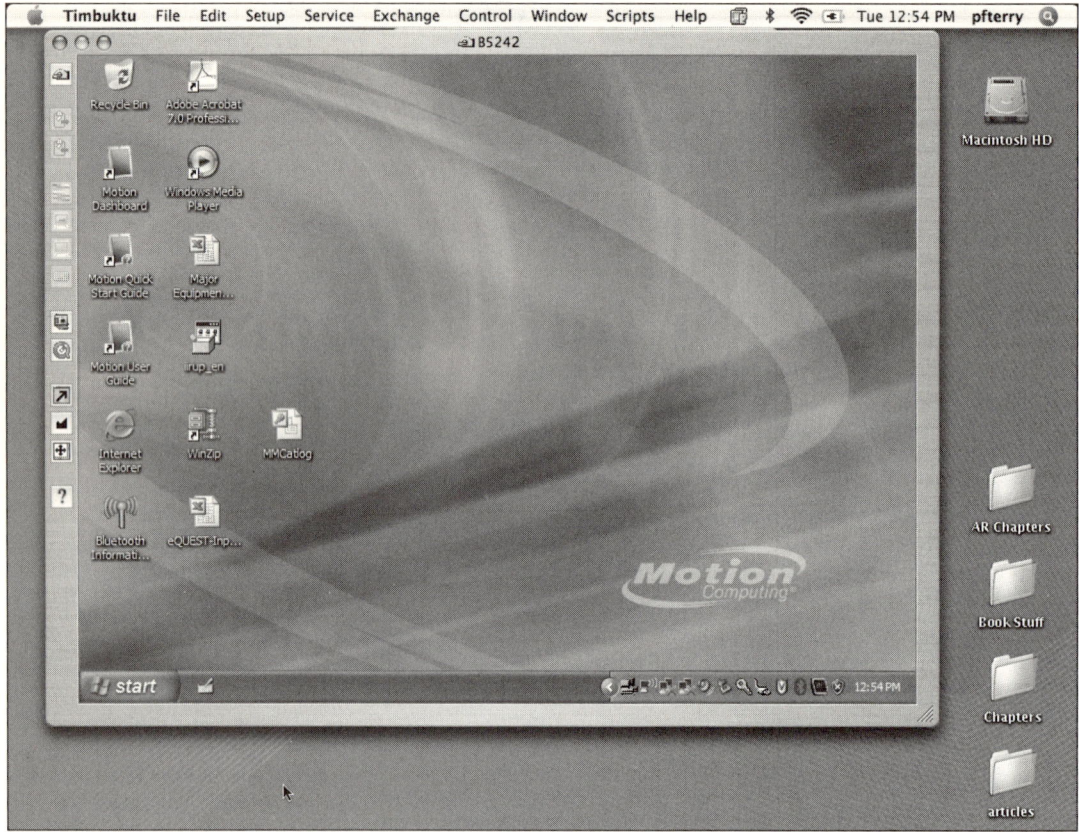

Figure 16-1

The Interface

The Timbuktu Quick Connect widget interface is straightforward. A prominently displayed text box holds the IP address of the Macintosh to which you want to connect (Figure 16-2). As you type its IP address, you'll see that the widget types ahead if you've connected with that machine before.

Clicking the Connect button or pressing the Return key after you've entered the IP address closes Dashboard, brings Timbuktu to the foreground, and prompts you for a name and password for the kind of connection that you are making (Figure 16-3).

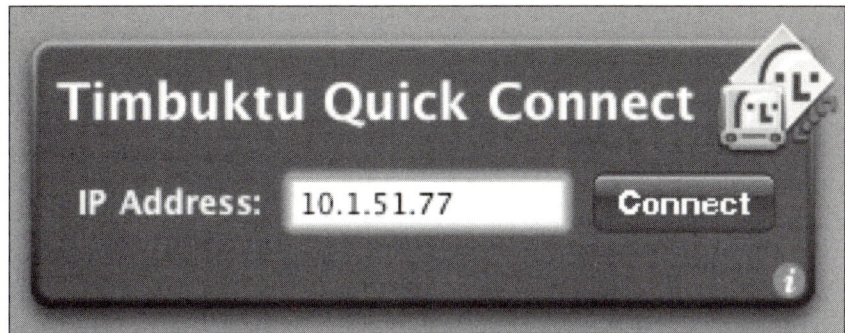

Figure 16-2

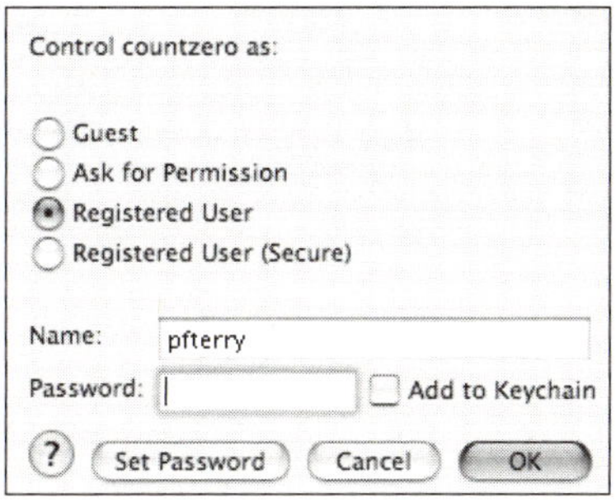

Control countzero as:

○ Guest
○ Ask for Permission
◉ Registered User
○ Registered User (Secure)

Name: pfterry
Password: | ☐ Add to Keychain
(?) (Set Password) (Cancel) (OK)

Figure 16-3

Once you have provided your password and clicked OK, you are logged in to the remote machine.

When you move your cursor over the front of the widget, you see the Information button in the lower-right corner. Clicking it flips the widget over (Figure 16-4) so you can see the preferences, instructions for use, and a copyright notice.

In addition to user configurable preferences, the back side also provides information about how the widget works. The preferences for the connection are the listed Timbuktu services. If the Control radio button is selected, entering the IP address of the remote machine and clicking the Connect button connects you to the remote machine. If the Send radio button is selected, entering the IP address of the remote machine and clicking the Connect button will prompt you for the password and then open a dialog where you can select files or type a message to send to the remote machine (Figure 16-5).

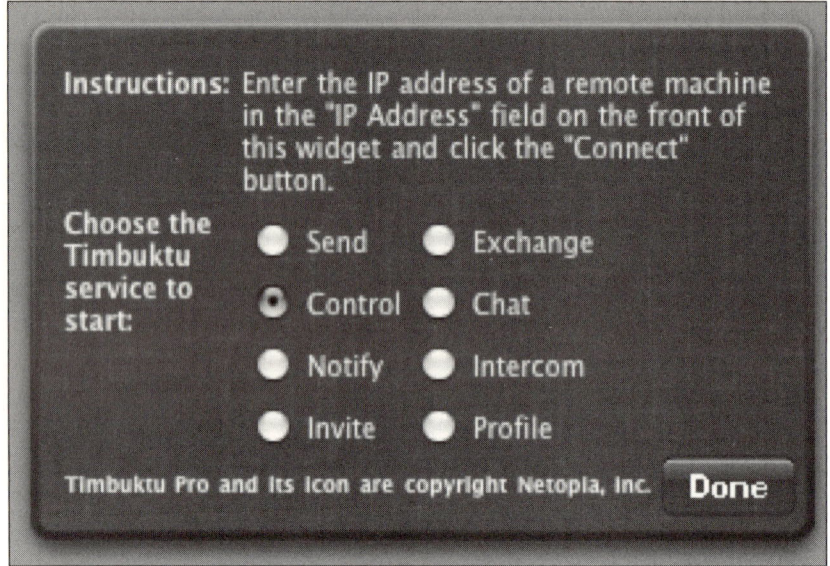

Figure 16-4

Figure 16-5

Timbuktu Quick Connect Internals

You can see the files that make up the Timbuktu Quick Connect widget by Control-clicking or right-clicking the widget and selecting Show Package Contents (Figure 16-6).

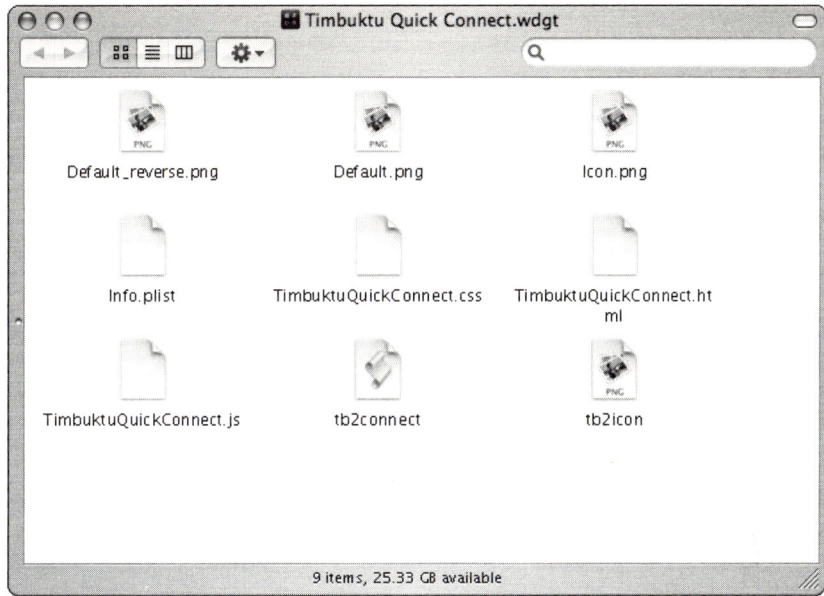

Figure 16-6

Like the Amazon Album Art widget, Timbuktu Quick Connect has an AppleScript as part of its bundle.

Info.plist

Because the widget needs to run the tb2connect AppleScript to connect with Timbuktu, the `AllowSystem` access key is set. This might seem to be unnecessary because the AppleScript is inside of the widget bundle, but the osascript command-line utility in the JavaScript that runs the AppleScript is part of the system. Setting the `AllowSystem` key gives the widget access to that utility.

```
<plist version="1.0">
<dict>
  <key>AllowSystem</key>
  <true/>
  <key>CFBundleIdentifier</key>
  <string>com.netopia.timbuktu.pro.widget.quickconnect</string>
  <key>CFBundleName</key>
  <string>Timbuktu Quick Connect Widget</string>
  <key>CFBundleDisplayName</key>
  <string>Timbuktu Quick Connect Widget</string>
  <key>CFBundleVersion</key>
  <string>1.0.2</string>
  <key>CFBundleShortVersionString</key>
  <string>1.0</string>
  <key>CloseBoxInsetX</key>
  <integer>12</integer>
  <key>CloseBoxInsetY</key>
```

245

```
        <integer>12</integer>
        <key>MainHTML</key>
        <string>TimbuktuQuickConnect.html</string>
    </dict>
</plist>
```

HTML/CSS

The HTML file contains the usual import of the CSS file and references to the JavaScript files. If you look below the front `<div>`, you see references to the Timbuktu Quick Connect functions: the `checkInput(theKeyPressed)`, the `ipAddressAutoComplete(theKeyPressed)`, the `launchTB2()`, and the `startTB2Connection()`.

```
<html>
  <head>
    <title>
      Timbuktu Quick Connect
    </title>
    <style type="text/css">
      @import "TimbuktuQuickConnect.css";
    </style>
    <script type="text/javascript" src="TimbuktuQuickConnect.js" charset="utf-
8"></script>
    <script type="text/javascript"
src="/System/Library/WidgetResources/AppleClasses/AppleButton.js" charset="utf-
8"></script>
    <script type="text/javascript"
src="/System/Library/WidgetResources/AppleClasses/AppleInfoButton.js" charset="utf-
8"></script>
    <script type="text/javascript"
src="/System/Library/WidgetResources/AppleClasses/AppleAnimator.js" charset="utf-
8"></script>
  </head>
  <body onLoad="setup();">
    <div id="front">
      <img id="backgroundImage" src="Default.png"></img>
      <img id="tb2Icon" src="tb2icon.png" onClick="launchTB2();"
onMouseover="highlightTB2Icon();" onmouseout="resetTB2Icon();"></img>
      <div id="title">Timbuktu Quick Connect</div>
      <div id="ipAddressFields">
        <table cellpadding="3">
          <tr>
            <td class="ipAddressLabel">
              IP Address:
            </td>
            <td>
              <input id="ipAddress" size="14" length="15" onKeyDown="return
checkInput(event);" onKeyUp="return ipAddressAutoComplete(event);">
            </td>
            <td>
              <div id="connectButton"></div>
            </td>
          </tr>
```

```
            </table>
        </div>
        <div id="infoButton"></div>
    </div>
```

Clicking the tb2Icon.png, for instance, executes the `launchTB2()` function, which launches Timbuktu if it isn't already running. If you look at the Default.png background image, you see that the tb2Icon.png overlays it. This selector in the CSS file sets its height and width to 50 × 50 pixels and positions it on the top and right edges of the Default.png.

```
#tb2Icon {
    position: absolute;
    top: 0px;
    right: 0px;
    height: 50px;
    width: 50px;
}
```

In addition to the `launchTB2()` function, the `checkInput(theKeyPressed)`, the `ipAddressAuto Complete(theKeyPressed)`, and the `findAddress(anAddress)` functions support the `launchTB2()` function. The `checkInput(theKeyPressed)` function validates the text as you enter it in the text box. The `findAddress(anAddress)` function tries to find an address from previous connections. The `ipAddressAutoComplete(theKeyPressed)` function uses the previous IP addresses and tries to autocomplete the address as you enter it.

The back `<div>` contains the information for the back side of the widget and preferences. The instructions are laid out using a table to create the hanging indent formatting. Each of the service buttons is incorporated as an input type=radio.

```
<div id="back">
    <img id="backgroundImage" src="Default_reverse.png"></img>
    <div id="mainContents">
      <table>
        <tr  valign="top">
          <td>
            <font class="preferencePaneFontLabel">
              Instructions:
            </font>
          </td>
          <td>
            <font class="preferencePaneFontText">
              Enter the IP address of a remote machine in the
              &quot;IP Address&quot; field on the front of
              this widget and click the &quot;Connect&quot;
              button.
            </font>
          </td>
        </tr>
        <tr valign="top">
          <td>
            <font class="preferencePaneFontLabel">
              Choose the Timbuktu service to start:
            </font>
```

```
            </td>
            <td>
              <table>
                <tr valign="top">
                  <td>
                    <input type="radio" name="serviceType" id="sendButton"
value="send" onClick="setDefaultService(this.value);">
                    <label for="sendButton"
onClick="selectDefaultService('sendButton');">
                      Send
                    </label>
                  </td>
                  <td>
                    <input type="radio" name="serviceType" id="exchangeButton"
value="exchange" onClick="setDefaultService(this.value);">
                    <label for="exchangeButton"
onClick="selectDefaultService('exchangeButton');">
                      Exchange
                    </label>
                  </td>
                </tr>
                <tr valign="top">
                  <td>
                    <input type="radio" name="serviceType" id="controlButton"
value="control" onClick="setDefaultService(this.value);">
                    <label for="controlButton"
onClick="selectDefaultService('controlButton');">
                      Control
                    </label>
                  </td>
                  <td>
                    <input type="radio" name="serviceType" id="chatButton"
value="chat" onClick="setDefaultService(this.value);">
                    <label for="chatButton"
onClick="selectDefaultService('chatButton');">
                      Chat
                    </label>
                  </td>
                </tr>
                <tr valign="top">
                  <td>
                    <input type="radio" name="serviceType" id="notifyButton"
value="notify" onClick="setDefaultService(this.value);">
                    <label for="notifyButton"
onClick="selectDefaultService('notifyButton');">
                      Notify
                    </label>
                  </td>
                  <td>
                    <input type="radio" name="serviceType" id="intercomButton"
value="intercom" onClick="setDefaultService(this.value);">
                    <label for="intercomButton"
onClick="selectDefaultService('intercomButton');">
                      Intercom
```

```
                </label>
              </td>
            </tr>
            <tr valign="top">
              <td>
                <input type="radio" name="serviceType" id="inviteButton"
value="invite" onClick="setDefaultService(this.value);">
                <label for="inviteButton"
onClick="selectDefaultService('inviteButton');">
                  Invite
                </label>
              </td>
              <td>
                <input type="radio" name="serviceType" id="profileButton"
value="profile" onClick="setDefaultService(this.value);">
                <label for="profileButton"
onClick="selectDefaultService('profileButton');">
                  Profile
                </label>
              </td>
            </tr>
          </table>
        </td>
      </tr>
      <tr  valign="top">
        <td colspan="2">
          <font class="preferencePaneCopyright">
            Timbuktu Pro and its icon are copyright Netopia,
            Inc.
          </font>
        </td>
      </tr>
    </table>
  </div>
  <div id="doneButton"></div>
</div>
</body>
</html>
```

The different font sizes for the label, the instructions, and the copyright notice on the back are all formatted in the CSS file. Each font style has its own selector.

```
/* Back elements */

#back {
  display: none;
}

#mainContents {
  position: absolute;
  top: 20px;
  left: 20px;
  bottom: 30px;
  right: 20px;
```

```
    }

    .preferencePaneCopyright {
        font: 8px "Lucida Grande";
        color: white;
        font-weight: bold;
    }

    .preferencePaneFontLabel {
        font: 10px "Lucida Grande";
        color: white;
        font-weight: bold;
    }

    .preferencePaneFontText {
        font: 10px "Lucida Grande";
        color: white;
    }

    #doneButton {
        position: absolute;
        bottom: 20px;
        right: 17px;
    }
```

The <div id="mainContents"> in the HTML file is the container for the content on the back side of the widget and is formatted using the mainContents selector in the CSS file.

JavaScript Functionality

The launchTB2() function that runs Timbuktu with a click on its icon uses the widget.openApplication() method and Timbuktu is listed in application identifier format for the defaults domain.

```
    function launchTB2() {
        widget.openApplication("com.netopia.timbuktu.pro");
    }
```

The widget's main function is the startTB2Connection(), which attempts to connect to Timbuktu whenever you enter an IP address and click the Connect button. The IP address is taken from the text box and passed to the tb2connect.scrpt.

The launchTB2() function called in the middle of this startTB2Connection() function starts Timbuktu if it isn't already running. This saves time because the application doesn't have to wait while Timbuktu starts up.

```
    function startTB2Connection() {
        var theAddress = document.getElementById("ipAddress").value;

        if (theAddress.length > 0) {
            // Add the address if it is not in the previous connections and a valid
            // key was pressed:
            if ((findAddress(theAddress) == false) && (validKeyPressed == true)) {
```

```
    previousConnections.push(theAddress);
     }

    launchTB2();

    widget.system("/usr/bin/osascript tb2connect.scpt " + defaultService + " " +
theAddress, null);
   }
 }
```

The AppleScript is a handler that takes the IP address and attempts to open a session with the remote computer using the service selected in the preferences. Each service that Timbuktu supports is included in the AppleScript and is linked to the appropriate preference on the back of the widget.

```
on run theParameters
   set theService to item 1 of theParameters as text
   set theAddress to item 2 of theParameters as text
   tell application "Timbuktu Pro"
     activate
     try
       if theService is "send" then
         make new outgoing flashnote connecting to internet address {internet
name:theAddress, platform:platform unknown} when rejected let user reenter
         return "Connected."
       else if theService is "exchange" then
         make new exchange session connecting to internet address {internet
name:theAddress, platform:platform unknown} when rejected let user reenter
         return "Connected."
       else if theService is "control" then
         make new control session connecting to internet address {internet
name:theAddress, platform:platform unknown} when rejected let user reenter
         return "Connected."
       else if theService is "chat" then
         make new chat session connecting to internet address {internet
name:theAddress, platform:platform unknown} when rejected let user reenter
         return "Connected."
       else if theService is "notify" then
         make new notify session connecting to internet address {internet
name:theAddress, platform:platform unknown} when rejected let user reenter
         return "Connected."
       else if theService is "intercom" then
         make new intercom session connecting to internet address {internet
name:theAddress, platform:platform unknown} when rejected let user reenter
         return "Connected."
       else if theService is "invite" then
         make new invite session connecting to internet address {internet
name:theAddress, platform:platform unknown} when rejected let user reenter
         return "Connected."
       else if theService is "profile" then
         make new profile session connecting to internet address {internet
name:theAddress, platform:platform unknown} when rejected let user reenter
         return "Connected."
       end if
     on error anError number -27
```

```
        return "User cancelled."
      end try
    end tell
  end run
```

The `ipAdressAutoComplete(theKeyPressed)` function tries to autoComplete the IP address as you enter it in the text box based on previous IP addresses that you've connected to.

```
function ipAddressAutoComplete(theKeyPressed) {
  alert("'" + String.fromCharCode(theKeyPressed.keyCode) + "' has a value of " +
theKeyPressed.keyCode.toString());
  var found = false;
  var i = 0;
  var ipAddressField = document.getElementById("ipAddress");
  var ipAddressFieldValue = document.getElementById("ipAddress").value;

  if ((theKeyPressed.keyCode != 46) && (theKeyPressed.keyCode != 8) &&
(previousConnections.length >= 1)) {
    // Look for the first one that matches:
    for (i=0; i<previousConnections.length; i++) {

      if
(previousConnections[i].toLowerCase().indexOf(ipAddressFieldValue.toLowerCase()) ==
0) {
        if (previousConnections[i] != ipAddressFieldValue) {
          ipAddressField.value = previousConnections[i];
          ipAddressField.setSelectionRange(ipAddressFieldValue.length,
ipAddressField.value.length);
        }
      }

    }
  }

}
```

Summary

Like the Amazon Album Art widget (Chapter 15), Timbuktu Quick Connect provides the user with a way to bypass steps in an application. Rather than open Timbuktu and look for the machine to which you want to connect, you can enter the IP address and connect directly to the Macintosh or PC on your network. Additionally, this widget demonstrates how easy it is to run AppleScripts from the command line and pass information from the JavaScript to the AppleScript.

iPhoto Mini

iPhoto is the digital equivalent of iTunes. It can download photos from most, if not all, digital cameras, and it helps you manage your library of digital photos. iPhoto has some editing features for adjusting the color and tone of photos, removing red-eye, and enhancing or retouching photos. iPhoto also has options that let you order prints of your photos and create a print album of photos. Anyone who has begun using a digital camera in place of their old Instamatic or SLR and is using iPhoto to store and organize digital photos knows how slow iPhoto can become as the libraries become large. Once again, a widget comes to the rescue. iPhoto Mini provides quick access to your digital photo library and provides an additional feature.

iPhoto Mini

Jesus de Meyer's iPhoto Mini widget gives access to your photo libraries without opening iPhoto. When you install it, iPhoto Mini automatically gets the path to your photo library, inserts the path into its preferences, and displays the first photo in your library. Each time iPhoto Mini loads, a photo in your iPhoto library is displayed.

The main benefit of iPhoto Mini is that it places your photo library only a keystroke away without running iPhoto, but it does have features that iPhoto doesn't have. iPhoto Mini has a "show random picture" feature that causes the widget to display a different picture each time you invoke Dashboard. Additionally, iPhoto Mini allows you to open a photo directly in an application from your iPhoto library. iPhoto's Share menu has an option that lets you email a selected photo or photos. Whenever you select Email from the Share menu, the Mail application is loaded and a new message is created with the selected photos attached. iPhoto Mini also lets you email photos directly from it without opening the iPhoto application, though you are limited to the current photo. It also lets you open photos in Preview, Safari, or an application that you choose.

The Interface

Pictures from your library dominate the interface of iPhoto Mini with the controls situated around the borders of the picture (Figure 17-1). The iPhoto icon in the upper-right corner of the widget allows you to open the application with just a click. The info button is in the upper-right corner instead of the lower-right corner, but that allows all of the photo controls to be grouped along the bottom border of the widget.

Figure 17-1

When you click the Albums menu, you see a list of albums that you have created. If you haven't created any Albums in iPhoto, the Albums menu contains the default albums. The number of pictures in the albums is displayed in parentheses (Figure 17-2).

Figure 17-2

When you click the Actions menu, you see a list of applications (Figure 17-3). Choosing an application from the list opens the photo you are currently viewing in that application. You can specify a different application using the Open in "custom" option at the bottom of the menu.

The left and right arrows at the bottom of the widget let you browse forward or backward in the album that you've selected. The Reload button rebuilds the album list after you have added albums in the iPhoto application. In the lower-right corner of the widget is the resize thumb control. iPhoto Mini supports resizing and maintains the proportions of the picture with the resize.

Figure 17-3

The back side of the widget contains widget preferences in addition to hot links to the edot studios web-site and a Donate button (Figure 17-4). The iPhoto Library text box contains the path to your iPhoto library. Should you need to move your library, you can change the path in the text box to point to the new location.

Figure 17-4

The Custom application name text box allows you to specify an application for the Open in "custom" Action menu. If you enter GraphicConverter in this text box, for instance, selecting Open in "custom" from the Actions menu opens the current photo in GraphicConverter. The Show random picture check-box, as mentioned earlier, causes iPhoto Mini to display a different picture from your albums each time Dashboard is invoked. Beyond the coolness factor, this feature is handy if you can post to your blog using email.

iPhoto Mini Internals

Looking inside the iPhoto Mini widget shows you the usual items (Figure 17-5). Worth mention are the AppleClasses and Images folders. The AppleClasses folder contains the latest versions of the AppleAnimator, AppleButton, and AppleInfoButton JavaScripts. These are included to solve problems with previous versions of 10.4 and provide backward compatibility.

Figure 17-5

The Images folder contains the bits that are used to build the widget from when it is resized. It also contains two versions of the iPhoto icon: in addition to the version that is displayed at the top of the widget, Jesus includes a highlighted version to display when your arrow is over the icon. An error image is also available when iPhoto Mini cannot find the iPhoto library (Figure 17-6).

Figure 17-6

Info.plist

When you look at the properties list for the widget, you see that only one access key is set. The `AllowFileAccessOutsideOfWidget` is set because iPhoto Mini needs access to the pictures in your directory. Because iPhoto Mini does not access any network or Internet resources, none of the other access keys is set.

```
<plist version="1.0">
<dict>
```

```xml
        <key>AllowFileAccessOutsideOfWidget</key>
        <true/>
        <key>BackwardsCompatibleClassLookup</key>
        <true/>
        <key>CFBundleDisplayName</key>
        <string>iPhotoMini</string>
        <key>CFBundleIdentifier</key>
        <string>com.edot-studios.widget.iphotomini</string>
        <key>CFBundleName</key>
        <string>iPhotoMini</string>
        <key>CFBundleShortVersionString</key>
        <string>1.2</string>
        <key>CFBundleVersion</key>
        <string>1.2</string>
        <key>CloseBoxInsetX</key>
        <integer>13</integer>
        <key>CloseBoxInsetY</key>
        <integer>13</integer>
        <key>Height</key>
        <integer>215</integer>
        <key>MainHTML</key>
        <string>iPhotoMini.html</string>
        <key>Plugin</key>
        <string>iPhotoLoader.widgetplugin</string>
        <key>Width</key>
        <integer>216</integer>
    </dict>
</plist>
```

You'll also notice the `BackwardsCompatibleClassLookups` key is set. This key provides backward compatibility for OS X 10.4.3 and later versions while maintaining forward compatibility. When Dashboard sees this key combined with a `<script>` tag referencing AppleClasses, it loads the AppleClass files in /System/Library/WidgetResources/ instead of the copy included in the widget. If the widget is installed on a 10.4.5 system, it uses the AppleClasses that shipped with that version of the system. If the widget is loaded on a 10.4 system, it uses the AppleClasses installed in the widget.

HTML/CSS

When you look at the iPhotoMini.html file, you can see the AppleClasses inside of the widget referenced at the top of the file to provide backward compatibility on older versions of Tiger.

```html
<!--
  © 2005, e dot studios

  License:
  YOU MAY USE THIS PROGRAM AT YOUR OWN RISK. WE ("E DOT STUDIOS") CANNOT BE HELD
  RESPONSIBLE FOR ANY DAMAGE THAT WAS CAUSED TO YOUR COMPUTER. THIS PRODUCT MAY NOT
  BE SOLD NOR MAY IT BE PLACED ON ANY REMOVABLE MEDIA WITHOUT FIRST CONTACTING THE
  AUTHOR. YOU ARE ALLOWED TO MAKE 1 (ONE) COPY FOR BACK UP PURPOSES, INTERNET BACK UP
  OR UPLOADING THIS PRODUCT TO AN INTERNET DRIVE OR SERVER IS PROHIBITED.
```

```
The source code is provided as is. You are not allowed to modify or reuse the
code without first contacting the author. This is also true for any plugins that
are used.

  Contact: contact@edot-studios.com
-->

<html>
  <head>
    <style type="text/css">
      @import "iPhotoMini.css";
    </style>
    <script type="text/javascript" src="iPhotoMini.js" charset='utf-8'/>
    <script type='text/javascript' src='AppleClasses/AppleInfoButton.js'
charset='utf-8' />
    <script type='text/javascript' src='AppleClasses/AppleAnimator.js'
charset='utf-8' />
    <script type='text/javascript' src='AppleClasses/AppleButton.js' charset='utf-
8' />
  </head>
```

In the body section of the HTML file, you see the "build widget" comment. Each of the <div>s in this section references a corresponding selector in the "widget image parts" section of the CSS file.

```
<body onload="init();">
  <div id="front">
    <!-- build widget -->
    <div id="top">
      <div id="top_left_corner"></div>
      <div id="top_edge">
        <div id="title">iPhoto Mini</div>
      </div>
      <div id="top_right_corner">
        <div id='infoButton'></div>
      </div>
    </div>

    <div id="middle">
      <div id="left_edge"></div>
      <div id="inner"></div>
      <div id="right_edge"></div>

      <div id="photoWell">
        <img src="" id="photo" />
      </div>
    </div>

    <div id="bottom_left_corner"></div>
    <div id="bottom_edge"></div>
    <div id="bottom_right_corner"></div>

    <img id='resize' src='/System/Library/WidgetResources/resize.png'
onmousedown='mouseDown(event);'/>
```

For instance, the top portions of the widget are built with the `top_left_corner`, `top_edge`, and `top_right_corner` selectors.

```css
#top_left_corner {
  position: absolute;
  top: 0px;
  left: 0px;
  bottom: 0px;

  width: 28px;

  background-image: url("Images/top_left_corner.png");
  background-repeat: no-repeat;
}

#top_edge {
  position: absolute;
  top: 0px;
  left: 28px;
  right: 28px;
  bottom: 0px;

  background-image: url("Images/top_edge.png");
  background-repeat: repeat-x;
}

#top_right_corner {
  position: absolute;
  top: 0px;
  right: 0px;
  bottom: 0px;

  width: 28px;

  background-image: url("Images/top_right_corner.png");
  background-repeat: no-repeat;
}
```

Each of these selectors includes the PNG file from the Images directory inside of the widget. The iPhotoMini.css file also contains selectors for the sides and bottom of the widget. At the end of the "build widget" section of the HTML file, the resize.png in the WidgetResources directory is included to provide a thumb control for the live resizing feature.

The next section in the HTML file, the "add widget elements" section, contains the code for the widget controls and the preferences on the back side of the widget. The icon `<div>` at the beginning of the section has an `onclick` function to launch iPhoto whenever you click the icon.

```html
<!-- add widget elements -->
<div id="icon" onclick="widget.openApplication('com.apple.iPhoto');"></div>
```

The icon selector in the iPhotoMini.css file places the icon in the upper-left corner of the widget and references the image in the Images directory.

```
#icon {
  position: absolute;
  top: 0px;
  left: 0px;

  background-image: url("Images/iPhotoIcon.png");
  width: 32px;
  height: 32px;
}
```

The sections below icon `<div>` contain the code for the controls. The `onchange` function in the `popupMenu` `select` id calls the `popupChanged(this)` JavaScript function to display the list of iPhoto albums in the Albums menu. The `actionPopupMenu` `select` id contains the list of options for opening the photo and calls the `actionPopupChanged(this)` JavaScript function to load the applications.

```
      <img class="popupMenuImage" src="Images/popup_menu.png" />
      <div id="popupMenuText">Albums</div>
      <select id='popupMenu' onchange='popupChanged(this);'></select>

       <img class="actionPopupMenuImage" src="Images/action_popup_menu.png" />
       <select id='actionPopupMenu' onchange='actionPopupChanged(this);'>
        <option value="">Select an action</option>
        <option value=""> </option>
        <option value="Preview">Open in Preview</option>
        <option value="Mail">Open in Mail</option>
        <option value="Safari">Open in Safari</option>
        <option value="custom">Open in "custom"</option>
      </select>

      <div id="leftButton" onclick="prevImage();" ></div>
      <div id="rightButton" onclick="nextImage();" ></div>
      <div id="reloadButton" onclick="loadAlbums(true);" ></div>
    </div>
    <div id="back">
      <!--
      <div id="edotIcon" onclick="widgetOpenURL('http://www.edot-
studios.com');"></div>
      -->
      <div id="prefs">
         iPhoto Library: <input type="text" id="libPath" /><br />
         Custom application name: <input type="text" id="customApp" /><br />
         <input type="checkbox" id="randomPic">Show random picture</input><br />
      </div>
      <div id="text_area">
         &copy; 2005 - <a href="#" onclick="widget.openURL('http://www.edot-
studios.com');">e dot studios</a>
      </div>
      <div id='donateButton'></div>
      <div id='doneButton'></div>
    </div>
  </body>
</html>
```

The `leftButton` and `rightButton` `<div>`s have the `onclick` functions for prevImage and nextImage to browse through the images in the albums. The `reloadButton <div>` has the `loadAlbums(true)` JavaScript function that rebuilds the list of iPhoto albums. Below these functions for the controls on the front of the widget, the preferences on the back side of the widget are included.

JavaScript Functionality

The iPhotoLoader plugin is central to the functionality of the iPhoto Mini widget. It reads the AlbumData.xml file to get the list of albums, can build paths to iPhoto's library directories by reading the preferences file, and creates the path where one isn't specified by assuming the default location in the user's directory. Because it can get all of the album information, it provides the widget with all of the information about the number of photos and the number and names of the photo albums. The JavaScript functions to browse the pictures in the albums don't directly call the plugin, but they make use of the information it provides. The global variables `gCurrentImageIndex` and `gNumberOfImages` in the `prevImage` and `nextImage` functions are populated with information from the plugin.

```
function prevImage() {
  --gCurrentImageIndex;

  if (gCurrentImageIndex < 0)
     gCurrentImageIndex = gNumberOfImages-1;

  changeImage(gCurrentImageIndex);
}

function nextImage() {
  ++gCurrentImageIndex;

  if (gCurrentImageIndex > (gNumberOfImages-1))
    gCurrentImageIndex = 0;

  changeImage(gCurrentImageIndex);
}
```

Because the iPhotoLoader plugin reads the AlbumData.xml file, it is able to read the list of albums and get the number of photos in each album. The `loadAlbums(reset)` function is responsible for building or rebuilding the album information.

```
function loadAlbums(reset) {
  if (iPhotoLoader) {
    if (reset) {
      var result = iPhotoLoader.buildAlbums();

      if (!result) {
        changeImage(-1);
      } else {
        var menuDiv = document.getElementById("popupMenu");
        var totalAlbums = iPhotoLoader.numberOfAlbums();

        menuDiv.options.length = 0;

        for (var i = 0; i < totalAlbums; i++) {
```

261

```
            var albumName = iPhotoLoader.nameOfAlbumAtIndex(i);
            var imagesCount = iPhotoLoader.numberOfPhotosInAlbum(albumName);

            menuDiv.options[i] = new Option(albumName+" ("+imagesCount+")",
    albumName);
        }

        menuDiv.options[0].selected = true;

        popupChanged(document.getElementById("popupMenu"));
      }
    } else {
      if (widget.preferenceForKey("randomPic") && iPhotoLoader) {
        gCurrentImageIndex =
Math.random()*iPhotoLoader.numberOfPhotosInAlbum(gCurrentAlbum);
        changeImage(gCurrentImageIndex);
      }
    }
  }
}
```

The iPhotoLoader plugin also helps load the current photo in the application selected from the Action menu. The `openInApp(appName)` function gets the path to the photo inside of the iPhoto directories and launches the application with the path to the photo.

```
function openInApp(appName) {
  if (iPhotoLoader) {
    var normalPath = unescape(gImage.src);
    var path = normalPath.split("://")[1];

    iPhotoLoader.openImageAtPathWithApp(path, appName);
  }
}
```

The `actionPopupChanged()` function gets the name of the custom application from the preferences and then calls the `openInApp()` function to give the custom application the path to the photo.

```
function actionPopupChanged(el) {
  var value = el.options[el.selectedIndex].value;

  if (value != undefined && value != "") {
    if (value == "custom")
      value = widget.preferenceForKey("customApp");

    openInApp(value);
  }

  el.options[0].selected = true;
}
```

Toward the end of the JavaScript file is the section that handles resizing the widget. It contains the `mouseDown` and `mouseUp` event handlers that make live resizing possible. The `mouseDown` handler is called whenever the resize control is clicked; it registers the handlers for the drag and the `mouseUp` at the end of the drag, and it records the size of the window.

```
/* RESIZING */

var growboxInset;

function mouseDown(event) {
  document.addEventListener("mousemove", mouseMove, true);
  document.addEventListener("mouseup", mouseUp, true);

 growboxInset = {x:(window.innerWidth - event.x), y:(window.innerHeight -
event.y)};

    event.stopPropagation();
    event.preventDefault();
}

function mouseMove(event) {
  var x = event.x + growboxInset.x;
    var y = event.y + growboxInset.y;

    document.getElementById("resize").style.bottom = 17;

  if (y <= 215)
    y = 215;

  if (x <= 216)
    x = 216;

  window.resizeTo(x,y);

  var frontDiv = document.getElementById("front");
  front.style.height = window.outerHeight;
  front.style.width = window.outerWidth;

  var photoDiv = document.getElementById("photo");
  var newHeight = y-38-30;
  var newWidth = x;

  var ratio = newWidth/newHeight;

  photoDiv.style.height = newHeight;
  photoDiv.style.width = newWidth;

  gImageMaxHeight = newHeight;
  gImageMaxWidth = newHeight*ratio;

  imageLoaded();

  event.stopPropagation();
    event.preventDefault();
}

function mouseUp(event) {
    document.removeEventListener("mousemove", mouseMove, true);
    document.removeEventListener("mouseup", mouseUp, true);
```

```
        event.stopPropagation();
        event.preventDefault();
    }
```

The `mouseMove` function is called as the window is resized. It tracks the size of the drag and resizes the window accordingly. The function also calculates the ratio between the original size of the window and the resized window and adjusts the picture to fit in the resized window.

The `mouseUp` hander at the end of the section removes itself and the `mouseMove` function so they will not continue to be called with any additional clicks or drags.

Summary

Like the Amazon Album Art widget, iPhoto Mini makes use of iPhoto's libraries and adds missing features. By allowing you to open the photos directly in Mail, Safari, Preview, and another application, iPhoto Mini saves you the effort of either saving the picture to another directory or searching through the iPhoto directories to find the file. The ability to show a random picture from your albums is one of those great touches that adds polish and sets iPhoto Mini apart from other widgets.

iTunes Connection Monitor

One of the features of iTunes is that you can share your music with other users on your network. This is much easier than sharing CDs, but the feature has its drawbacks. If you quit iTunes while someone is listening to your music, it will tell you that users are connected (Figure 18-1), but it doesn't tell you which users. Even though iTunes is up to version 6.0, identifying the connected audiophiles has never been added to iTunes.

iTunes Connection Monitor

As he has with an increasing number of applications, Jason Yee provides missing functionality, and then some, in a widget: iTunes Connection Monitor. The widget provides two views of the connections to your shared music. It provides a list of users who are listening to music in your shared music library and shows you which songs they are listening to.

While not as elaborate as some widgets, iTunes Connection Monitor does follow the Apple notion of a widget that does one thing very well.

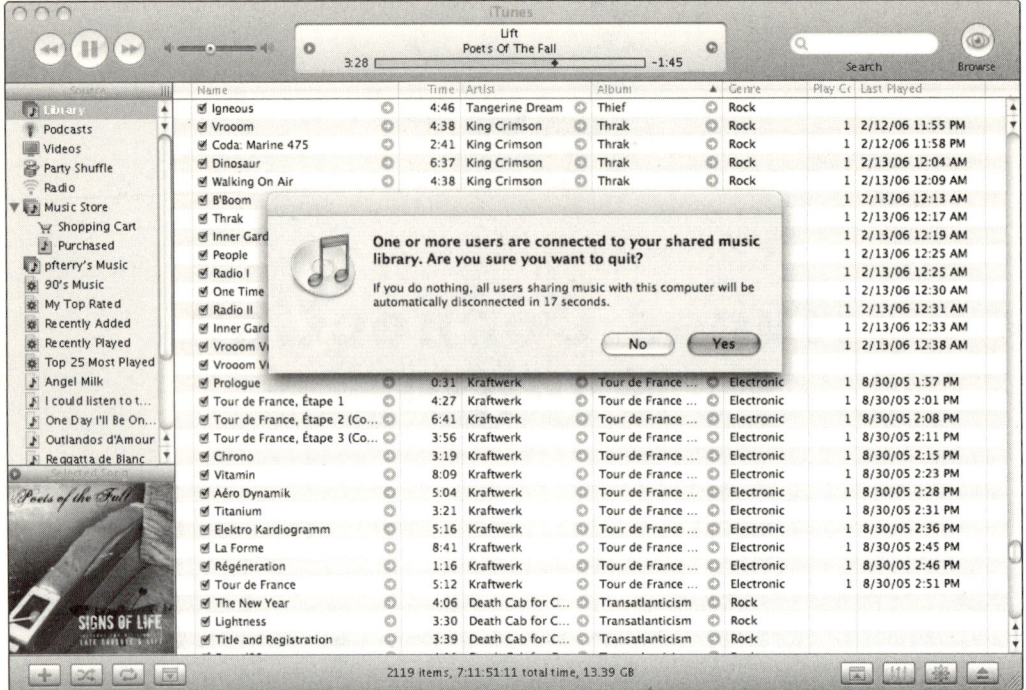

Figure 18-1

The Interface

The iTunes Connection Monitor may have the simplest interface of all the widgets you have looked at. It has two sides as most widgets do. The front side has a listing of users connected to your shared music library (Figure 18-2). The widget checks for connections each time you invoke Dashboard, but the reload button at the lower right of the widget will check again.

Figure 18-2

The back side of the widget doesn't contain the widget's preferences, but is another view of connections to your shared music library (see Figure 18-3). This view shows you the songs that the connected users are listening to.

Figure 18-3

iTunes Connection Monitor Internals

When you show the contents of the iTunes Connection Monitor, you may think this is the simplest widget you have ever seen (Figure 18-4). What you'll immediately notice is that iTunes Connection Monitor does not have plugins, multiple JavaScripts, multiple images, or localized files. The Images directory contains only the flipper graphic and the front and back PNG files for the widget.

Part of the reason for this simplicity may be that while iTunes is scriptable using AppleScript, none of the commands allows you to see the connected users or the songs they are listening to.

Because the AppleScript dictionary in iTunes doesn't support these functions (small surprise, given that they aren't available in the application itself), Jason has to use a Unixy approach to get the information.

Figure 18-4

Info.plist

In the Info.plist file, notice that only the `AllowSystems` access key is set. When you look at the JavaScript, you'll see that the widget needs the `AllowSystems` access key enabled because it uses a command-line utility called lsof, which provides a list of all of the open files on your Macintosh.

```
<plist version="1.0">
<dict>
  <key>AllowMultipleInstances</key>
  <false/>
        <key>AllowSystem</key>
        <true/>
  <key>CFBundleIdentifier</key>
  <string>com.argon18.widget.itcm</string>
  <key>CFBundleName</key>
  <string>iTCM</string>
        <key>CFBundleDisplayName</key>
        <string>iTCM</string>
  <key>CFBundleShortVersionString</key>
  <string>1.6</string>
  <key>CFBundleVersion</key>
  <string>1.6</string>
  <key>DefaultImage</key>
  <string>Default</string>
  <key>Height</key>
  <integer>203</integer>
  <key>MainHTML</key>
  <string>itcm.html</string>
  <key>Width</key>
  <integer>164</integer>
</dict>
</plist>
```

HTML/CSS

The CSS and JavaScript files are imported at the top of the HTML file. The front and back sides of the widget are very similar. The span on the front of the widget contains the text "Searching," which is replaced with the list of the IP addresses of computers when the JavaScript has run the command to gather the connected users. If you have a hosts file configured, the IP addresses are replaced with the machine host names. The span on the back of the widget also contains the text "Searching." This is replaced with the list of songs playing when the JavaScript has run the command to gather them.

```
<html>
<head>
  <style type="text/css">@import "itcm.css";</style>
  <script type="text/javascript" src="itcm.js" charset="utf-8"></script>
</head>
<body>
  <div id="front">
    <img span="backgroundImage" src="Images/Default.png">
    <span id="connections">Connected Users: Searching...</span>
    <img id="flipper" src="Images/flipper.png" onclick='flip("front")'>
  </div>
```

```
    <div id="back">
      <img span="backgroundImage" src="Images/Default2.png">
      <span id="songs">Songs Playing: Searching...</span>
      <img id="flipper" src="Images/flipper.png" onclick='flip("back")'>
    </div>
  </body>
</html>
```

For both the front and the back, the current visible `<div>` is passed as a parameter as a notification to flip to the other.

The connections selector in the itcm.css file sets the style for the list of IP addresses or machine names. The font line in the CSS file has multiple sizes and fonts to give Dashboard more than one option for rendering the widget if one or two of the fonts aren't available. Notice that in addition to the three listed sans-serif faces — Verdana, Arial, and Helvetica — Jason has included the generic font face sans-serif.

```
body {
  margin: 0;
}

#connections {
  font: 10px/12px Verdana,Arial,Helvetica,sans-serif;
  color: #FFFFFF;
  position: absolute;
  top: 35px;
  left: 20px;
  right: 20px;
}

#songs {
  font: 10px/12px Verdana,Arial,Helvetica,sans-serif;
  color: #FFFFFF;
  position: absolute;
  top: 35px;
  left: 20px;
  right: 20px;
}

.backgroundImage {
  position: absolute;
  top: 0px;
  left: 0px;
}

#flipper {
  position: absolute;
  bottom: 5px;
  right: 5px;
}

#back {
  display: none;
}
```

269

The flipper selector toward the bottom of the CSS file determines where the flipper button appears on the widget. It is set for five pixels from the right and five pixels from the bottom of the widget.

JavaScript Functionality

Even though it lacks user configurable preferences, the iTunes Connection Monitor does store a preference. If you open the widget-com.argon18.widget.itcm.plist file (Figure 18-5), you'll see the solitary whichside preference.

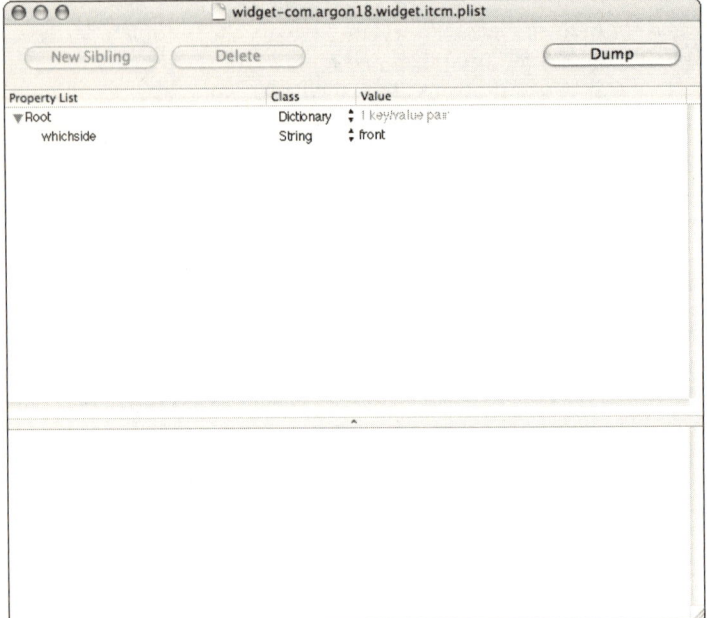

Figure 18-5

This preference is the side of the widget — either front or back — that was open the last time Dashboard was open. The flip(side) function determines whether the front or the back side was open and writes the name of the side to the whichside parameter.

```
if(window.widget) {
    widget.onshow = onshow;
    widget.onremove = onremove;
}

function onshow() {
    // called whenever widget is shown after first run
    searching();
    load_info();
}

function onremove() {
```

```
      // whenever widget is removed, unload preference
      widget.setPreferenceForKey(undefined,"whichside");
    }

    function getside() {
      // load side preference
      var whichside = widget.preferenceForKey("whichside");
      if(!whichside || whichside.length == 0) {
        widget.setPreferenceForKey("front","whichside");
        var whichside = widget.preferenceForKey("whichside");
      }
      return whichside;
    }

    function flip(side) {
      if(side == "front") {
        var front = document.getElementById("front");
        var back = document.getElementById("back");
        widget.setPreferenceForKey("back","whichside");
      } else {
        var front = document.getElementById("back");
        var back = document.getElementById("front");
        widget.setPreferenceForKey("front","whichside");
      }

      if(window.widget) {
        widget.prepareForTransition("ToBack");
      }

      searching();

      front.style.display="none";
      back.style.display="block";

      if(window.widget) {
        setTimeout('widget.performTransition();', 0);
        setTimeout("load_info();",1);
      }
    }

    function searching() {
      var side = getside();
      if(side == "front") {
        var msg = document.getElementById("connections");
        msg.innerText = "Connected Users: Searching...";
      } else {
        var msg = document.getElementById("songs");
        msg.innerText = "Songs Playing: Searching...";
      }
    }
```

The word "Searching" is a placeholder for the user's IP address and songs playing. When the information is collected, the JavaScript replaces the "Searching" text with the list of IP addresses or the user names.

The `load_info()` function does the heavy lifting for discovering iTunes users. `lsof` is a command-line utility that lists the open files on your Macintosh. This means that if a file is open, the utility lists the files in the same way that the ls command does. Entering a simplified version of the command used in the widget in Terminal, for instance, gives you a listing of the currently open music files:

```
[offhook:~] pfterry% lsof -F -c iTunes | egrep .mp3
n/Users/pfterry/Music/iTunes/iTunes Music/Compilations/10 Years In The Life [Disc
1]/1-02 Relativity (Transeau's Excursion).mp3
```

lsof, in the `load_info()` function, is passed the b switch to build the device file and the F switch to specify a character list. The results of that lsof are piped to grep, which looks for the 'daap->' in the output. The outputString undergoes a replacement to get only the users and the machine IP addresses.

```
function load_info() {
  var side = getside();
  if(side == "front") {
    // load front side
    var syscall = widget.system("lsof -b -F -itcp:daap | grep 'daap->'", null);
    if(syscall.outputString !== undefined) {
      // process netstat return info
      syscall.outputString = syscall.outputString.replace(/\S*->/g,'');
      syscall.outputString = syscall.outputString.replace(/:\S+/g,'');
      var ipArray = syscall.outputString.match(/\S+/g);
      ipArray = ipArray.sort()

      // clean duplicates, empties, and localhost entries
      var ipList = new Array();
      var previous = "";
      for(var i=0; i<ipArray.length; i++) {
        if((ipArray[i].length > 0) && (ipArray[i] != previous)) {
          ipList[ipList.length] = ipArray[i];
        }
        previous = ipArray[i];
      }

      var return_info = "Connected Users: " + ipList.join(", ");
    } else {
      // netstat was empty
      var return_info = "Connected Users: No Users Connected";
    }
    var msg = document.getElementById("connections");
    msg.innerText = return_info;
  } else {
    // load back side
    var syscall = widget.system("lsof -F -c iTunes | egrep
'(\\.aac|\\.mp3|\\.wav|\\.aiff|\\.m4a|\\.m4p|\\.m4b)'", null);
    if(syscall.outputString !== undefined) {
      // process lsof return info
      var regex1 = /.+\//g;

      // split output
      var songlist = syscall.outputString.replace(regex1,", ");
      var return_info = "Songs Playing: " + songlist.replace(", ","");
```

```
    } else {
      var return_info = "Songs Playing: No Songs Playing";
    }
    var msg = document.getElementById("songs");
    msg.innerText = return_info;
  }
  return true;
}
```

The next portion of the JavaScript cleans up the list of connected users. It creates an empty array and then walks the list of connections to remove any duplicates or localhost entries. The array is then joined to create a flat list of connections and appended to the "Connected Users:" text. If the listing is empty, the "Connected Users: No Users Connected" is used.

The JavaScript for the back side of the widget uses lsof to get a listing of songs by grepping for files ending in one of the standard audio formats and assigns it to the variable syscall. That listing is processed using a regular expression (regex1 = /.+\//g;) and the songlist is built. After a replacement, the songlist is appended to the "Songs Playing:" text and inserted into the widget using msg.innerText.

Summary

Though you might not expect it, the iTunes Connection Monitor gets the information about who is connected to your music library and which songs they are playing by using elements of a Unix shell script. That function in the JavaScript is able to get the information from the shell and report the IP addresses and the users.

More Widgets

RSS feeds began as a resource description framework (RDF) for describing the metadata of a website. RDF was designed as a way to make it easier for developers to create search engines. The metadata contained the site map, the keywords, and the dates of updates among other things. RDF developed into Rich Site Summary (RSS) and became an XML format for publishing content on the Web. What started as a means of publishing information for search engines is now incorporated into current versions of browsers so you can subscribe to a feed and get the latest information from a site directly in your browser.

RSS feed widgets make an easy case for a widget application because they provide the latest information from a website and you don't have to launch your browser to get it. An interesting twist is that individual widgets are being created for feeds from individual websites rather than more generic RSS feed widgets that can take in feeds from a number of sources.

More Widgets

Jesus de Meyer's More Widgets is one of those RSS feed widgets and it is pointed at Apple's Dashboard Downloads page. It retrieves and parses the information about the latest widgets uploaded to Dashboard Downloads, and shows the listings from the other groupings on the site. Unlike a number of RSS feed widgets, More Widgets also presents the details about the selected widget.

The Interface

The parsed content of the RSS feed is presented in the scrolling content area of the widget. The Recent listing shows the name of the widget and the date that it was uploaded to the Dashboard Downloads site. The other selectable lists provide the same views that you would see on the Dashboard Downloads website.

Figure 19-1

Clicking the Dashboard icon takes you to the Dashboard Downloads page. This widget demonstrates how to use all of the widget space for functionality. When you move your pointer over the icon, it is highlighted. The gear menu next to the icon lets you choose a category of widgets from a pop-up menu. The Category that you've selected from the Dashboard Downloads page is displayed at the bottom of the widget panel. Additionally, the widget has a search field.

Clicking the widget name in the list of widgets displays the description of the widget from the Dashboard Downloads website (Figure 19-2). Most RSS feed widgets display a listing of articles in the feed and then send you off to read the article when you click the article title. More Widgets displays the information about the widget so you can decide whether you want to download it before you leave Dashboard.

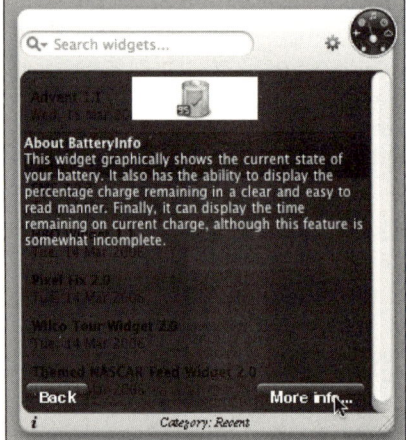

Figure 19-2

After you have read the information about the widget, you can click the Back button to return to the listing of widgets. If you want to download the widget, you can click the More Info button. Dashboard is closed and Safari launches and takes you to the widget's page at Dashboard Downloads.

More Widgets allows you to browse the Dashboard Downloads site without loading a browser. The widget uses the same categories as the site, and the menu at the top of the widget allows you to switch between them (Figure 19-3).

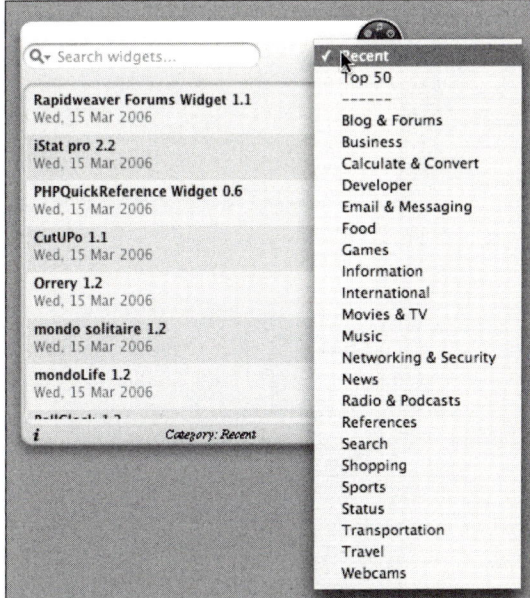

Figure 19-3

The search text box at the top of More Widgets (Figure 19-4) closes the widget and takes you to the search page at Dashboard Downloads with your search term already applied. The search box also returns the most recent searches you've conducted.

When you click the info button at the bottom of the widget (Figure 19-5), you see the back side of the widget with the credits and Donate and Done buttons. (Notice the Dashboard icon just visible behind the background in the upper-left corner.)

Figure 19-4

Figure 19-5

More Widgets Internals

When you show the contents of More Widgets, you see the usual set of widget files (Figure 19-6). Because this widget is resizable, the separate images are used to build the widget and give you more control over the interface. The Default.png file is what Dashboard uses to display the widget background when you first add the widget to Dashboard. After that, the Default.png isn't referenced again.

Figure 19-6

Info.plist

The properties list has the `AllowNetworkAccess` key set so the widget can retrieve the RSS feed from Apple's website. The `BackwardsCompatibleClassLookup` is also set so the widget can be used on earlier versions of Tiger.

```
<dict>
    <key>AllowNetworkAccess</key>
    <true/>
    <key>BackwardsCompatibleClassLookup</key>
    <true/>
    <key>CFBundleDisplayName</key>
    <string>More Widgets</string>
    <key>CFBundleIdentifier</key>
    <string>com.edot-studios.widget.morewidgets</string>
    <key>CFBundleName</key>
    <string>More Widgets</string>
    <key>CFBundleVersion</key>
    <string>1.2</string>
    <key>CloseBoxInsetX</key>
    <integer>13</integer>
    <key>CloseBoxInsetY</key>
    <integer>13</integer>
    <key>MainHTML</key>
    <string>MW.html</string>
</dict>
</plist>
```

HTML/CSS

You can see the Apple Classes inside of the widget bundle referenced at the top of the file to provide backward compatibility on older versions of Tiger.

```
<html>
    <head>
        <title>More Widgets</title>
        <style type="text/css">
            @import "MW.css";
        </style>

        <script type="text/javascript" src="MW.js" charset='utf-8'/>
        <script type='text/javascript' src='AppleClasses/AppleScrollArea.js'
charset='utf-8'/>
        <script type='text/javascript' src='AppleClasses/AppleScrollbar.js'
charset='utf-8'/>
        <script type='text/javascript' src='AppleClasses/AppleAnimator.js'
charset='utf-8'/>
        <script type='text/javascript' src='AppleClasses/AppleButton.js'
charset='utf-8'/>
        <script type='text/javascript' src='AppleClasses/AppleInfoButton.js'
charset='utf-8' />
        <script type='text/javascript' src='Stretcher.js' charset='utf-8' />
    </head>
    <body onload="init();">

    <!-- Front Panel -->
```

In the Front `<div>`, you can see that the widget saves your last ten search terms. You can also see the values listed for categories on Apple's site. The `changeCategory()` JavaScript function in MW.js changes the feed based on the selection you make from this pop-up menu. Below that, the `gotoDashboardSite()` function is attached to the `onmousedown` event and is called whenever you click the Dashboard icon on the widget.

```
        <div id="front">
            <div id="top">
                <div id="top_left">
                </div>
                <div id="top_middle">
                </div>
                <div id="top_right">
                </div>

                <input id='search' type="search" placeholder="Search widgets..."
results="10" autosave="searches" onsearch="searchWidget(this)" />

                <img class="categoryPopupImage" src="Images/gear.png" />
                <select onChange="changeCategory(this.selectedIndex)"
id="categoryPopup">
                    <option value="home">Recent</option>
                    <option value="top50">Top 50</option>
                    <option value="">------</option>
```

```
                    <option value="blogs_forums">Blog & Forums</option>
                    <option value="business">Business</option>
                    <option value="calculate_convert">Calculate & Convert</option>
                    <option value="developer">Developer</option>
                    <option value="email_messaging">Email & Messaging</option>
                    <option value="food">Food</option>
                    <option value="games">Games</option>
                    <option value="information">Information</option>
                    <option value="international">International</option>
                    <option value="movie_tv">Movies & TV</option>
                    <option value="music">Music</option>
                    <option value="networking_security">Networking & Security</option>
                    <option value="news">News</option>
                    <option value="radio_podcasts">Radio & Podcasts</option>
                    <option value="references">References</option>
                    <option value="search">Search</option>
                    <option value="shopping">Shopping</option>
                    <option value="sports">Sports</option>
                    <option value="status">Status</option>
                    <option value="transportation">Transportation</option>
                    <option value="travel">Travel</option>
                    <option value="webcams">Webcams</option>
                </select>

                <div id='dashSite' onmousedown='gotoDashboardSite()'></div>
            </div>
            <div id="list">
                <div id="list_left">
                </div>
                <div id="list_middle">
                </div>
                <div id="list_right">
                </div>
            </div>
            <div id="bottom">
                <div id="bottom_left">
                </div>
                <div id="bottom_middle">
                    <div id="status"></div>
                </div>
                <div id="bottom_right">
                </div>
            </div>
```

Toward the bottom of the HTML file are the `contentParent` and `contentScrollArea` `<div>`s for the content area where the items in the feeds are displayed. Below the content area `<div>`s are the details `<div>`s. Whenever you select a widget in the list, the detailed information about the widget is displayed in the detail pane that these `<div>`s specify.

```
<div id="contentParent">
        <div id="contentScrollArea">
            <div id="content"></div>
        </div>
```

```
                <div id="contentScrollbar"></div>
        </div>

        <div id="detailsParent">
            <div id="details_top">
                <div id="details_top_left">
                </div>
                <div id="details_top_middle">
                </div>
                <div id="details_top_right">
                </div>
            </div>
            <div id="details_inner">
                <div id="details_inner_left">
                </div>
                <div id="details_inner_middle">
                </div>
                <div id="details_inner_right">
                </div>
            </div>
            <div id="details_bottom">
                <div id="details_bottom_left">
                </div>
                <div id="details_bottom_middle">
                </div>
                <div id="details_bottom_right">
                </div>
            </div>
            <div id="detailsInnerParent">
                <div id="detailsScrollArea">
                    <div id="details"></div>
                </div>
                <div id="detailsScrollbar"></div>
            </div>
            <div id="buttons">
                <div id="cancelButton"></div>
                <div id="moreInfoButton"></div>
            </div>
        </div>

        <div id='infoButton'></div>
        <img id='resize' src='/System/Library/WidgetResources/resize.png'
onmousedown='mouseDown(event);'/>
    </div>
    <div id="back">
        <div id="credits">
            RSS Feed provided by <a href="#"
onclick='widget.openURL("http://www.apple.com/")'>Apple</a><br />
            Widget created by <a href="#" onclick='widget.openURL("http://www.edot-
studios.com/")'>e dot studios</a><br />
            <p class="copy">
            &copy; 2006 - e dot studios
            </p>
        </div>
```

```
            <div id="donateButton"></div>
            <div id='doneButton'></div>
        </div>
        </body>
</html>
```

If you open the Images directory (Figure 19-7), you'll see the individual graphics corresponding to the
`<div>`s.

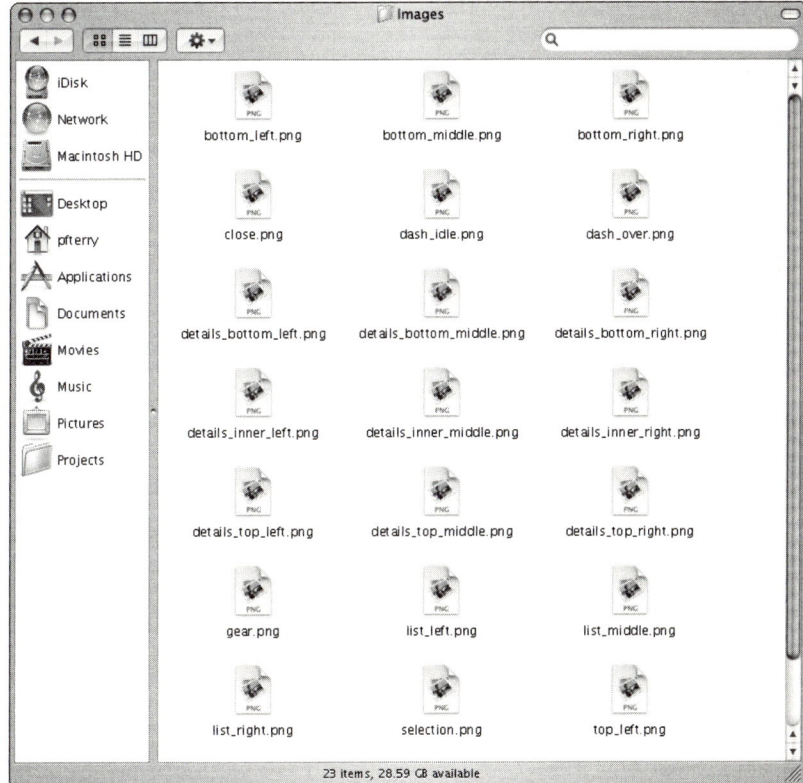

Figure 19-7

In the MW.css file, the comment line "Details" indicates where the selectors are for the details `<div>`s.
Taking the selectors for the top row, you can see that they reference the tiles for the details area on the
widget.

```
/* DETAILS */

#detailsParent {
    position: absolute;
    top: 50px;
    bottom: 30px;
    left: 0px;
```

```
        right: 0px;

        display: none;
        opacity: 0.0;
}

#details_top {
    position: absolute;
    top: 0px;
    left: 0px;
    right: 0px;

    height: 7px;
}

#details_top_left {
    position: absolute;
    top: 0px;
    bottom: 0px;
    left: 0px;

    width: 18px;

    background-image: url("Images/details_top_left.png");
    background-repeat: no-repeat;
}

#details_top_middle {
    position: absolute;
    top: 0px;
    bottom: 0px;
    left: 18px;
    right: 19px;

    background-image: url("Images/details_top_middle.png");
    background-repeat: repeat-x;
}

#details_top_right {
    position: absolute;
    top: 0px;
    bottom: 0px;
    right: 0px;

    width: 19px;

    background-image: url("Images/details_top_right.png");
    background-repeat: no-repeat;
}
```

The details content selectors are for the space where the details about each widget will be displayed. They specify the font and font size to use for the content, the amount of padding to set the margins, and the alignment of the paragraphs.

```
/* Details content */

#detailsInnerParent {
    position: absolute;
    top: 0px;
    bottom: 0px;
    left: 10px;
    right: 10px;

    font-family: "Lucida Grande";
    font-size: 0.6em;
    text-align: center;
    color: #fff;
}

#details {
    position: absolute;
    top: 0px;
    bottom: 25px;
    left: 0px;
    right: 19px;

    padding-top: 5px;
    padding-left: 5px;

    overflow: hidden;
}

#details p.text {
    text-align: left;
}

#buttons {
    position: absolute;
    left: 15px;
    right: 27px;
    bottom: 1px;
}

#cancelButton {

}

#moreInfoButton {
    position: absolute;
    right: 5px;
    bottom: 0px;
}
```

JavaScript Functionality

The MW.js file is neatly divided into sections for variables and initialization, functions, XML parsing, building the list, and resizing the widget.

285

The `changeCategory(index)` function gets the appropriate listing for the category that you select from the Category pop-up menu. The first five lines are variables for tacking items associated with changing the category. The first variable holds the category that has been selected from the pop-up menu. The `listDiv` variable holds the listing of widgets. The `statusDiv` contains the status of the widget. It displays either the name of the currently selected category or, as you can see later in this function, a "Loading..." message while it fetches the content. The value and name variables contain the value that you selected from the category pop-up and the display name associated with that value.

```
function changeCategory(index) {
    var selectionDiv = document.getElementById("categoryPopup");
    var listDiv = document.getElementById("content");
    var statusDiv = document.getElementById("status");

    var value = selectionDiv.options[index].value;
    var name = selectionDiv.options[index].text;

    widget.setPreferenceForKey(index, "selectedIndex");

    if (value && value != "") {
        //listDiv.innerText = "";
        statusDiv.innerText = "Loading...";

        gCategoryName = name;

        loadXMLDocument(gAppleDashFeedURL+value+"/recent.rss");
    }
}
```

The `widget.setPreferenceForKey(index, "selectedIndex")` takes the selected category and writes it to the preferences file. By doing this, the next time you open Dashboard, More Widgets remembers your selection and gets the latest feed for it. The if statement at the end of the function sets the status to "Loading..." and gets the Recent widgets feed from the Dashboard site using the `loadXMLDocument` function.

The `loadXMLDocument` function is in the XML Parsing set of functions in MW.js. The functions in this section of the JavaScript take the contents of the RSS feed from the Apple Dashboard site and produce the listings for the More Widget's content area. The `loadXMLDocument(url)` begins retrieving the Dashboard RSS feed using the XMLHttpRequest object which is from the WebKit, with the line `xmlRequest = new XMLHttpRequest()`. The following lines in the function begin processing the request by setting the header that will be sent, setting the mime type to XML, and making an open request. The `processXMLRequest()` function checks that the DOM tree was read successfully — the number 4 signals the completion of the transaction. If the DOM tree was read successfully, the function calls the `parseXMLDocument(xmlRequest.responseXML)` function with the response from the RSS feed.

```
/* XML Parsing */

var xmlRequest;

function loadXMLDocument(url) {
    url += "?uselessParam" + (new Date()).getTime();

    if (xmlRequest) {
```

```
            xmlRequest.abort();
            xmlRequest = null;
        }

    xmlRequest = new XMLHttpRequest();

    xmlRequest.onreadystatechange = processXMLRequest;
    xmlRequest.setRequestHeader("Cache-Control", "no-cache");
    xmlRequest.overrideMimeType("text/xml");
    xmlRequest.open("GET", url, true);
    xmlRequest.send(null);
}

function processXMLRequest() {
    if (xmlRequest.readyState == 4) {
        parseXMLDocument(xmlRequest.responseXML);
    }
}
```

The parseXMLDocument() function begins by calling the findChild function from the WebKit, which walks the DOM tree of the XML response. For each node that it finds on the tree, this parse function gets the description, link, content, and publication date of the widget and adds it to the array. When it is through walking the tree, it calls the build() function.

```
function parseXMLDocument(xmlData) {
    var rssElement = findChild(xmlData, 'rss');
    if (!rssElement) {
        //alert("no rss tag found!");
        return;
    }

    if (gItemsList) {
        delete gItemsList;
        gItemsList = null;
    }
    gItemsList = new Array();

    var channelElement = findChild(rssElement, 'channel');
    if (!channelElement) {
        //alert("no channel tag found!");
        return;
    }

    for (var element = channelElement.firstChild; element != null; element =
element.nextSibling) {
        if (element.nodeName = 'item') {
            var title = findChild(element, 'title');

            if (title != null) {
                var desc = findChild(element, 'description');
                var link = findChild(element, 'link');
                var html = findChild(element, 'content:encoded');
                var pubDate = findChild(element, 'pubDate');
```

```
                        gItemsList.push(new Array(title.firstChild.nodeValue,
        desc.firstChild.nodeValue, link.firstChild.nodeValue, html.firstChild.nodeValue,
        ((pubDate == null) ? "" : pubDate.firstChild.nodeValue)));
                }
            }
        }

        build();

        var statusDiv = document.getElementById("status");
        statusDiv.innerText = "Category: "+gCategoryName;

        gContentScrollArea.refresh();
    }

    function findChild (element, nodeName) {
        var child;

        for (child = element.firstChild; child != null; child = child.nextSibling) {
            if (child.nodeName == nodeName)
                return child;
        }

        return null;
    }
```

The `build()` function creates the HTML listing of widgets. It creates an unordered list and places each of the widgets as an item in that list. It also incorporates a `mouseUp` event to show the details of the widget whenever you click a widget in the list.

```
    function build() {
        var div = document.getElementById("content");
        var html = new String();

        if (gItemsList.length > 0) {
            html += "<ul>";
            for (var i = 0; i < gItemsList.length; i++) {
                var type = (i % 2) ? "even" : "odd";

                html += "<li id='item"+i+"' class='"+type+"'
    onmouseup=\"showDetails("+i+")\" >";
                html += "<div id='listTitle'>"+gItemsList[i][gFeedItemTitle]+"</div>";
                html += "<div
    id='listDate'>"+parseDateItem(gItemsList[i][gFeedItemDate])+"</div>";
                html += "</li>";
            }
            html += "</ul>";
        } else {
            html += "No items!";
        }

        div.innerHTML = html;
    }
```

The showDetails(itemNr) function displays the details of the widget whenever you click the widget name in the scrolling list. This function gets the selected item and sets the background color to show that it has been selected. It gets the details of the selected widget, creates the HTML that is used to display the details information, and sets the details area to the HTML. The details window that covers the widget window is created using the details selectors in the MW.css file. The details graphics are stored in the Images directory.

```
function showDetails(itemNr) {
    var itemDiv = document.getElementById("item"+itemNr);

    if (gSelectedItem != null) {
        if (gSelectedItem != itemDiv) {
            gSelectedItem.style.background = "none";
            gSelectedItem.style.backgroundColor = gSelectedItem.bgColor;
            gSelectedItem.url = "";
        }
    }

    gSelectedItem = itemDiv;
    gSelectedItem.bgColor = itemDiv.style.backgroundColor;
    gSelectedItem.url = gItemsList[itemNr][gFeedItemLink];

    itemDiv.style.background = "url(Images/selection.png)";

    var detailsDiv = document.getElementById("details");
    var html = new String();

    html += getWidgetImageURL(gItemsList[itemNr][gFeedItemContent])+"<br />";
    html += "<p
class=\"text\">"+getWidgetFullDescription(gItemsList[itemNr][gFeedItemContent])+"</
p>";
    detailsDiv.innerHTML = html;

    gAnimator = new AppleAnimator(500, 25, 0, 1, detailsFader);
    gAnimator.start();
}
```

Summary

Like other RSS feed widgets, More Widgets allows you monitor an RSS feed without using your browser. More Widgets takes XML data from Apple's website and parses it to produce the scrolling list of widgets that are available at Dashboard Downloads. It does this using the XMLHttpRequest object and parsing the XML information that is returned. You are also able to get basic information about the widgets listed at Dashboard Downloads without launching a browser.

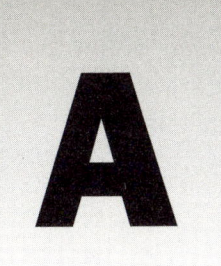

Answers to Exercises

Chapter 1

1. Cheetah and Puma, respectively. Give yourself bonus points if you loaded the Wikipedia widget from Apple's Dashboard website and opened Dashboard to retrieve this information.

2. The widget installer moves the copy you double-click into your widget folder. This means you will have to move it out to make changes. You may want to copy your widget from your development area to the desktop and install that copy.

3. Old Unix hands write paths that start at the root level of your personal account with a tilde, as in ~/Library/Widgets/. This is much shorter than typing the full path in terminal: /Users/<yourlogin>/Library/Widgets/. Why is this important? Since widgets can call shell scripts, you need to remember this distinction in your HTML and JavaScript files. More on paths in a latter chapter.

Chapter 2

1. As your high school English teacher might have told you, there is no wrong answer to this question. Or more accurately, there are any number of right answers. GraphicConverter, for example, has a Caliper Rule tool that lets you take measurements within your graphics.

2. The FlightTracker widget has an AllAirports.js file. This should have been a pretty easy guess that you could then confirm with Show Package Contents. If you tried to use Spotlight to find the file, you may have noticed that you can't search inside of bundles.

3. You can see this kind of folder organization if you look inside of the Weather widget. The folder hierarchy is:

```
/Weather/Images/
/Weather/Images/Icons/
/Weather/Images/Icons/moonphases/
/Weather/Images/Minis/
```

The images inside of the directories are referenced with a *relative path*, that is, the path is given relative to the current directory.

```
Images/Icons/
Images/Icons/moonphases/
Images/Minis/
```

In the case of a widget, the paths are given relative to the mainHTML file, Weather.html. If you open the Weather.html, Weather.js, and Weather.css files, you see absolute path references starting at the root level of the Weather folder similar to the listing above.

The opposite of a relative path is an absolute path, which starts at the root level of your hard drive. The path to the Weather.html file in an absolute form is /Macintosh HD/Library/Widgets/Weather.wdgt/ Weather.html.

Chapter 3

1. You enter a property in the Info.plist file that points to it.

2. No, because the widget object isn't supported in Safari.

3. Use BBEdit's Open Hidden File feature or copy the widget out to a folder where you have write permissions and do the editing there.

Chapter 4

1. UTF-8 is a variable-length character-encoding scheme for Unicode. The name stands for 8-bit Unicode Transformation Format.

2. No. If you do use an ID selector with the value "radar" more than once in your widget, the getElementByID() will not work correctly.

3. You can use the <div> tag to associate the style with the back side and preferences of your widget.

Chapter 5

1. Dashboard intercepts any alert messages and sends them to console.log.

2. PID stands for Process ID. Every program on an OS X machine has an entry in the system's process list and is assigned a unique process ID. A smaller ID number indicates that the process started running close to boot time. You can see the running processes in Activity Monitor or, using Terminal, in top.

3. Step through code, one line at a time, and examine the variable's values.

Chapter 6

1. Use the black info button graphics in the AppleClasses folder. Whenever possible, use the graphics in WidgetResources. This ensures compatibility when your widgets are installed on other users' Macs.

2. You may not have clearly delineated what is on the front side of the widget from what is on the back side. Always keep the contents of the front or back within their respective <div>s.

3. Your widget's preferences file is an XML file that you can open with any text editor or with Apple's Property List Editor to examine the contents.

Chapter 7

1. Leave one preference item in the file.

2. Dashboard isn't really a process. If you get information on any of the widgets, you'll see that they are owned by the Dock (Figure A-1).

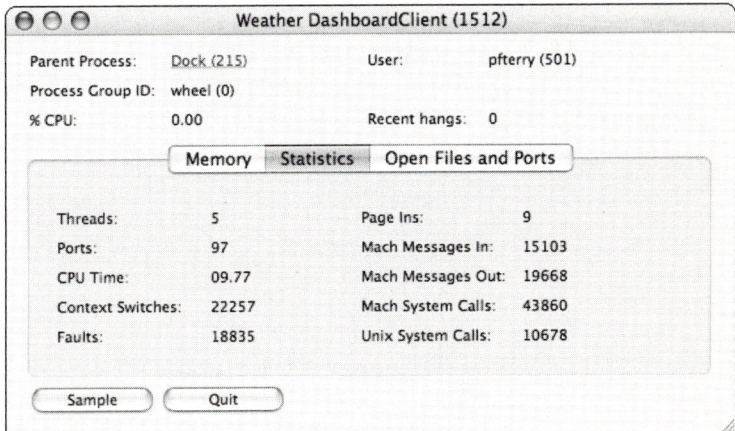

Figure A-1

3. Clicking in the widget's close box or removing it in the Widget Manager.

Chapter 8

1. Live resizing is also called relative resizing.

2. Relative resizing is typically used for widgets that display RSS feeds.

3. Apple's scrollbar classes are stored in the WidgetResources directory.

Chapter 9

1. You can use the getData method with the ondrop and onpaste events only.

2. You pass the information in the event variable.

3. It doesn't take any parameters.

Chapter 10

1. You call the `cancelDefault()` method.

2. The `event.stopPropagation()` method doesn't take any parameters.

3. Arguably, drag and drop was introduced with the Trashcan in Macintosh OS 1.0.

Chapter 11

1. You will want to use the `widget.system()` method in asynchronous mode. The Unix traceroute utility shows you the Internet path from your Macintosh to the computer or network resource that you are accessing. As it finds each router on its way to that Internet computer, it writes the IP address and information about each device to stdout. It is common for traceroute to take more than a minute or two to find the network path to that computer and it may time out. For this reason, you should allow the widget to continue to run while traceroute is running, and you should specify that the handler get each line and display it in your widget.

2. You would use the `AllowInternetPlugins` access key.

3. You may, but it is overkill. The more appropriate access key is the `AllowFileAccessOutsideOfWidget`. This key provides your widget with the maximum amount of access that it needs.

Chapter 12

1. Widget plugins are part of the widget bundle. WebKit plugins reside in the /Library/Internet Plug-ins/ directory.

2. No, they can be left in the /Library/Internet Plug-ins/ directory. They are called and automatically loaded whenever Dashboard is activated.

3. They use too much memory.

Additional Dashboard Programming Information

This appendix contains pointers to additional sources of Dashboard programming information. For the latest information about changes to Dashboard or WebKit, always check Apple's Developers' site. You will find most of the information that you need on Apple's website, but you can find other sources in blogs and forums with a quick search on Google.

Guides, Tutorials, and Specifications

Apple maintains a site for OS X developers at `http://developer.apple.com` where you can find the Dashboard, Safari, and WebKit programming documents listed below. Most of these documents can be downloaded as PDF files. In addition to Dashboard, Safari, and WebKit-related documents and technical notes, you'll also find information about Human Interface Guidelines and creating universal binaries for the new Intel Macs as well as other programming guides.

Apple Human Interface Guidelines (HIG)

To learn more about the human interface, read Apple's Human Interface Guidelines.

```
http://developer.apple.com/documentation/UserExperience/Conceptual/OSXHIGuide
lines/index.html?http://developer.apple.com/documentation/UserExperience/
Conceptual/OSXHIGuidelines/XHIGUsingTechnologies/chapter_8_section_6.html
```

The HIG describes how to create an application with a consistent user interface. Be sure to read the "High Level Design Guidelines for Widgets" section.

Dashboard Reference

The Dashboard reference contains information not included in the tutorial.

```
http://developer.apple.com/documentation/AppleApplications/Reference/Dashboard_Ref/
index.html?http://developer.apple.com/documentation/AppleApplications/Reference/
Dashboard_Ref/DashboardRef/chapter_1_section_1.html
```

This reference describes the JavaScript objects available to widgets as well as the interfaces for configuring and extending a widget.

Dashboard Tutorial

The Dashboard tutorial is the main source of information for widgets.

```
http://developer.apple.com/documentation/AppleApplications/Conceptual/Dashboard_
Tutorial/index.html?http://developer.apple.com/documentation/AppleApplications/
Conceptual/Dashboard_Tutorial/Introduction/chapter_1_section_1.html
```

The tutorial walks you through the basics of creating widgets to more advanced topics. It describes all of the components, events, and access keys for creating widgets.

Debugging Dashboard Widgets

If your widget has bugs, you may want to refer to this guide.

```
http://developer.apple.com/technotes/tn2005/tn2139.html
```

This technical note (TN2139) discusses debugging strategies, tips, and tricks for Dashboard widgets.

Developing Dashboard Widgets

For a brief overview of developing widgets, refer to this page at Apple's website.

```
http://developer.apple.com/macosx/dashboard.html
```

This information is scattered throughout the tutorial and other technical notes, but this is a good starting point.

Dynamic HTML and XML: The XMLHttpRequest Object

If you are creating a widget that works with RSS feeds, this document is your best source of information.

```
http://developer.apple.com/internet/webcontent/xmlhttpreq.html
```

This note describes how to use the XMLHttpRequest Object to connect your widget directly to an XML source to update your widget's information in the background without reloading the page.

Safari JavaScript Reference

For information about using JavaScript in Safari, refer to this reference.

```
http://developer.apple.com/documentation/AppleApplications/Reference/SafariJSRef/
index.html#//apple_ref/doc/uid/TP40001482
```

This reference describes Apple's JavaScript extensions to Safari and the WebKit.

Safari Document Object Model Overview

This guide provides a brief introduction to the Document Object Model.

```
http://developer.apple.com/documentation/Cocoa/Conceptual/WebKit_DOM/index
.html?http://developer.apple.com/documentation/Cocoa/Conceptual/WebKit_DOM/
01introduction.html
```

This is a 30,000-foot introduction to Apple's implementation of the WebKit Document Object Model. It primarily provides links to Apple and W3C DOM specifications and documents.

Safari JavaScript Programming Topics

If your widget makes use of the Document Object Model, you may want to refer to this guide.

```
http://developer.apple.com/documentation/AppleApplications/Conceptual/SafariJS
ProgTopics/index.html?http://developer.apple.com/documentation/AppleApplications/
Conceptual/SafariJSProgTopics/Tasks/DOM.html
```

This collection of programming topics describes how to use the DOM from JavaScript. In particular, it talks about drawing to the canvas, using the Pasteboard from JavaScript, and using Objective-C from JavaScript.

Safari HTML Reference

Because Dashboard and Safari share the WebKit HTML additions, you may want to refer to this guide.

```
http://developer.apple.com/documentation/AppleApplications/Reference/SafariHTMLRef/
index.html?http://developer.apple.com/documentation/AppleApplications/Reference/
SafariHTMLRef/Introduction.html
```

This reference describes every HTML tag and property supported by Safari and WebKit.

Universal Binaries Programming Guidelines

The Universal Binaries Programming Guidelines document the coding changes that need to be made to applications so they can run on the new Intel-based Macintosh computers.

```
http://developer.apple.com/documentation/MacOSX/Conceptual/universal_binary/index
.html?http://developer.apple.com/documentation/MacOSX/Conceptual/universal_binary/
universal_binary_intro/chapter_1_section_1.html
```

Because widgets are mainly composed of HTML, CSS, and JavaScript, they will be able to run on the new Intel-based Macs. If your widget contains a plugin, however, you need to compile your plugin as a universal binary. This guide describes how to build or modify Mac OS X applications so they will run on either PowerPC or Intel-based Macs.

Introduction to WebKit Plugin Programming Topics

For information about WebKit plugins, refer to this document.

```
http://developer.apple.com/documentation/InternetWeb/Conceptual/WebKit_PluginProg
Topic/index.html?http://developer.apple.com/documentation/InternetWeb/Conceptual/
WebKit_PluginProgTopic/WebKitPluginTopics.html
```

This collection of programming topics primarily describes the WebKit plugin architecture and explains how compiled plugins work inside of WebKit applications like Safari.

Mailing Lists

Mailing lists are the best source of current information about programming topics and assistance when you are having problems.

```
http://lists.apple.com/mailman/listinfo/dashboard-dev
```

Currently only one mailing list is devoted to Dashboard widgets. Apple hosts the Dashboard Developers mailing list and you can sign up at this address. The list routinely discusses Dashboard programming problems and bugs and is frequented by one of the Apple Dashboard engineers.

Other Resources

Because widgets are mostly based on open standards technologies, you will be able to find many non-Mac-specific sources of information for HTML, XHTML, CSS, and JavaScript.

MacTech Magazine

MacTech magazine may be the last Macintosh programming magazine around. It has been publishing articles for over 20 years and has always been on the cutting edge of Macintosh programming trends. The articles are aimed at the beginning to intermediate programmer and cover everything from AppleScript, Carbon, and Cocoa development to web scripting languages and Macintosh technologies. Go to their website (www.mactech.com/) for more information.

Websites

Any listing of websites is sure to be made obsolete by paper publication timelines, so it is better just to point to the main Dashboard websites that are the most active.

Apple Dashboard Downloads

This website (`www.apple.com/downloads/dashboard/`) is the main source for the latest widgets. If you're wondering whether someone has created the widget that you are thinking about writing, this is the first place to stop. As these pages are being written, there are close to 2,000 widgets.

Dashboard Lineup

Dashboard Lineup (`www.dashboardlineup.com/`) is a combination blog, widget repository, and community forums.

Dashboard Widgets

Dashboard Widgets (`www.dashboardwidgets.com/`) is a regularly updated blog that also has forums.

MacDevCenter

MacDevCenter (`www.macdevcenter.com/`) is part of the O'Reilly network. It contains a collection of regular articles and blogs that occasionally include Dashboard articles or programming topics.

Mac OS X Hints

This website (`www.macosxhints.com`) is the best source of hints for OS X with daily postings. It has a number of hints about Dashboard and widgets.

MacTech

MacTech is the online presence of the paper magazine. The website (`www.mactech.com/`) contains loads of information for the Macintosh programmer including news, articles, and sample code. Besides providing programming information and code, MacTech will keep you informed about programming directions.

Widget Distribution

Now that you've written a widget — or two — you may be ready to go beyond emailing them to a few of your closest friends. You may be ready to share them with the world. This appendix talks about the best places to upload your widgets and some of the issues of distribution.

Where to Post Your Widget

Shrinkwrap software is almost a thing of the past. Small developers no longer have to worry about dealing with distributors, paying for media duplication and packaging, and producing the right number of packages for brick-and-mortar stores. All of those expensive distribution methods have been replaced by Web distribution. You can put up a website and let everyone know that your widgets are available. In some cases, you don't even have to put up a website.

Apple

To get the most exposure, Apple's Dashboard Downloads page is probably the best place to upload your widgets. Other widget collections are available in addition to individual developer's sites, but Dashboard Downloads is perhaps the single place that everyone goes to look for new widgets. It is a well-known central repository, it has submission guidelines at `www.apple.com/downloads/dashboard/submit/index.html` (Figure C-1), and all of the widgets are checked before they are placed for download.

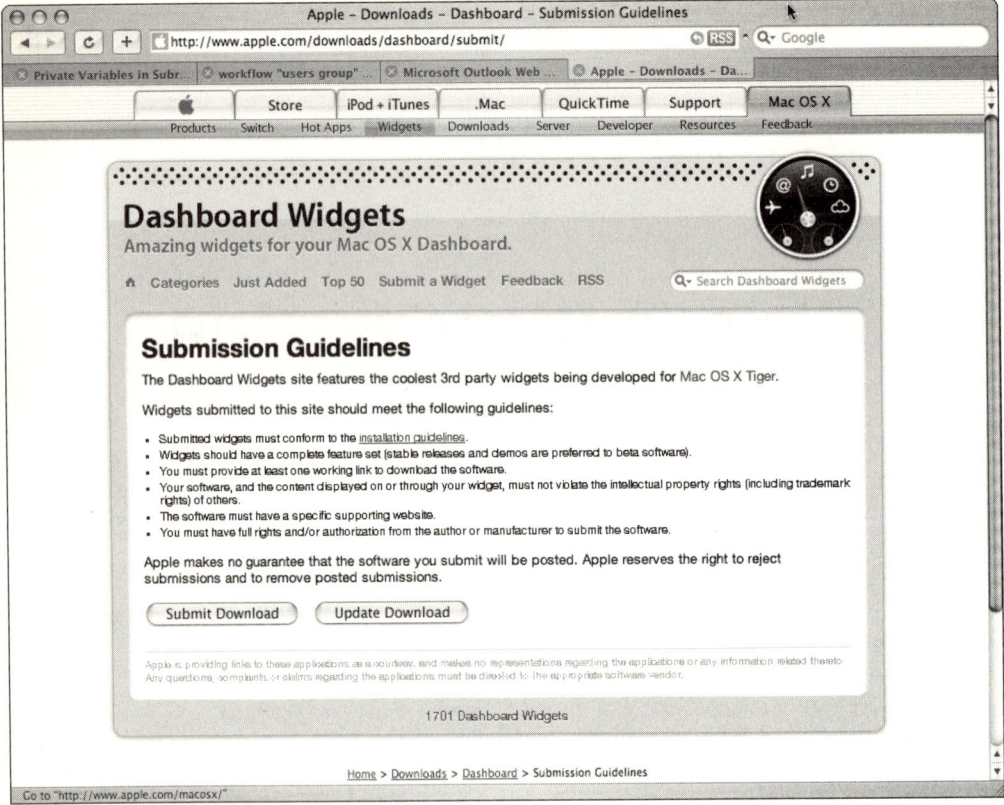

Figure C-1

However, Apple can't be your only distribution point, because you must provide one working link to download the software. The submission guidelines also point out that the widget must have a supporting website. You must have full rights to distribute the widget and must not have violated the intellectual property rights of others. Your widget should also have a complete feature set, but you'd never release betaware, would you?

Other Websites

In addition to Apple's Dashboard Downloads, you can find other locations on the Internet where you can post your widgets. As noted in Appendix B, Dashboard Widgets (`www.dashboardwidgets.com/`) is a good community site in addition to being a well-organized showcase of widgets. Dashboard Widgets has a submissions form that isn't as restrictive as Apple's, and your widgets will be reviewed before placed for download.

The most obvious place to post your widgets is on your personal website. It may not get as much traffic as Apple's, but you can provide support and additional information about your widget. If you don't have a personal website, you can get a .Mac account where you can share files or you can probably get a website through your ISP. Just remember, however, that if your widgets are popular, you may exceed the monthly bandwidth limitations.

Should You Charge for Your Widget?

This is a complicated question. While some people frown on charging for widgets, widgets are software. The more useful widgets are, the greater the likelihood that users will pay for them. If you've spent a great deal of time on the design and functionality of your widget, and it looks like a professional piece of software, go for it.

Some developers have already decided to charge, but on a *donationware* basis, which is similar to shareware but not as demanding. If the user likes your widgets, he can make a donation through PayPal or Kagi as an incentive to keep you working on widgets. You can also disable some features until the user makes a donation and receives a registration code. Widget Machine's NotePad, for example, has a time-out feature and stops working once you have used it longer than the specified time.

One thing to keep in mind is that widgets are based on open standards and are not compiled software. Anyone can examine your code unless you move the important functionality into a plugin.

Post It!

Okay, you've created a widget, you've run it though the testing gauntlet with friends or your QA lab, and you've fixed all of the bugs and even added some additional features. You are ready to upload it, but what do you need to do first?

Getting Ready to Post

Whether you choose to use a .Mac account or another personal website, you'll need to make certain that the widget installs properly whenever the user downloads it. This would be worth a little testing time.

You'll need to make an archive of your widget to upload it. You can do this by Control-clicking or right-clicking on your widget in the Finder and selecting the Create archive of . . . command from the contextual menu. This creates a ZIP file that you'll be able to upload to your web server. When you download the widget from your website using Safari, it is automatically expanded and you are prompted to install the widget. It is placed in your /Library/Widgets/ folder, Dashboard is opened, and you are prompted to keep the widget or remove it. You may want to test the download and install process with Firefox to see if the download functions the same way. If it doesn't and the user has to manually install your widget, you may want to include that information on the download page. Apple's Installation Guidelines (www.apple.com/downloads/dashboard/submit/installers.html) have text that you can add to your download page and covers automatic as well as manual installation.

In its Installation Guidelines (Figure C-2), Apple notes that if you want users to purchase the widget, complete a registration, or read an end-user license agreement, you should have them do this at your website before downloading the widget. These tasks are more easily accomplished through a website than through the widget. Always keep your users in mind and make downloading and installation as simple as possible.

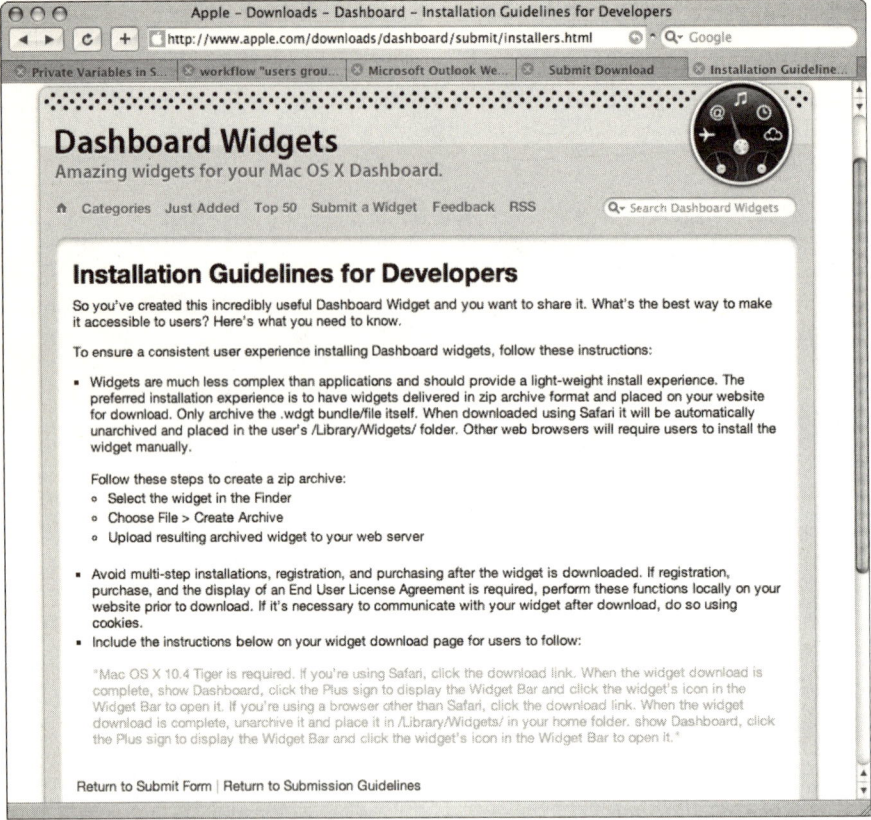

Figure C-2

Submitting to Apple's Dashboard Downloads

Now that you have prepared your widget to upload to widget collections and you have tested the download from your personal website, you are ready to submit the widget to Apple's Dashboard Downloads.

The submittal form (`www.apple.com/downloads/dashboard/submit/submit.html`) is straightforward and asks for contact and product information. You'll need to have a product summary and description for your widget in addition to version information, requirements, size, the download links, and a screenshot. Once you click the Submit button, you just have to wait until your widget has been reviewed and is available for everyone to download and begin submitting feature requests.

Index

I